TEXAS
The Dark Corner
of the Confederacy

TEXAS
The Dark Corner
of the Confederacy

Contemporary Accounts
of the Lone Star State in
the Civil War

EDITED BY B. P. GALLAWAY

Third Edition

University of Nebraska Press
Lincoln and London

© 1994 by the University of Nebraska Press
Manufactured in the United States of America.
The paper in this book meets
the mimimum requirements of American National
Standard for Information Sciences –
Permanence of Paper for Printed Library Materials,
ANSI Z39.48–1984.
Library of Congress Cataloging-in-Publication Data
Texas, the dark corner
of the Confederacy : contemporary accounts
of the Lone Star State
in the Civil War / edited by B. P. Gallaway. – 3rd ed.
p. cm. Includes bibliographical
references and index. ISBN 0-8032-2148-7 (cl.). –
ISBN 0-8032-7036-4 (pbk.)
1. Texas – History – Civil War, 1861-1865 – Sources.
I. Gallaway, B. P.
E850.9.T49 1994 973.7′464 – dc20
93-37186 CIP

Contents

MAPS

Preface to the Third Edition

In the summer of 1863, a twenty-two-year-old Southern belle named Kate Stone and her family came to Texas as refugees, driven from their plantation in northeastern Louisiana by fighting around Vicksburg. Long accustomed to the comfort, beauty, and charm of life among aristocrats, they were shocked by the backwardness, filth, and ugliness they encountered west of the Sabine. Within the short span of a few weeks, their luxurious world of plantation elegance was replaced by rough-hewn log cabins with dirt floors, homely and sweat-stained women, and lazy, unkempt, and largely illiterate frontiersmen in soiled buckskin and tattered homespun, some with dried tobacco juice matted in their beards.

"Oh the swarms of ugly, rough people," Kate wrote in her diary, "different only in degrees of ugliness." In her quest for an explanation, she concluded that there "must be something in the air of Texas fatal to beauty."

Kate's diary abounds with descriptions of barefoot women in unsightly hoop skirts attending church services; "a horrid decoction of burnt wheat" used as a substitute for coffee; brackish drinking water served in "halves of broken bottles"; cracked and broken dinnerware that had been washed in the waste-laden water of a duck pond; and swarms of "redbugs, fleas by the millions, and snakes gliding through the grass by hundreds." More than once Kate confided in her diary that she and her mother seemed to have found "the dark corner of the Confederacy."

Other visitors and newcomers to the Lone Star State during the Civil War decade recorded similar impressions. A young lady with a background somewhat similar to Kate's wrote that the jaws of Texas males always were so full of tobacco that they could not speak "without disagreeable consequences." An English officer who met Sam Houston on a train in South Texas observed that the hero of San Jacinto was an unsophisticated old man who "blew his nose with his fingers"; and a stage driver at Fort Belknap advised one of his passengers, "If you want to obtain distinction in *this* country, kill somebody."[1]

Not all travelers, visitors, and new residents agreed with this negative assessment of Texas and its people. An Illinois farm boy recently arrived in North Texas described the country south of Dallas as a beautiful land of "tall oaks, sparkling streams, and rolling hills." A traveler en route to California described residents of San Antonio as "intelligent, patriotic, and as good looking as any I have witnessed." Another traveler, who crossed Texas in 1863, concluded that Texans "had sort of a bon-homie honesty and natural courtesy and good nature . . . which was very agreeable." Even a captured Union soldier at Camp Ford, a Confederate prisoner-of-war camp near Tyler, wrote that his guards "did not drink . . . did not swear and did not gamble. They were watchful of us," he explained, "but they did everything kindly and with a willingness that greatly lessened our feeling of dependence." And even Kate Stone had to admit that the cascading colors of wildflowers that blanketed the rolling prairies of North Texas in the springtime were beautiful.

Which, then, is the more accurate assessment of the Lone Star State and its people during the Civil War? The answer has to be that travelers' descriptions of the land and its inhabitants varied widely according to the part of the state they saw, the time of year they visited, the people they encountered, and their own interests, prejudices, and backgrounds. When these descriptions are compared, generalized assessments become almost impossible because Civil War Texas was a land of physical, social, and ethnic contrasts which were often perplexing, occasionally pleasing, sometimes disgusting, but always captivating.

This book attempts to reconstruct a reasonably complete picture of Texas during those terrible years of secession and war through excerpts from firsthand descriptions of the state and its inhabitants written by people who were part of that picture. The selections are taken from diaries, journals, almanacs, official documents, speeches, reminiscences, and memoirs. Since most Texans and some of the state's visitors did not possess an appreciable measure of literacy, the excerpts are not always models of flawless composition. Nevertheless, most appear exactly as written although in some instances the editor found it necessary to make a few minor changes in the interest of clarity, continuity, and congruity. Ellipses within and at the ends of sentences designate the omission of words or phrases. Full lines of ellipses indicate that one or more sentences have been omitted. The editor's corrections, comments, and clarifications are enclosed in brackets.

The excerpts are presented, as nearly as possible, in chronological sequence, but some effort has been made to group them geographically. The titles and introductions that preface the excerpts were added by the editor to set the stage for the accounts, reveal something of their nature and content, and occasionally explain the significance of the source from which they were taken. It is hoped that this collection captures something of the life and spirit of wartime Texas.

In compiling these readings I am indebted to many individuals and institutions. First, I acknowledge a tremendous debt of gratitude to my late mentor and major professor at the University of Texas at Austin, H. Bailey Carroll. It was he who first introduced me to the fabulous treasures to be found in dusty archives and special collections. Llerena Friend, former director of Eugene C. Barker Texas History Center and its archives at the University of Texas at Austin, and Dorman H. Winfrey and James Day, former directors of the Texas State Library and Archives, respectively, generously assisted in the location of primary sources vital to my project. Joe B. Frantz, then editor of the *Southwestern Historical Quarterly,* and the late Rupert N. Richardson, editor of the *West Texas Historical Association Year Book,* graciously granted permission to use essential materials from their publications. I also am indebted to the family of the late Don H. Morris, former president and first chancellor of Abilene Christian University, and to the late Harold B. Simpson, founder and director of the Confederate Research Center in Hillsboro, for granting access to their family archives and special collections. I would also like to acknowledge a great debt of gratitude to Alwyn Barr, chairman of the history department at Texas Tech University, who for this third edition has updated his remarkable historiographical essay on Civil War Texas which initially appeared in the Winter 1964 issue of *Texas Libraries.* John L. Robinson, chairman of the history department at Abilene Christian University, and the late Ernest Wallace, a distinguished professor of history at Texas Tech University for over forty years, provided obscure manuscripts and made helpful suggestions. Finally, I am forever grateful to Vernon Williams, whose computer expertise and technical assistance were vital to the preparation of this third edition, and to Dawn Alexander Tepe, who labored over the revised manuscript with more skill and love than its editor deserved.

NOTE

1. Llerena B. Friend, "The Texan of 1860," *Southwestern Historical Quarterly* 62 (July 1958): 5; A. J. L. Fremantle, *Three Months in the Southern States: April–June, 1863* (New York: John Bradburn, 1864), pp. 77–85.

Introduction

The Lone Star State was a land of paradoxes during the war years. Her diverse social and economic structure was greatly complicated by a highly variegated topography, an erratic climate, an unequal distribution of wealth, and a rapidly increasing population. According to the *Eighth Census of the United States* in 1860, the total population was 604,215. The figure included 182,566 slaves, 355 free African Americans, and a "foreign" population of 43,422. Brazoria County was the wealthiest county in the state and also the one containing the largest number of slaves. Only 21,878 Texans were slaveholders and almost half owned three slaves or less. Only two Texas planters claimed two hundred slaves or more, and only one of these, D. C. Mills of Brazoria County, claimed more than three hundred.

By 1860 counties had been organized as far west as the one hundredth meridian and along the valley of the lower Rio Grande; the western interior was unorganized, unsettled, and very unhealthy. Human life was especially cheap west of a frontier line of settlement that extended roughly along the western fringe of the Western Cross Timbers, through the Hill Country west of San Antonio, and southwest to the Rio Grande settlements. The heart of the organized section was the southeastern cotton-producing region, where the wealthy gentry and larger plantation owners were concentrated. Small "corn and pork farms" dotted the landscape north and east of the major cotton-producing regions and extended as far west as the Western Cross Timbers. Southwest of the German settlements and beyond the rolling Hill Country were thousands of wild mustangs and wild, unbranded longhorn cattle. The size of the horse and cattle herds diminished somewhat from 1856 to 1858 and during the early years of the Civil War because of the shortage of water caused by prolonged drought. It was only after the unusually frigid winter of 1864 that near normal rainfall returned to Southwest Texas. During the drought many South Texas streams became dry arroyos. Travelers told of sun-bleached skeletons of wild horses and longhorn cattle lining dry creek beds, adding to an already desolate and eerie landscape.

In general, conditions in Texas were rougher and more primitive than in other Confederate states. When the Civil War began, Texas was still essentially a log cabin frontier. Although the Mexican inhabitants along the southwestern border built their houses out of adobe, and the German residents of the Hill Country lived in sturdy houses occasionally built from native limestone, the vast majority of Anglo-Celtic frontiersmen fashioned their dwellings out of rough, hand-cut logs. There were some sawmills in the pine forests of East Texas, but most pioneer farmers in the central and western portions of the state cut their own logs and lived in homemade cabins. A few Texans on the High Plains lived in temporary sod houses, but most preferred and eventually completed shanties of wood and adobe. Because timber was in such short supply, some High Plains residents hauled hardwood logs from as far away as the Oklahoma Cross Timbers. Soldiers at Fort Phantom Hill and Fort Chadbourne, struggling for survival in the sun-baked Central Denuded Region of West Texas, hauled logs from the Concho River region, the lower Colorado River basin, or the valley of the Western Cross Timbers southwest of Fort Worth. Log cabins tended to be warm and inviting havens for raccoons and rattlesnakes; but rough-hewn logs, when available, continued to serve as the favorite building material for frontier Texans, just as they had been for the pioneers in the Great Pine Forest of the East.

Since less than 5 percent of the population lived in urban centers, Texas was essentially a land of innumerable villages, frontier forts, trading posts, sprawling ranches, and isolated farming communities. By 1860, however, the state did possess several sizable towns. The largest population concentrations were at San Antonio and Galveston, each claiming populations approaching ten thousand. Houston, Austin, New Braunfels, Marshall, and about fourteen other settlements boasted more than one thousand inhabitants. Almost one-third of the free population in urban centers was foreign-born, many having come directly from their homelands to Texas to become merchants, craftsmen, teamsters, or laborers. The best buildings in the towns were usually hotels, such as the Tremont House in Galveston, the Menger Hotel on Alamo Plaza in San Antonio, and the Swenson Building (Avenue Hotel) in Austin. The Swenson Building, completed the same year as the magnificent new capitol building, was called "an ornament to the City" by the *Texas State Gazette*.

Roads between the towns were bad, and occasionally travelers "went astray upon cattle-paths" and found themselves miles from their destination. Except for Galveston, where some of the most traveled avenues were surfaced with shells, the streets of Texas towns were unpaved and became quagmires during rainy weather.

Although Galveston had long been the commercial center of the coast, the city of Houston rapidly was becoming the railroad capital of the state (see map 1). Trains that arrived in Houston in 1860 were on definite schedules, and construction crews steadily extended steel track deeper and deeper into the undeveloped interior. The Buffalo Bayou, Brazos, and Colorado, commonly called the Harrisburg Railroad, stretched all the way to Alleyton near the Colorado River. The Houston and Texas Central had reached Navasota and Millican in the Brazos River valley, and a branch line was already completed into Brenham from Hempstead. Construction crews for the Texas and New Orleans Railroad, completing a line from Houston to Beaumont, expected to finish their task within a few months. A team of "scientific engineers" was in the process of calculating the cost of constructing a ship channel through Buffalo Bayou to Galveston Bay, opening Houston to oceangoing commerce. Steamboats ran between Houston and Galveston, carefully scheduled to make connections with vessels arriving from New Orleans. The economic future of Houston and the entire Texas Gulf Coast seemed bright on the eve of secession.

Such was the physical stage on which the Civil War drama was enacted. The news of John Brown's raid on Harpers Ferry and of Abraham Lincoln's election to the presidency greatly magnified the average Texan's anxiety and sectional hatred. By the time the state Secession Convention convened in Austin early in 1861, many Texans were nearly in a frenzy. Several destructive fires of unknown origin in Dallas, Denton, and Waxahachie were interpreted as proof that subversive abolitionists or Kansas Jayhawkers were at work in the Lone Star State. Vig-

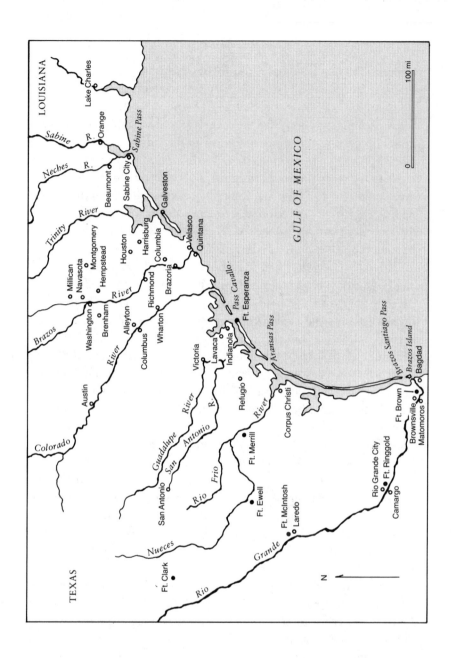

Map 1. The Texas Coast.

ilante bands and secret organizations immediately sprang up to deal with the unseen terror. Strangers were attacked, travelers were threatened, and "troublemaking" slaves and suspected Yankee sympathizers were lynched. A chilling incident that took place in Breckenridge demonstrated the extent of the mass hysteria. A traveling salesman, caught with several copies of Hinton Rowan Helper's *Impending Crisis of the South* in his wagon, was securely bound and suspended by his ankles from a large oak tree. His coal oil–soaked wagon then was driven under him and set afire. The hapless victim, whose only crime was possession of literature used by the Republican party campaign in 1856, was burned alive.

The state convention passed the secession ordinance on February 1, 1861, by a vote of 171 to 6, and this action received popular sanction three weeks later by a vote of 46,129 to 14,698. Only nineteen counties could claim slim majorities opposing secession, largely in the rolling Hill Country northwest of Austin, where many Germans lived, and along the Red River in North Texas, which contained clusters of free-soil immigrants from the Old Northwest.

The struggle over secession was bitter, and prominent Texans lined up on both sides. David G. Burnet, E. M. Pease, J. W. Throckmorton, George and John Hancock, E. J. Davis, and A. J. Hamilton sided with Sam Houston in a futile effort to keep the Stars and Stripes flying over the state. Objecting hotly to the "imbecility" of national leaders in the North who preached "the debasing doctrine of the equality of all men," Texas secessionists such as Judge O. M. Roberts, Alfred M. Hobby, A. P. Gallaway, Edward M. Ross, and George M. Flournoy strove to remove the state from the "shackles" of union.[1]

When Texas voters sanctioned secession by a margin of more than three to one, the Secession Convention turned its attention to expelling Federal troops from the state and taking possession of U.S. forts strategically situated across the Indian frontier of West Texas. But resistance was expected; there were twenty-one Federal installations garrisoned by approximately twenty-seven hundred U.S. troops, under the command of U.S. Major General David E. Twiggs in San Antonio. A Committee of Public Safety, acting on orders from the Secession Convention, demanded that Twiggs surrender all Federal military property to state officials. Ben McCulloch, a veteran of the Texas Revolution, assembled a force of adventurers, Indian fighters, and other "enraged volunteers" and stormed into San Antonio. Surprisingly, Twiggs, having resigned his command but unable to obtain instructions from Washington, surrendered all Federal troops, posts, and supplies without offering even token resistance. Ben McCulloch's brother Henry received the surrender of all Federal posts in North Texas while another Texas fire-eater named John S. "Rip" Ford assumed command of Federal installations in the southern part of the state. U.S. troops began leaving Texas almost immediately; but when President Lincoln issued a call for volunteers after the firing on Fort Sumter, Federal troops still in Texas were apprehended as prisoners of war.

Texas was far removed from most of the major battlefields of the war, but the state was confronted with the fourfold problem of providing men for military service at home and in other theaters, defending the Gulf Coast against Federal attack, stamping out internal subversion, and protecting frontier residents from Indians, bushwhackers, and *renegadoes*. Governor Francis R. Lubbock, who defeated Edward Clark in the race for the state's highest office in 1861, and Pendleton Murrah, who defeated T. J. Chambers in 1863, were chief executives who labored tirelessly in support of the "glorious cause." The Texas legislature responded by establishing a military board, which was authorized to dispose of U.S. bonds held by the state and to levy special taxes to secure revenue for the purchase of military supplies. Confederate notes and treasury warrants were given official sanction, and all able-bodied men were ordered to enroll for frontier defense, subject to being mustered into Confederate service if needed. A few Texas units, assigned to frontier defense, spent most of the war within the boundaries of the state. Others, such as Nicholas C. Gould's Twenty-Third Cavalry, patrolled the Indian Frontier of Southwest Texas until the Red River Campaign of 1864 and then, with all other available units, was shifted to Arkansas and Louisiana. Others, including the famous Frontier Regiment of the Texas Rangers, were transferred to Confederate service and fought largely east of the Mississippi. John Bell Hood's Texas Brigade – perhaps the most famous of all Texas units – fought with Robert E. Lee's Army of Northern Virginia in six of the bloodiest battles of the war, including Antietam and Gettysburg.

When the war began, the eyes of most Texans were focused on New Mexico, where John R. Baylor, commander of the Second Texas Rifles, launched one of the most ambitious Confederate campaigns of the western war. Having occupied all the Federal posts between Brownsville and El Paso, Baylor and his troops pushed into the upper Rio Grande region of New Mexico. Baylor's operations were prompted by his hope, shared by Richmond officials, that a Confederate West might be established all the way to the Pacific Ocean. On August 1, 1861, Baylor issued a proclamation forming the Confederate Territory of Arizona, which included, on paper at least, all of Arizona and New Mexico south of the thirty-fourth parallel. To help secure Confederate control of the region, Brigadier General Henry Hopkins Sibley, who had organized three regiments in San Antonio, moved into New Mexico in December 1861.

But Southern dreams of a Confederacy that extended to the Pacific were quickly shattered. Federal troops from California and Colorado poured into the upper Rio Grande Valley to oppose the westward expansion of the Confederacy. Baylor, having proclaimed himself military governor of Confederate Arizona, stationed ragtail garrisons all across the district as far west as Tucson. Small-scale but sometimes bitter fighting spotted the region until an important Confederate supply train was destroyed in the battle of Apache Canyon in New Mexico on March 26, 1862. Because it was impossible to live off the country in this desolate region, the loss of essential supplies was a disaster for the Confederates. Two days later, Confederate "manifest destiny" received its death blow in the battle of Johnson's Ranch, near Glorieta Pass in New Mexico. The Confederate troops won the field, but their desperate need for supplies forced Sibley's withdrawal. Shortly thereafter, Baylor and Sibley made the decision to evacuate New Mexico. Dreams of a Confederate port on the Pacific were thus snuffed out by the success of Federal arms and the failure of Confederate logistics. Since the fighting around Glorieta Pass was the Confederacy's final effort to expand westward, it has been called the "Gettysburg of the West." News of the collapse of Southern imperial dreams in the West caused little stir among Richmond officials, who were preparing for a tremendous battle in western Tennessee between U. S. Grant's forces and Confederate troops under the command of Albert Sidney Johnston (who coincidentally had served as secretary of war for the Republic of Texas, 1838–1840).

This bloody clash, known as the battle of Shiloh, ended in Confederate defeat and cost the life of General Johnston. Partly as a result of heavy Confederate losses in this battle, friction developed between

Texas officials and the Richmond government. These disputes were of considerable value to the North in its efforts to reduce the western Confederacy. Texas leaders, like officials in other Confederate states, were devoted to the compact theory of government and demanded that a state's right of self-determination be respected at all costs.

The first major clash took shape when the Texas legislature passed a law exempting from Confederate military service all persons serving in defense of the state. Richmond authorities refused to honor the Texas law. Confederate conscription laws, which eventually called all white men between the ages of seventeen and fifty, were hated by most Texans and were openly flouted, frequently with the blessing of state officials. The Texan disgust with Confederate conscription grew mightily, especially after Shiloh. Changes in the program effected by the Confederate Congress did little to dispel claims that it was unfair, unreasonable, and contradictory. One provision of the conscription law – commonly known by Confederates as the "twenty-nigger law" – deferred persons owning twenty or more slaves from military service. Other provisions permitted the hiring of substitutes and exempted many professional classes, such as mail carriers and college professors, whose work could hardly be classified as essential. Many prospective recruits for Confederate service either rushed to join state units serving on the frontier or sought refuge in Mexico. Neither Richmond nor officials in Austin won this dispute, and it did much to undermine the Confederate war effort.

Another dispute with Richmond involved another essential Texas resource: cotton. Richmond agents seized Texas cotton, converted it into Mexican specie or foreign bills of exchange, and then purchased vital supplies for the Confederacy. The demand for cotton in the North and in England reached an all-time high in 1863, and international cotton buyers along the Rio Grande stood ready to pay top prices for raw cotton. The Texas Military Board, created by an act of the legislature in January 1862, also impressed cotton, but planters were required to surrender only part of their crop and could sell the remainder for their own profit. Nevertheless, despised impressment teams from Richmond not only took possession of all cotton available but forced Texas planters to accept worthless Confederate notes and "cotton certificates" as full payment. By the time the Confederate fortress city of Vicksburg, Mississippi, fell in the summer of 1863, most state officials and many private citizens were aware of the growing anti-Richmond sentiment that was

spreading rapidly among the citizens of the Lone Star State. This growing isolationist impulse sprang largely from popular dissatisfaction with
Confederate conscription and "unreasonable impressment" of Texas
cotton.

The cotton shortage in the North was one reason for repeated Union
attempts to invade and conquer Texas beginning in 1862. Texas was the
Confederacy's largest cotton-producing state, as the New England textile interests were well aware. When textile manufacturers felt the pinch
of the cotton shortage and sickened at the sight of their empty spindles,
they complained to Washington that they faced ruin. Manufacturers of
cotton goods demanded that Lincoln order an immediate invasion of the
Lone Star State. They were supported by several influential New York
banking houses, vocal Texas Unionists, and at least three members of
Lincoln's cabinet. For the most part, Lincoln turned a deaf ear. Certainly
he was correct in his belief that Texas cotton was not sufficiently vital to
the U.S. war effort to justify a full-scale invasion of the Lone Star State;
but no doubt this persistent pressure, in addition to his determination to
make the Union blockade as effective as possible, accounts for his sanction of a few feeble and largely unsuccessful military thrusts against
Texas during the first two years of the war.

The Federal blockade, flimsy and inadequate in the beginning because of the dearth of vessels available for the purpose, was applied to
the Texas coast early in July 1861 and within a few months was seriously
curtailing the state's commerce. It was more than 35 percent effective by
the end of the year and rapidly becoming painful for Texas cotton merchants. Enterprising Texas businessmen soon discovered a significant
loophole in the blockade by shipping cotton through Bagdad, a sleepy
little village near the mouth of the Rio Grande on the Mexican side of
the river (see map 1). The area around Bagdad was converted into a
thriving international cotton market despite a treacherous offshore
sandbar that hampered loading operations. When Lieutenant Colonel
A. J. L. Fremantle arrived there in April 1863, he found the village itself
just "a few miserable wooden shanties," but he observed that seventy
ships were lying at anchor "outside the bar." He described the area
around Bagdad as a veritable beehive of activity with "endless bales of
cotton" stacked along the coast for "an immense distance."[2]

Galveston, the state's chief center of maritime commerce, was the first
to attract U.S. blockading vessels. The USS *South Carolina* arrived in

Texas waters in the summer of 1861, and other Federal vessels were quick to follow. By winter, blockading squadrons were patrolling the entire length of the coast from Sabine Pass to Padre Island. Early in 1862, Confederate shore installations at Galveston were bombarded, twelve commercial vessels found near Galveston Island were captured or destroyed, and foreign vessels in Galveston Bay were temporarily seized or driven away. Fearing an invasion, the Secession Convention in Austin ordered coastal fortifications strengthened. Defense works at Sabine Pass, Matagorda Island, Galveston, Aransas Pass, and Brazos Santiago were bolstered and newly organized, poorly equipped, and inexperienced artillery units assigned to various points along the coast. After the U.S. schooner *Sam Houston* moved in and engaged Galveston's shore batteries in May, small-scale but successful Federal landings took place all along the Texas coast from Sabine City to Aransas Pass. Corpus Christi was threatened by a halfhearted amphibious invasion in August, but Confederate troops were successful in repelling the invaders. Several Federal landing parties swarmed ashore near Galveston, Sabine Pass, and Indianola, but these beachheads soon were abandoned either voluntarily or under pressure from Confederate forces.

Federal troops hurled their might at the strategic ports at Sabine Pass and Galveston and enjoyed their greatest success there. After landing at Sabine Pass in September, a large Federal force destroyed coastal fortifications, captured Fort Griffin, occupied Beaumont, and demolished an important railroad bridge across Taylor Bayou. It was early the following year before constant pressure from Confederate troops forced Union troops to withdraw. In these skirmishes, Confederate forces inflicted only light casualties on the enemy, but they capped their victory by capturing two Union vessels that were standing guard in the narrows of the pass below Fort Griffin.

The Confederate recapture of Galveston just a few weeks earlier was even more impressive. Early in October 1862, a Union fleet, including the famous gunboat *Harriet Lane,* sailed into Galveston Harbor and held it until the city could be occupied by Union troops two months later. Then, on New Year's Eve, Major General John B. "Prince John" Magruder, who had replaced Paul O. Hébert as the Confederate commander of Texas, launched a joint land and sea operation against the Federals which has been called "the wildest New Year's Eve party that Galveston has ever had." Magruder's troops captured the *Harriet Lane* and another Federal vessel, took six hundred prisoners, and reestablished Confederate control over the city.

After the last Federal troops were driven from Sabine Pass and Galveston, the entire Texas coast was once again under Confederate control. General Magruder took precautions to keep it that way. Coastal fortifications were again strengthened and the number and quality of Confederate units assigned to coastal defense increased. During the months that followed, there were several naval encounters off the coast, occasional bombardments of Confederate shore installations, and periodic clashes between blockade runners and blockading vessels, but no further attempts were made to invade Texas until after the fall of Vicksburg.

When Union forces captured Vicksburg and secured control of the Mississippi River in the summer of 1863, discerning Texans realized that the sun of the Confederacy was beginning to set. News of Lee's defeat at Gettysburg arrived in Texas about the same time as news of the fall of Vicksburg. This double disaster gave rise to a hopelessness that many Texans felt but refused to admit. The entire length of the Mississippi was patrolled by Union gunboats, isolating Texas and the other states of the Confederate Trans-Mississippi from the rest of the Confederacy. Additional isolation was imposed by the increasing effectiveness of the Union blockade. Confederate General E. Kirby Smith, commander of the Trans-Mississippi Department, found himself virtually a dictator over Confederate territory cut off from the rest of the world. General Smith called a conference of Trans-Mississippi governors in Marshall, Texas. While it was in session, the U.S. War Department ordered General Nathaniel P. Banks, commanding in Louisiana, to begin a new series of amphibious assaults against Texas. Once again, the North's shortage of cotton contributed to this order. Perhaps more important, Lincoln had become convinced that there was a distinct possibility that E. Kirby Smith might reach some understanding with a French puppet government that had been established in Mexico City in violation of the Monroe Doctrine.

Accordingly, on September 7, 1863, a Federal fleet once again approached Sabine Pass. Southern defenses were considered weak there, and if naval vessels were able to silence shore batteries, the Federals could effect landings, strike inland to occupy Beaumont again, and then capture the Texas and New Orleans Railroad, which connected with

Houston. Fort Griffin was manned by Company F of the First Texas Heavy Artillery, commanded by Captain F. H. Odlum. Since Odlum was not present, Lieutenant Dick Dowling, the second in command, ordered his men to hold their fire while the Federals completed their bombardment of coastal fortifications. The next day, as the Union flotilla moved into the narrows preparing to land troops, Dowling ordered his six largely undamaged artillery pieces to open fire. Within forty-five minutes, the Confederates sank two gunboats, damaged another, and drove away the transports containing an invasion force of more than five thousand troops. The Confederates suffered no casualties, and they claimed that their rapid fire had almost melted the barrels of their cannon. Dowling and his men, including Irish stevedores recruited in Houston and Galveston, took 350 prisoners, killed almost 100 men, and captured large quantities of weapons and supplies. Kirby Smith considered the battle of Sabine Pass little more than a Federal feint, but official U.S. records reveal that this attack was a major military operation aimed at occupying the Lone Star State.[3]

In October, Banks made another attempt to capture Sabine Pass by moving up the Bayou Teche across southern Louisiana, but Magruder and his Texans were more than ready for him. The Sabine Pass–Beaumont region was overflowing with Confederate artillery, infantry, and cavalry, waiting to engage Banks's forces. Using black labor from surrounding plantations, Magruder erected elaborate fortifications, even tearing up the track of the Texas and New Orleans Railroad to secure building materials. In December, as an added precaution in the event Banks should break through the Sabine Pass–Beaumont defenses, Magruder ordered the San Antonio and Mexican Gulf Railroad destroyed, all the line's cars wrecked, and two steam engines dismantled and rendered unfit for service. Faced with the possibility of another defeat, or at best an expensive victory that could cost him the Republican presidential nomination he hoped to receive the following summer, Banks gave the order to withdraw to New Orleans after only light skirmishes with Confederate cavalry.

Following the abortive Bayou Teche offensive, the Federals shifted their attention to the southern tip of Texas. A successful amphibious landing was made at Brazos Santiago on November 2, 1863, and the Santiago bar became a base of operations for almost five thousand Federal troops. General Hamilton P. Bee, Confederate commander in

Brownsville, had only about twelve hundred troops to try to repel the invaders. Forced to withdraw, Bee adopted a "scorched earth" policy, left Brownsville in flames, and retreated upriver toward Rio Grande City. Federal forces entered the city four days later and occupied the smoldering ruins of Fort Brown. Soon thereafter, other Union forces effected successful landings farther up the coast at Pass Cavallo, Indianola, Port Lavaca, and Corpus Christi. Within a few months, the Federals planted almost eight thousand troops on Texas soil. Banks's forces were scattered along the Rio Grande from Brownsville to Rio Grande City and along the southeastern coast, extending from Brazos Santiago to the mouth of the Colorado River. Except for Sabine Pass and Galveston, the Union controlled all major ports along the length of the Texas coast. The Confederate cotton trade through Brownsville was halted, Federal control of the lower Rio Grande assured, and the possibility of French cooperation with E. Kirby Smith diminished. Confederate cotton had to be shipped through Laredo, 235 miles upriver from Brownsville, or through Eagle Pass, 90 miles still farther upstream. The only Confederate hope of halting the Federal march up the Rio Grande rested on the narrow shoulders of Colonel John Salmon "Rip" Ford and his four hundred tired, unpaid, and undisciplined troops, who faced the enemy totally without logistical support. In March 1864, news arrived in Austin that a small Federal force was at the gates of Laredo and the fall of this border hamlet was expected at any moment. Union troops occupied Laredo five days later.

The spring of 1864, the high tide of Federal success in the halfhearted campaign to conquer Texas, was for Texans the beginning of a period of extreme suffering that was to last until the end of the war. The news from all fronts was bad. General Ulysses S. Grant had almost cleared Tennessee of Confederate resistance, and General William T. Sherman had marched across the entire state of Mississippi almost unopposed. In addition, there were other problems of immediate concern to Texans on the home front: Banks had just launched another massive thrust toward Texas by ascending the Red River through Louisiana, and Federal blockading squadrons had all but sealed off the Texas Gulf Coast. Texas fighting men were forced to leave their almost destitute families to rush into Louisiana to meet the most recent threat.

The shortage of essential commodities on the home front as a result of the blockade reached critical proportions. Many items such as paper, tea, coffee, and dinnerware were not available at any price. The scarcity of weapons, tools, horses, mules, articles of clothing, and most foods contributed further to the fears, wretchedness, and discomfort of Texas residents. The shortage of salt in some localities prompted enterprising Texans to dig up the earthen floors of their smokehouses to leach the soil for saline drippings. Hard money had all but disappeared except along the upper Rio Grande. Confederate money was almost without value, and it appeared only a matter of time before high taxes coupled with runaway inflation would destroy the state's economy. One woman paid ninety dollars in Confederate currency for a yard and a half of denim. Shoes, when available, cost thirty dollars a pair. Watermelons sold for five dollars each. Medical supplies, perhaps the most pressing need, were impossible to obtain in most localities. Commodities readily available before the war – purgatives, opium, whiskey, turpentine, quinine, and calomel – had disappeared by the spring of 1864. Malnutrition, diarrhea, dysentery, virulent erysipelas, and various digestive disorders were widespread. Suffering and death from these and other diseases became commonplace. Cholera broke out in San Antonio, smallpox was reported in several counties in East Texas, and a yellow fever epidemic, common along the coast, struck Galveston during the summer. These home-front conditions contributed greatly to the large-scale desertion of Texas soldiers during the last two years of the war.

When Banks launched his Red River campaign in Louisiana, another serious deficiency became apparent to residents of Texas – the critical shortage of manpower for military service. All available troops, not essential for holding the enemy at bay in Texas, were ordered to Arkansas and Louisiana. Texas African Americans were pressed into military service to build barricades and repair railroads and highways, but they were not trusted with firearms and therefore never served as soldiers, except occasionally and ineffectively during the final days of the war. Governor Murrah transferred all troops detailed to noncombatant jobs to combat duty and initiated an impressment program which forced old men, beardless boys, bushwhackers, deserters, and all types of shirkers into military service. A factor of importance, although scarcely noticed by those who feared inadequate protection at home, was the steady reduction in the number of Federal troops in the state. Many Federal units, fighting in Texas or assigned to garrison duty in occupied regions of the state, were transferred to Berwick Bay in Louisiana to participate in

Banks's "big push" up the Red River. The size and effectiveness of Confederate units remaining in the state were also reduced, and it was largely the deterioration of Federal military strength that made subsequent Confederate victories along the lower Rio Grande possible.

The Red River campaign was the largest, most formidable military assault directed against the Confederate Trans-Mississippi Department. Its success might well have terminated all Confederate resistance west of the Mississippi River. The operation, which lasted from March 12 to May 20, has been called one of the most costly and destructive campaigns of the war. Union losses in killed, wounded, and missing were probably in excess of eight thousand, if losses in both Arkansas and Louisiana are included. Confederate losses during the same period were certainly in excess of six thousand. Although small when compared with major campaigns east of the river, the success of Confederate arms in the Red River campaign bolstered the morale of Trans-Mississippi residents, providing a measure of hope where otherwise there was none.

Working closely with Henry W. Halleck, Lincoln's small-minded general in chief, Banks began planning the campaign early in 1864. General William T. Sherman, commanding a Federal army in Mississippi, agreed with Banks that the campaign was worthwhile, but both he and U. S. Grant opposed using Federal troops needed east of the Mississippi. Eventually, Sherman agreed to furnish Banks with ten thousand men, but he stipulated that these troops were not to be taken beyond Shreveport and must be returned to his department no later than April 15. On March 12, General Banks, in command of some twenty-seven thousand men and a fleet of gunboats, moved up the Red River hoping to effect a merger with other Federal forces entering Louisiana from Missouri and Arkansas. It was estimated that a grand total of thirty-five thousand infantry and about eight thousand cavalry, supported by a powerful flotilla of gunboats, took part in the invasion.

A frantic Kirby Smith made appeals for manpower and dispatched all available units to intercept the Federal invaders. He instructed General Richard Taylor, Confederate commander in western Louisiana, and General Sterling Price, Confederate commander in Arkansas, to prepare for a major, last-ditch battle, which he expected somewhere in the vicinity of Shreveport. During the weeks that followed, General Price, in command of several thousand Confederate cavalry, stopped the Federal columns crossing Arkansas near Camden, and General Taylor's army, composed of approximately eleven thousand Confederate troops, all but routed Banks's forces at Mansfield, Louisiana, early in April.

General Banks was hampered in his operations by the time limit imposed by Sherman and by lack of coordination between Federal forces in Arkansas and Louisiana, but he was defeated by tenacious opposition, poor communications, bad weather, and plunging water levels in the Red River brought about by the absence of spring rains. Plagued by logistical problems, shallows in the river, and a rash of sniping by local inhabitants, Banks's mighty invasion, intended to impress party leaders in the North, bogged down and became a hopeless nightmare. Actually, his commanders were successful in regrouping their forces after the near rout at Mansfield and fought to a draw at Pleasant Hill on April 9, but Banks decided that evening to abandon the operation and return to New Orleans. Many of the horrors of his retreat downriver are recorded in the letters of Union soldiers who wrote home about water moccasins, mosquitoes, quicksand, wreckage in the river, and decomposing bodies either "floating downstream" or lodged "near the river bank" with "buzzards picking at them." There is no doubt that the "crooked, narrow, and turbid" river became a place of terror for retreating Federals. As one fleeing soldier observed, the "high banks furnished the most favorable positions for artillery and . . . the deadly sharpshooter."[4]

There was a brighter and sometimes humorous side to this otherwise tragic and ugly campaign. In spite of overwhelming hardships, many Texas soldiers took time for jokes and merriment. On one occasion, Confederate forces captured a regiment of New York Zouaves, dressed in their baggy red-flannel, bloomerlike pantaloons. When the captives were marched into the Confederate encampment, the Texas troops gasped in mock disbelief. The Texans threw down their weapons and swore that they would quit and go home rather than fight women. Evidently some of the Zouaves failed to realize that the Texas boys were jesting, for they earnestly insisted that they were men and not women.

Meanwhile, Colonel Ford, facing Federal troops considerably diminished in number on the Rio Grande, began to enjoy considerable success in his quest to drive the enemy from Texas soil. The drastic reduction in troop strength and the desolate nature of the country combined to convince Federal garrisons occupying dirty adobe hamlets that their presence was of little value to anyone. Ford noted that the Federals displayed a welcome disinclination to give their lives fighting for these remote river settlements. Once the Federal retreat down the Rio Grande began, it escalated rapidly. After a small skirmish, Ford's ragamuffin army reoccupied Laredo on April 15, just six days after Banks gave his order to begin the Red River withdrawal almost a thousand miles to the northeast. During the weeks that followed, Ford and his cavalry nipped at the heels of the retreating Federals. The Confederates seized a handful of little mud hut settlements along the Rio Grande, including Los Angeles, Los Ojuelos, and Comitos north of Rio Grande City. Then for ten days following the capture of Comitos, torrential rains fell, ending an extended drought but converting the Rio Grande Valley into a steaming hell. Ford's Texans were sullen and mutinous, for they lived in the brush without shelter, and they were tired, hungry, sick, and desperately in need of supplies. A few days later, when they stormed into Rio Grande City, they found the town deserted. Ford's soldiers were sorely disappointed that the retreating Federals left nothing behind that might be of use to them. The shortage of food for his men and forage for his animals forced Ford to take drastic and illegal measures. He dispatched a raiding party across the river, where Mexican cotton was seized, converted into Mexican coin, and used to purchase essential supplies. Few Civil War commanders solved their logistical problems with more daring and reckless abandon.

As the Texas colonel pushed downriver toward Brownsville, his little army increased in size. Each week, bands of ragged, hungry Texans and Mexicans rode into his encampments. Many were border ruffians and Mexican *renegadoes* willing to fight as long as they were winning and in preference to starving or trying to live off the desolate country. Some were deserters from garrisons around San Antonio; others were refugees from the political dislocations in Mexico. By the end of May 1864, Ford had almost a thousand tough, dirty, unruly, and surly troops riding under his banner. Suffering from recurring malaria, Ford often found it difficult to stay in the saddle, but somehow he managed to continue in pursuit of his rapidly retreating enemy.

On June 21, Ford's cavalry fought an engagement at Las Rucias ranch house, forcing the Federals to withdraw, capturing large quantities of supplies, and opening the road to Brownsville. Soon the Confederates were skirmishing north of Fort Brown, with the city of Brownsville the prize for the victor. Once again, the Union forces withdrew after only token resistance, and Ford's devil-may-care Texans entered the city and occupied the partially burned-out fort. During the months that followed, the Federals continued their retreat under pressure from the Confederates and temporarily abandoned the Texas mainland, entrenching themselves on Brazos Island.

At this point, both sides may have expected officials in Washington and Richmond to arrange a peace settlement, for fighting almost ceased in South Texas. The Federals, ensconced behind their fortifications on Brazos Island, and the Confederates, confident in their control of the mainland, measured one another carefully. For more than six months both sides waited, with only an occasional skirmish to break the monotony. Desertion again became a major problem among the Confederates as news filtered in of Lincoln's reelection, Sherman's march through Georgia, and Grant's siege of Richmond. Those who remained watched and waited and sought to keep informed about battles elsewhere. There was some intrigue between the Federals on Brazos Island and Mexican officials in Matamoros during the last months of 1864, and there was minor skirmishing between Ford's boys and Union patrols south of Brownsville, but there was little change in the stalemate until the spring of 1865. By that time wholesale desertion had greatly weakened Confederate strength on the mainland, and Federal patrols were ranging throughout South Texas as far north as San Antonio.

All former Confederate able-bodied soldiers in Texas who had been captured and who had been released after they signed paroles promising never to bear arms against the United States were declared exchanged by Texas officials and ordered to report to their units. For the most part, the people of Texas, suffering from shortages of everything and facing starvation and disease, had lost their will to fight. Even though Governor Pendleton Murrah promised deserters that they would be granted full pardon if they returned to their units, the military strength of the state continued to ebb. During the late spring, a small Federal invasion force in Louisiana again began moving up the Red River toward Texas, and several thousand Federal reinforcements landed on Brazos Island at the mouth of the Rio Grande. Only a few small and depleted Confederate units could be mustered to face these new threats to the state. Although most Texans were unaware of it, Lee's badly mauled Army of Northern Virginia had been driven out of its Petersburg fortifications and was slowly being encircled by U. S. Grant's forces near Appomattox in Virginia.

The Federals on Brazos Island launched a spring offensive during the last weeks in March, swarmed onto the Texas mainland once again, and engaged isolated pockets of Ford's Texans scattered across the South Texas wasteland. What at first was thought to be a massive invasion slowly became a series of largely impotent thrusts at Confederate installations. Both sides were sick of fighting in this God-forsaken country, and the consequences of victory seemed almost as repugnant as the consequences of defeat. It must have occurred to Federal officers that victory would require them to move farther into the desolate interior, accomplishing little except to expose Union supply lines to additional harassment from Ford's cavalry. Perhaps they concluded that remaining near their base of supply was preferable to facing additional hardships and dangers by stretching their supply lines. At any rate, Ford and his undermanned units at Fort Brown hurled repeated attacks against the invaders and once again enjoyed a measure of success. Scattered skirmishes of little significance occurred during the first weeks of April, and then, forty-nine months after the war began at Fort Sumter, the final armed encounter of the conflict was fought in Texas. Ironically, it was a Confederate victory. Ford and his Texans engaged a Federal force on the afternoon of May 13, 1865, at Palmito ranch house, not far from Brownsville. Many of the Federal troops were forced to return to their Brazos Island refuge. After the smoke of combat had cleared, Ford learned from captured Union soldiers that Lee had surrendered almost five weeks earlier.

The news of Lee's capitulation, followed by news of the surrender of Confederate generals Joseph E. Johnston in North Carolina and Richard Taylor in Alabama, spread across the Lone Star State slowly. Texans were glad the war was over, but the humiliation of defeat and anticipation of an uncertain future under Yankee rule filled them with apprehension. Governor Murrah, Kirby Smith, and John Magruder urged the people of the Trans-Mississippi to continue fighting until aid could be secured from England or France, but the Federal war of attrition had taken its toll, and fighting men in Texas were largely unable or unwilling to continue the hopeless struggle. All military units were pitifully understrength and woefully ill-equipped, and Confederate and state forces in Texas numbered about fifteen thousand men. About three thousand were around Galveston and Houston while the rest were in scattered garrisons in Corpus Christi, Hempstead, Sabine Pass, Marshall, Austin,

San Antonio, and Brownsville. About this time a conference of Trans-Mississippi governors convened in Marshall, where E. Kirby Smith rejected an invitation to surrender his department on the same terms that Lee had accepted from Grant. Smith and other Confederate leaders hoped to secure a guarantee of immunity for themselves and others in the Trans-Mississippi who had borne arms against the Union, but they soon learned that they had nothing with which to bargain. The same leaders who had argued so strenuously that secession was inherent in the very nature of the U.S. Constitution now voiced opinions on the "rights of the states in the Union." Some die-hard states' righters demanded that state conventions "settle all questions" concerning each state's proper relationship within the Union. This could be accomplished quickly, they insisted, with as little interference as possible from Washington. This was essentially the demand made by the Marshall convention, but it was sternly rejected by U.S. General John Pope.[5]

By the end of May, General Smith had accepted the bitter fact that any attempt to continue fighting in the Trans-Mississippi would be futile. Having already made arrangements for a formal surrender of his department while in New Orleans, he signed terms of capitulation on board the U.S. warship *Fort Jackson* in Galveston Harbor on June 2. Military personnel were to be paroled to return to their homes, and Confederate property was to be surrendered to Federal authorities. The final flame of Confederate authority west of the Mississippi flickered out as General Smith attached his name to the document.

NOTES

1. Ernest Wallace, *Texas in Turmoil* (Austin: Steck-Vaughn, 1965), pp. 60–63; Dudley G. Wooten, ed., *A Comprehensive History of Texas, 1685–1898*, 2 vols. (Dallas: William G. Scarff, 1898), 2:104–106; and Ernest W. Winkler, ed., *Journal of the Secession Convention of Texas, 1861* (Austin: Austin Printing Co., 1912).

2. A.J.L. Fremantle, *Three Months in the Southern States: April–June 1863* (New York: John Bradburn, 1864; reprint, Lincoln: University of Nebraska Press, 1991), p. 9.

3. U.S. War Department, *The War of the Rebellion: A Compilation of the Official Records of the Union and Confederate Armies*, 130 vols. (Washington, D.C.: U.S. Government Printing Office, 1880–1901), Ser. I, vol. 26, pt. 1, pp. 287–297, 673, and 695–697.

4. S. C. Jones, *Reminiscences of the Twenty-Second Iowa Volunteer Infantry: Giving Its Organization, Marches, Skirmishes, Battles, and Sieges as Taken from the Diary of Lieutenant S. C. Jones of Company A* (Iowa City, 1907), p. 68, microfiche copy in Abilene Christian University Library; see also A. H. Plummer, *Confederate Victory at Mansfield* (Mansfield: United Daughters of the Confederacy, 1969), pp. 37–38.

5. Wallace, *Texas in Turmoil,* pp. 139–140.

Recollections of a North Texas Boyhood

David Carey Nance was only nine years old when he came to Texas in 1852 to help work a farm his father had purchased on the blackland prairies southwest of Dallas. In the following excerpt from his unpublished recollections, which he wrote in about 1924, he describes his life and labor in early Texas and the dangers of living on the periphery of civilization. Frontier living was hard, and because his father was in poor health and he was the oldest son, young Nance had to assume responsibilities and perform tasks that were challenging and difficult even for adults. His recollections provide insights into pioneer farm life, a boy's personal interests and thoughts, and the meager educational opportunities available at this time in North Texas. There were few opportunities for recreation, and the occasional chance to attend a "pay" school was a welcome change from the demanding routines of farm life. David Nance, however, sought an education with an eagerness that belies his years. He spent what little spare time he had teaching himself to read and write. He constructed wooden water buckets, churns, washtubs, and other essential household items from red cedar cut from the hills overlooking the blackland prairies and used the money from the sale of these items to pay itinerant teachers for a few days of precious instruction during the summer months. These descriptions make this brief excerpt rewarding reading for students of Texas history; the interest of many readers may be enhanced when they learn that David Nance was the grandfather of Don Morris, the first chancellor of Abilene Christian University.

Source: David Nance, "Theological Treatise with Autobiographical Sketch" (n.d.), in Jimmy Lawson's private collection of the David Carey Nance papers. Used by permission.

I was born in Cass County, Illinois on February 2, 1843 . . . and in 1852 came with my father to Dallas County, Texas, then a wild waste. Indians and Buffalos were plentiful at that time about Ft. Worth, while Bear, Panther, Wildcats, Foxes and so on, were numerous here on the old home in Texas which till now has been my home ever since. Here on the John Kiser Survey my father bought the land in December 1852, but did not obtain written title for some years afterward.

Father did not have good health; and I, being the eldest child then 9 years of age, was his only helper. But a home had to be built, for there were none for rent.

Here we plowed up the heavy sod, made and hauled the Red Cedar rails and fenced the farm with great ox teams. We planted and cultivated the crops when the soil was dry, and plowed the sod when it rained, and hauled the rails and fenced it in the winter.

Of course one of my tender years could not help much, but I did what I could, and was always busy. In the winter of 1853–4 when I was ten past, my daily morning task was to shuck and shell a large water bucket full of corn, and feed the sheep. This I did day by day with my own bare little hands, and then turn out the flock, and with dog, and my little lunch I took the flock out on the open prairie to graze and kept them till time to bring them home in the evening. This we had to do to save the sheep from the wolves; and even then they would kill a few. Thus we cared for the sheep and cattle, grew the crops, and built the home, adding a few acres year by year, till the great civil war came in 1861.

But for all these hardships, including fathers ill health, he was a great reader, and I, a studious boy. But as with every one else in those days, it was work, work, all the time, and few schools. Sometimes we would have a summer school of two or three months, and even then these were a grand treat to me; for of necessity they were rudimentary, and I loved books. I went to these schools, and used my oportunities well. They were "pay schools," and most every one was poor. And during odd days from the farm work, when there was no school, I learned the coopers art; and built cedar churns, washtubs, and water buckets, and sold them to our neighbors. This gave me a few dollars of my own, and with these dollars I bought books, and borrowed others, and read them. Father was good to me, and encouraged me all he could.

And thus I kept abreast of my neighbor boys in my few days at school till the war came. But I never read fiction. I read good books or none, even then and the Bible was one I loved and read.

But like all boys in Early life, I loved adventure, so that when the first call came for volunteer troops I was crazy to go yes, Crazy, for that is the only way to describe a boys sentiment when he is anxious to go to war. He is crazy, and if he goes he will see it so himself if he lives that long.

Well, I went, and learned my lesson, and I learned it well; so that no second trial was needed. In September 1861, I enlisted in what was later known as the 12th Texas Cavalry under Colonel W. H. Parsons of Waco, all young men of about my age.

[That David Nance survived the war at all is nothing short of phenomenal. As a member of Parsons's Regiment fighting in Arkansas in the summer of 1862, he was seriously wounded three times in the battle of Cache River in Woodruff County. The next year, while working in a gunpowder manufacturing plant near Waxahachie, Texas, he miraculously survived an explosion and fire that destroyed the plant and killed two men working with him. Then during General Nathaniel Banks's Red River invasion of the Confederate Trans-Mississippi Department in 1864, Nance received two more serious wounds while fighting with his unit in Louisiana. Nevertheless, Nance lived a long and useful life and died peacefully at his farm in Dallas County in the summer of 1925.]

1856–1857

San Antonio before the War

A Journey Through Texas, the second volume in Frederick Law Olmsted's famous trilogy describing his tours of the antebellum South, was actually written from his brother's field notes. Olmsted (1822–1903) was a successful journalist, a talented artist, an expert in horticulture, an imaginative engineer, a brilliant and stimulating man of letters, and a dedicated conservationist and naturalist. He spent a lifetime fighting the forces of decay, pollution, blight, and destruction in an effort to preserve such natural havens as Central Park, Prospect Park, Yosemite, and other "thriving manifestos of nature." Frederick Law Olmsted was, in effect, the father of urban planning in the United States. He possessed a tremendous store of talent, a broad variety of interests, and a probing curiosity.

He was fascinated by everything he saw, and his descriptions are alive with the excitement of his detailed observations. The excerpt below taken from his *Journey Through Texas*, focuses on his and his brother's visit to San Antonio in 1857. It is the best description of antebellum San Antonio extant.

Source: Frederick Law Olmsted, *A Journey Through Texas* (New York: Dix, Edwards, and Company, 1857), pp. 147–160.

We had hardly . . . [begun our journey] when one of our [German] table companions [from New Braunfels] came up on the road behind us, also on his way to San Antonio. He joined us, by our invitation, and though we found some difficulty in mutual comprehension, added much to our pleasure and information.

The distance to San Antonio, by the shortest road, is about thirty miles. The old road follows up a creek bottom, and houses, sheltered by live-oaks, stand thick along it, each in the centre of a little farm, having a broad open range of pasture before it. We left these and the hills beyond them, to the right, and went in a straight course out upon the open prairies. The grass had, in many places, been recently burned, giving the country a desolated surface of dead black monotony.

The trees were live-oaks and even these were rare. The groundswells were long, and so equal in height and similar in form, as to bring to mind a tedious sea voyage, where you go plodding on, slow hour after slow hour, without rising a single object to attract the eye.

At noon we crossed the Cibolo (pronounced by Texans "Sewilla"), a creek which has the freak of here and there disappearing in its course for miles, leaving its bed dry, except during freshlets. Here were several settlements, almost the only ones on the day's route. Not very far away, however, are, in several places, Germans, who have built neat stone houses out upon the prairie away from any running water, depending entirely upon wells.

Seven miles from San Antonio we passed the Salado, another small creek, and shortly after, rising a hill, we saw the domes and white cluster dwellings of San Antonio below us. We stopped and gazed long on the sunny scene.

The city is closely-built and prominent, and lies basking on the edge of a vast plain, through which the river winds slowly off beyond where the eye can reach. To the east are gentle slopes toward it; to the north a long gradual sweep upward to the mountain country, which comes down within five or six miles; to the south and west, the open prairies, extending almost level to the coast, a hundred and fifty miles away.

There is little wood to be seen in this broad landscape. Along the course of the river a thin edging appears especially around the head of the stream, a short ride above the city. Elsewhere, there is only limitless grass and thorny bushes.

These last, making *chapparal,* we saw as we went further on, for the first time. A few specimens of *mesquit* (algarobbia glandulosa) had been pointed out to us; but here the ground shortly became thickly covered with it. This shrub forms one of the prominent features of Texas, west of San Antonio. It is a short thin tree of the locust tribe, whose branches are thick set with thorns, and bears, except in this respect, a close resemblance to a straggling, neglected peach-tree. Mixed with other shrubs of a like prickly nature, as an undergrowth, it frequently forms, over acres together, an impenetrable mass. When the tree is old, its trunk and roots make an excellent fire-wood; but for other purposes it is almost useless, owing to its bent and tortuous fibre. A great value is said to lie in its gum, which, if properly secured, has been pronounced equal to gum-arabic in utility.

By a wall of these thorns the road is soon closed in. Almost all the roads of entrance are thus lined, and so the city bristles like the porcupine, with a natural defense. Reaching the level, we shortly came upon the first house, which had pushed out and conquered a bit of the chapparal. Its neighbor was opposite, and soon the street closed in.

The singular composite character of the town is palpable at the entrance. For five minutes the houses were evidently German, of fresh square-cut blocks of creamy-white limestone, mostly of a single story and humble proportions, but neat, and thoroughly roofed and finished. Some were furnished with the luxuries of little bow-windows, balconies, or galleries.

From these we enter the square of the Alamo. This is all Mexican. Windowless cabins of stakes, plastered with mud and roofed with rivergrass, or "tula"; or low, windowless, but better thatched houses of adobe (gray, unburnt bricks), with groups of brown idlers lounging at their doors.

The principal part of the town lies within a sweep of the river upon the other side. We descend to the bridge, which is close down upon the water, as the river, owing to its peculiar source, never varies in height or temperature. We irresistibly stop to examine it, we are so struck with its beauty. It is of a rich blue and pure crystal, flowing rapidly but noiselessly over pebbles and between reedy banks. One could lean for hours over the bridge-rail.

From the bridge we enter Commerce street, the narrow principal thoroughfare, and here are American houses, and the triple nationalities break out into the most amusing display, till we reach the main plaza. The sauntering Mexicans prevail on the pavements, but the bearded Germans and the sallow Yankees furnish their proportion. The signs are German by all odds, and perhaps the houses, trim-built, with pink window-blinds. The American dwellings stand back, with galleries and jalousies and a garden picket-fence against the walk, or rise, next door, in three-story brick to respectable city fronts. The Mexican buildings are stronger than those we saw before but still of all sorts, and now put to all sorts of new uses. They are all low, of adobe or stone, washed blue and yellow, with flat roofs close down upon their single story. Windows have been knocked in their blank walls, letting the sun into their dismal vaults, and most of them are stored with dry goods and groceries, which overflow around the door. Around the plaza are American hotels, and new glass-fronted stores, alternating with sturdy battlemented Spanish walls, and [these] confronted by the dirty, grim, old stuccoed stone cathedral, whose cracked bell is now clunking for vespers in a tone that bids us no welcome, as more of the intruding race who have caused all this progress on which its traditions, like its imperturbable dome, frown down.

SAN ANTONIO

We have no city except perhaps New Orleans that can vie, in point of the picturesque interest that attaches to odd and antiquated foreignness, with San Antonio. Its jumble of races, costumes, languages and buildings; its religious ruins, holding to an antiquity for us indistinct enough to breed an unaccustomed solemnity; its remote, isolated, outposted situation, and the vague conviction that it is the first of a new class of conquered cities into whose decaying streets our rattling life is to be infused, combine with the heroic touches in its history to enliven and satisfy your traveler's curiosity.

Not suspecting the leisure we were to have to examine it at our ease, we set out to receive its impressions while we had the opportunity.

After drawing, at the Post-office window, our personal share of the dear income of happiness divided by that department, we strolled, by moonlight, about the streets. They were laid out with tolerable regularity, parallel with the sides of the main plaza, and are pretty distinctly shared among the nations that use them. On the plaza and the busiest streets, a surprising number of old Mexican buildings are converted, by trowel, paintbrush, and gaudy carpentry, into drinking-places, always labeled "Exchange," and conducted on the New Orleans model. About these loitered a set of customers, sometimes rough, sometimes affecting an "exquisite" dress, by no means attracting to a nearer acquaintance with themselves or their haunts. Here and there was a restaurant of a quieter look, where the traditions of Paris are preserved under difficulties by the exiled Gaul.

The doors of the cabins of the real natives stood open wide, if indeed they exist at all, and many were the family pictures of jollity or sleepy comfort they displayed to us as we sauntered curious about. The favorite dress appeared to be dishabille, and a free-and-easy, loloppy sort of life generally seemed to have been adopted as possessing, on the whole, the greatest advantages for a reasonable being. The larger part of each family appeared to be made up of black-eyed, olive girls, full of animation of tongue and glance, but sunk in a soft embonpoint, which added a somewhat extreme goodnature to their charms. Their dresses seemed lazily reluctant to cover their plump persons, and their attitudes were always expressive of the influences of a Southern sun upon national manners. The matrons, dark and wrinkled, formed a strong contrast to their daughters, though, here and there, a fine cast of feature and a figure erect with dignity, attracted the eye. The men lounged in roundabouts and cigarites, as was to be expected, and in fact the whole picture lacked nothing that is Mexican.

Daylight walks about the town yielded little more to curiosity. The contrast of nationalities remained the chief interest. The local business is considerable, but carried on without subdivision of occupation. Each of a dozen stores offers all the articles you may ask for. A druggest or two, a saddler or two, a watchmaker and a gunsmith ply almost the only distinct trades. The country supplied from this centre is extensive but very thinly settled. The capital owner here is quite large. The principal accumulations date from the Mexican war, when no small part of the many millions expended by government were disbursed here in payment to contractors. Some prime cuts were secured by residents, and no small portion of the lesser pickings remained in their hands. Since then the town has been well-to-do, and consequently accumulates a greater population than its position in other respects would justify.

The traffic, open and illicit, across the frontier with interior Mexico, has some importance and returns some bulky bags of silver. All the principal merchants have their agencies on the Rio Grande, and throw in goods and haul out dollars as opportunity serves. The transportation of their goods forms the principal support of the Mexican population. It is this trade, probably, which accounts for the large stocks which are kept, and the large transactions that result, beyond the strength of most similar towns.

All goods are brought from Matagorda Bay, a distance of 150 miles, by ox-teams, moving with prodigious slowness and irregularity. In a favorable season, the freight-price is one-and-a-quarter cents per lb., from Lavacca. Prices are extremely high, and subject to great variations, depending upon the actual supply and the state of the roads.

Cash is sometimes extremely scarce in the town. The Mexican dollars are sent forward to a good market. Government brings its army-stores direct from the coast. But some hay, corn, and other supplies are contracted for in the region, and from this source, and from the leavings of casual travelers and new emigrants, the hard money for circulation is derived. Investments at present are mostly in lands. There are no home-exports of the least account. Pecan-nuts, and a little course wool, are almost the only items of the catalogue. The wealth and steady growth of the town depend almost entirely upon the rapid settlement of the adjacent country.

A scanty congregation attends the services of the battered old cathedral. The Protestant church attendance can almost be counted upon the fingers. Sunday is pretty rigidly devoted to rest, though most of the stores are open to all practical purposes, and the exchanges keep them up a brisk distribution of stimulants. The Germans and Mexicans have their dances. The American[s] resort to fast horses for their principal recreation.

We noticed, upon a ruined wall, the remains of a placard, which illustrates at the same time a Yankee shrewdness in devoting a day to grief, without actual loss of time, and the social manners of the people:

"RESOLUTIONS ON THE DEATH OF
THE HON. DANIEL WEBSTER."

"Be it resolved by the Board of Aldermen of the city of San Antonio, in Common Council assembled, that, by the death of the late Daniel Webster, the people are plunged in mourning, and in testimonial of our grief, we sincerely join with other cities and towns of our country in requesting a suspension of labor, and the closing of all places of business, on Sunday, *the 10th inst.,* from 10 o'clock A.M. to 4 o'clock P.M., and that all flags in the city be displayed at half-mast, and minute guns fired through the day."

The town of San Antonio was founded in 1730 by a colony of twelve families of pure Spanish blood, from the Canary islands. The names of the settlers are perpetuated to this day by existing families which have descended from each, such as Garcia, Flores, Navarro, Garza, Yturri, Rodriquez. The original mission and fort of San Antonio de Valero dates from 1715, when Spain established her occupancy of Texas.

THE MISSIONS

Not far from the city, along the river, are these celebrated religious establishments. They are of a similar character to the many scattered here and there over the plains of Northern Mexico and California, and bear a solid testimony to the strangely patient courage and zeal of the old Spanish fathers. They pushed off alone into the heart of a savage and unknown country, converted the cruel brutes that occupied it, not only to nominal Christianity but to actual hard labor, and persuaded and compelled them to construct these ponderous but rudely splendid edifices, serving, at that time, for the glory of the faith, and for the defense of the faithful. . . .

The Alamo was one of the earliest of these establishments. It is now within the town, and in extent, probably, a mere wreck of its former grandeur. It consists of a few irregular stuccoed buildings huddled against the old church, in a large court surrounded by a rude wall; the whole used as an arsenal by the U.S. Quartermaster. The churchdoor opens on the square and is meagerly decorated by stucco mouldings, all hacked and battered in the battles it has seen. Since the heroic defense of Travis and his handful of men in '36, it has been a monument not so much to faith as to courage.

The Mission of Concepcion is not far from the town, upon the left of the river. Further down are three others, San Juan, San José and La Espada. On one of them is said to have been visable, not long ago, the date, "1725." They are in different stages of decay, but all are real ruins, beyond any connection with the present weird remains out of the silent past.

They are of various magnificence, but all upon a common model, and of the same materials rough blocks of limestone, cemented with a strong gray stucco. Each has its church, its convent, or celled house for the fathers, and its farm-buildings, arranged around a large court, entered only at a single point. Surrounding each was a large farm, irrigated at a great outlay of labor by aqueducts from the river.

The decorations of the doors and windows may be still examined. They are of stucco, and are rude heads of saints, and mouldings, usually without grace, corresponding to those described as at present occupying similar positions in Mexican churches. One of the missions is a complete ruin, the others afford shelter to Mexican occupants, who ply their trades, and herd their cattle and sheep in the old cells and courts. Many is the picturesque sketch offered to the pencil by such intrusion upon falling dome, tower, and cloister.

THE ENVIRONS

The system of aqueducts, for artificial irrigation, extends for many miles around San Antonio, and affords some justification for the Mexican tradition that the town not long ago contained a very much larger population. Most of these lived by agriculture, returning at evening to a crowded home in the city. These water-courses still retain their old Spanish name "acequias." A large part of them are abandoned, but in the immediate neighborhood of the city they are still in use, so that every garden-patch may be flowed at will.

In the outskirts of the town are many good residences recently erected by Americans. They are mostly of the creamy limestone, which is found in abundance near by. It is of a very agreeable shade, readily sawed and cut, sufficiently durable, and can be procured at a moderate cost. When the grounds around them shall have been put in correspondence with the style of these houses, they will make enviable homes.

THE SAN ANTONIO SPRING

There are, besides the missions, several pleasant points for excursions in the neighborhood, particularly those to the San Antonio and San Pedro

Springs. The latter is a wooded spot of great beauty but a mile or two from the town, and boasts a restaurant and beer-garden beyond its natural attractions. The San Antonio Spring may be classed as of the first water among the gems of the natural world. The whole river gushes up in one sparkling burst from the earth. It has all the beautiful accompaniments of a smaller spring, moss, pebbles, seclusion, sparkling sunbeams, and dense overhanging luxuriant foliage. The effect is overpowering. It is beyond your possible conceptions of a spring. You cannot believe your eyes, and almost shrink from sudden metamorphosis by invaded nymphdom.

BATHING

The temperature of the river is of just that agreeable elevation that makes you loth to leave a bath, and the color is the ideal blue. Few cities have such a luxury. It remains throughout the year without perceptible change of temperature, and never varies in height or volume. The streets are laid out in such a way that a great number of houses have a garden extending to the bank, and so a bathing-house, which is in constant use. The Mexicans seem half the time about the water. Their plump women especially are excellent swimmers, and fond of displaying their luxurious buoyancy. The fall of the river is such as to furnish abundant water-power, which is now used but for a single corn-mill. Several springs add their current to its volume above the town, and that from the San Pedro below. It unites, near the Gulf, with the Guadalupe, and empties into Espiritu Santo Bay, watering a rich, and, as yet, but little-settled country. The soil in the neighborhood of the city is heavy and sometimes mixed with drifts of limestone pebbles and deposits of shell, but is everywhere black and appears of inexhaustible fertility if well cultivated and supplied with moisture. The market-gardens belonging to Germans, which we saw later in the season, are most luxuriant. The prices of milk, butter and vegetables are very high, and the gains of the small German market-farmers must be rapidly accumulating.

TOWN LIFE

The street-life of San Antonio is more varied than might be supposed. Hardly a day passes without some noise. If there be no personal affray to arouse talk, there is some Government train to be seen, with its hundreds of mules, on its way from the coast to a fort above; or a Mexican ox-train from the coast, with an interesting supply of ice, or flour, or matches, or of whatever the shops find themselves short. A Government express clatters off, or news arrives from some exposed outpost, or from New Mexico. An Indian in his finery appears on a shaggy horse, in search of blankets, powder and ball. Or at the least, a stagecoach with the "States," or the Austin, mails, rolls into the plaza and discharges its load of passengers and newspapers.

The street affrays are numerous and characteristic. I have seen for a year or more a San Antonio weekly, and hardly a number fails to have its fight or its murder. More often than otherwise, the parties meet upon the plaza by chance, and each, on catching sight of his enemy, draws a revolver and fires away. As the actors are under more or less excitement, their aim is not apt to be of the most careful and sure; consequently it is, not seldom, the passers-by who suffer. Sometimes it is a young man at a quiet dinner in a restaurant who receives a ball in the head, sometimes an old negro woman returning from market who gets winged. After disposing of all their lead, the parties close to try their steel, but as this species of metallic amusement is less popular, they generally contrive to be separated ("Hold me! Hold me!") by friends before the wounds are mortal. If neither is seriously injured, they are brought to drink together on the following day, and the town waits for the next excitement.

Where borderers and idle soldiers are hanging about drinking places, and where different races mingle on unequal terms, assassinations must be expected. Murders, from avarice or revenge, are common here. Most are charged upon the Mexicans, whose passionate motives are not rare, and to whom escape over the border is easiest and most natural.

The town amusements of a less exciting character are not many. There is a permanent company of Mexican mountebanks, who give performances of agility and buffoonery two or three times a week, parading before night in their spangled tights with drum and trombone through the principal streets. They draw a crowd of whatever little Mexicans can get adrift, and this attracts a few sellers of whiskey, *tortillas* and *tamaules* (corn, slapjacks and hashed meat in cornshucks), all by the light of torches making a ruddily picturesque evening group.

The more grave Americans are served with tragedy by a thin local company, who are death on horrors and despair, long rapiers and well oiled hair, and for lack of a better place to flirt with passing officers, the city belles may sometimes be seen looking on. The national background of peanuts and yells is not, of course, wanting.

A day or two after our arrival, there was the hanging of a Mexican. The whole population left the town to see. Family parties, including the grandmother and the little negroes, came from all the plantations and farms within reach, and little ones were held up high to get their share of warning. The Mexicans looked on imperturbable.

San Antonio, excluding Galveston . . . [Olmsted thought the yellow fever epidemics in Galveston had given San Antonio a slight population edge], is much the largest city of Texas. After the Revolution, it was half deserted by its Mexican population, who did not care to come under Anglo-Saxon rule. Since then its growth has been rapid and steady. At the census of 1850, it numbered 3,500; in 1853, its population was 6,000; and in 1856, it is estimated at 10,500. Of these, about 4,000 are Mexicans, 3,000 Germans, and 3,500 Americans. The money-capital is in the hands of the Americans, as well as the officers and the Government. Most of the mechanics and the smaller shopkeepers are German. The Mexicans appear to have almost no other business than that of carting goods. Almost the entire transportation of the country is carried on by them, with oxen and two-wheeled carts. Some of them have small shops for the supply of their own countrymen, and some live upon the produce of farms and cattle ranches owned in the neighborhood. Their livelihood is, for the most part, exceedingly meagre, made up chiefly of corn and beans.

1858

El Paso before the War

W. W. Mills arrived in El Paso in 1858 and lived there for the next forty years except for brief interludes. During the Civil War years he opposed secession, was arrested as a Union spy, and eventually served as a lieutenant in the United States Army. His description of old El Paso remains the most complete and absorbing ever written. The following excerpt deals with life in the Adobe City just before the Civil War.

Source: W. W. Mills, *Forty Years at El Paso, 1858–1898*, ed. Rex W. Strickland (El Paso: Carl Hertzog, 1962), pp. 5–26. Reprinted by permission.

El Paso is situated on the Rio Grande River, in the extreme west corner of Texas, within a mile of that river, which forms the boundary between Texas and Mexico, and very near to New Mexico on the north and on the west.

The altitude is 3,700 feet and the climate is mild, pleasant and healthful. El Paso was then a small adobe hamlet of about three hundred inhabitants, more than three-fourths of whom were Mexicans. Nearly all that portion of the village or "ranch" south of San Antonio and San Francisco streets was then cultivated in vineyards, fruit trees, fields of wheat and corn and gardens, for at that time and for years later there was an abundance of water in the Rio Grande all the year round, and El Paso was checkered with acequias (irrigation ditches).

At the head of El Paso street, near the plaza, where the main acequia ran, there were several large ash and cottonwood trees, in the shade of which was a little market where fruit, and vegetables, and fowls, and mutton, and venison, and other articles were sold. We had no regular meat market.

To one of these trees some enterprising citizen had nailed a plank, which for years served as a bulletin board where people were wont to tack signed manuscripts giving their opinions of each other. Here Mrs. [Mary Elizabeth] Gillock, who kept the hotel . . . notified the "Publick" when her boarders refused to pay their bills, and here, in 1859, I saw my brother Anson nail the information that three certain citizens were liars, etc., and here, just ten years later, I gave the same information regarding B. F. Williams. Foolish? Perhaps.

The flouring mill of Simeon Hart, about a mile above the village, was the chief individual enterprise in the valley, and ground the entire wheat crop from both sides of the river, and supplied flour to all the people and the military posts.

The proprietor, a man of wealth and influence, staked all and lost all in the Confederate cause.

The dam which supplied water to this mill had been constructed two hundred years ago by the people of the Mexican side of the river, who kept it in repair for all these years without asking any assistance from the people of the Texas side, although they generously divided the water with us.

The patience and industry displayed by this people in repairing and rebuilding this dam, when washed away by annual floods, can only be compared to that of beavers.

The Texas bank of the Rio Grande was then (1858) only a short distance south of where the Santa Fe depot now stands, but just how far south it is impossible for me . . . to tell, though I have been often asked to testify as to where the river bed was then, and in later years. It found its present bed more or less gradually by erosion and revulsion during these years, and left very few landmarks.

The bed of the river was narrower then than now, and many cottonwood trees grew upon each bank.

At the end of El Paso street was the ferry, where pedestrians crossed in small canoes, and vehicles and wagon trains in larger boats. Sometimes, when the spring floods came, it was impossible for any one to cross for several days.

Be it remembered there was not a railroad or telegraph station within a thousand miles of us. The business houses, with one exception, were on El Paso street, and around the little plaza.

My brother Anson and I each built homes at El Paso before the war, he on San Francisco and I on San Antonio street. The post office was on the west side of El Paso street, facing the head of San Antonio street, and in this same large room there was also a whiskey saloon, a billiard table, and several gambling tables. . . . This room and the street in front of it were the favorite shooting grounds of the sporting men, and others, and here took place many bloody encounters. . . . The graveyard was convenient, being on one of the hills on what is now known as "Sunset Heights." At one time there were more people buried there who had died by violence than from all other causes. When I state that the writer of these pages sometimes read the burial service there over the remains of our departed countrymen, it may be imagined how sadly we were in need of spiritual guidance. Every citizen, whatever his age or calling, habitually carried a six-shooter at his belt, and slept with it under his pillow. . . .

The Mexican population, now nearly all passed away by death or removal, were of a much better class than those who came in later with the advent of the railroads. . . .

The villages below El Paso were more prosperous then than now, because their population is agricultural and the lack of water in the river in recent times has caused great discouragement and even distress. The same was true of Juarez, Mexico, just opposite El Paso, then called Paso del Norte.

The county seat was first at San Elezario, twenty-two miles below El Paso, with fifteen hundred population, and later at Ysleta, with twelve hundred population (nearly all Mexicans), and still later at El Paso. Court proceedings and arguments to juries and political speeches were then made in the Spanish language.

Fort Bliss, garrisoned by regular United States troops, situated at the place now called East El Paso, was considered by army officers and their families as one of the most desirable posts in the whole country, and several officers who subsequently held very high rank during the Civil War had been stationed there. There was another fort, called Quitman, seventy miles below El Paso, on the river, and a chain of military posts from there to San Antonio. The nearest posts in New Mexico were Fort Fillmore, forty miles to the north, near Las Cruces, and Fort Craig, one hundred miles still further north toward Santa Fe.

As to hunting, there were at that time comparatively plenty of wild deer, turkeys, wild geese, ducks and mountain quail on the mountains and in the valley, and I got my share of them.

. . . .

Of the Americans then at El Paso, some had left wives, or debts, or crimes behind them in "the States," and had not come to the frontier to teach Sunday school. But there were good people here also, and for the few who were capable of doing business and willing to work, the opportunities were as good then and as profitable as they have ever been since that time. The products of the mines, crudely worked, in northern Mexico, were brought to El Paso and exchanged for merchandise or money. The military posts (forts) in . . . [the Trans-Pecos region] and southern New Mexico were supplied with corn, flour, beef, hay, fuel, etc., by El Paso merchants and contractors.

The Overland Mail Company then operated a weekly line of mail coaches, drawn by six animals, between St. Louis and San Francisco. The time between these two cities was usually twenty-six days, the distance being 2,600 miles. These splendid Concord coaches (now almost gone out of use) carried the United States mail, for a Government subsidy, and usually four to nine through passengers, besides the driver and "conductor." Changes of animals were made at "stations" built of rock or adobe, every twenty-five to forty miles, or wherever the company could find a stream, or spring, or water-hole. These coaches traveled day and night, in all kinds of weather.

El Paso was at this time (1858) the terminus of two other important stage routes – one from Santa Fe, New Mexico, and the other from San Antonio, Texas. These were in every particular so similar to the greater "Overland" route that a description is unnecessary. There was also a stage line to Chihuahua.

. . . .

In order that the importance of these mail routes and other enterprises on this frontier may be appreciated, I must here state a fact which may seem strange to some of my readers. At that time this whole frontier was in the actual possession of savage Indians. The Americans and Mexicans were secure only near the military posts, or villages, or settlements, and when they traveled from place to place, they traveled in companies strong enough for defense, or at night and by stealth, trusting to Providence, or luck, each according to his faith.

The men who, for whatever reasons, had made their way to this distant frontier, were nearly all men of character; not all of good character, certainly, but of positive, assertive individual character, with strong personality and self-reliance. (The weaklings remained at home.) Many of them were well bred and of more than ordinary intelligence, and maintaining the manners of gentlemen. Even the worst of these men are not to be classed with the professional "toughs" and "thugs" who came later with the railroads. . . .

Common trials and dangers united the two races as one family, and the fact that one man was a Mexican and another an American was seldom mentioned, and I believe as seldom thought about. Each man was esteemed at his real worth, and I think our estimates of each other's characters were generally more correct than in more artificial societies.

Spanish was the language of the country, but many of our Mexican friends spoke English well, and often conversations, and even sentences, were amusingly and expressively made up of words and phrases of both languages.

To the traveler, who had spent weeks crossing the dry and desert plains, this valley, with the grateful humidity of the atmosphere, the refreshing verdure, the perfume of the flowering shrubs, the rustling of the leaves of the cottonwood trees, and their cool shade, and in the spring or summer, the bloom of the many fruit trees, or the waving of grain fields, were all like a sight or breath of the Promised Land!

The people, the peasantry, were content and happy. To them, with their simple wants, it was a land of plenty. The failure of water in the Rio Grande has sadly changed all this. It may be said that this valley and the things here described were not in themselves beautiful, but only appeared so by contrast with the barren country over which the wanderer had traveled; and this may be true, but it is not wise to analyze too severely the things that give us pleasure. They are few enough at best.

Our currency was the Mexican silver dollar, then at par, and the Mexican ounce, a gold coin worth sixteen dollars.

There were no banks, and no drafts or checks except those given out by the paymasters and quartermasters of the United States Army. Everybody loaned money when he had it, but only for accomodation. . . .

It was no unusual thing for merchants to loan large quantities of their goods, bales of prints and muslin and sacks of sugar and coffee to their neighbor merchants, to be repaid in kind when their wagon train arrived.

Carriages and buggies were considered as almost community property, and the man who refused to lend them was considered a bad neighbor. Everybody had credit at "the store," and everybody paid up sooner or later.

. . . .

In spite of privations, our little village seemed to have an unaccountable fascination for every one who saw it, refined American ladies as well as the less fastidious and sterner sex. This was my El Paso. To me it was like the Deserted Village to Goldsmith.

1859

Across Texas on
the Butterfield Trail

Albert Deane Richardson, a correspondent for the *Boston Journal* and later Horace Greeley's *New York Tribune*, traveled by stage across Texas during the fall of 1859 recording his impressions of the inhabitants, economy, culture, and wildlife of the Lone Star State. The beauty of the rolling countryside west of Fort Belknap and the curiosities of frontier living failed to overshadow the revulsion he occasionally felt as he came to understand the barbaric character of the Texas environment. Richardson was horrified at a stage stop on the Brazos when his stage driver explained that instant celebrity status was obtained "in *this* country" if "you . . . kill somebody." Later he labeled the region beyond the Concho a "shoreless ocean of desolation" and observed that Texans took on the appearance of "moving arsenals" in order to survive. Although the Boston tourist evidently secured much of his information concerning the Comanches from talkative white inhabitants who sometimes tended to "stretch the truth," his description of the Penateka Comanches has become a classic. His account of these nomadic warriors on horseback, whom he called "Tartars of the desert" and "destroying angels of the frontier," is perhaps the most colorful ever written about these Indians.

Richardson's excellent powers of observation and his breezy, fluid, and flamboyant style, demonstrated to the fullest in the following excerpt from *Beyond the Mississippi,* which he published in 1866, make it apparent why he was successful both as a journalist and as an author. Unfortunately, his personal life left much to be desired. While working at his desk in the *Tribune* office just three years after publishing *Beyond the Mississippi,* he was fatally shot by his fiancée's former husband. The deathbed marriage that followed made national headlines, and the ceremony was performed by the flamboyant Brooklyn preacher Henry Ward Beecher. Richardson's killer, a drunken Tammany Hall politician named David McFarland, was subsequently acquitted of the murder charge through the efforts of powerful Tammany lawyers.

The excerpt from *Beyond the Mississippi* which follows contains Richardson's account of his journey over part of the Butterfield Trail from Colbert's Ferry on the Red River near Sherman to the famous Horsehead Crossing on the Pecos River (see map 2). At the latter point he abandoned his Butterfield stage and boarded another coach, which took him into Mexico over another ancient artery of early travel, the Chihuahua Trail. That portion of the Butterfield Trail which Richardson traveled and describes below was a part of the old wagon road over which the U.S. government operated the first transcontinental mail service from Tipton, Missouri, to San Francisco, California. In its entirety, the Butterfield Trail extended 2,795 miles across seven states. To government surveyors it was better known as the Ox-Bow or Horse-shoe route; but the portion that spanned Texas was known first as the Old Military Road or Marcy Trail be-

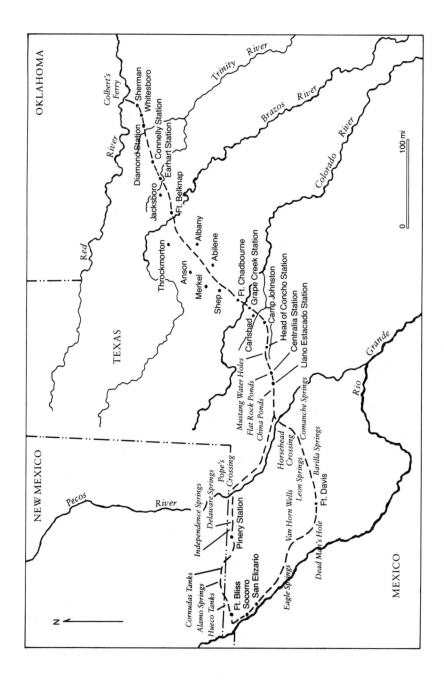

Map 2. The Butterfield Mail Route. (From the *Southwestern Historical Quarterly* 61 (July 1957): 3. Reprinted with permission.)

cause it had been laid out by Captain Randolph B. Marcy of the United States Army in 1849 and then as the Butterfield Trail after the Butterfield company initiated round-trip passenger service in 1858.

The John Butterfield Overland Mail Company, named after the company's first president, was formed in 1857 as an amalgamation of four express companies, including Wells Fargo. The line had been in operation for about one year when Richardson made his sightseeing tour. The stage in which he rode was probably one of 250 Concord coaches that had been purchased by the company several months earlier. The mail was placed under the driver's seat or in a leather "boot" at the rear of the coach, and passengers rode inside, with the driver and "shotgun" guard perched on the driver's box above. The cost of a through ticket to California was $200, but since Richardson went only part of the way, he probably paid only about half that amount. Certainly stage travel was not for the sensitive, the physically delicate, or the weakhearted. Passengers were bounced around in shameless fashion and fed dollar-a-plate meals at dusty "stop" stations along the way. The typical meal consisted of tainted pork, jerked beef, or wild game, tough hardtack, and black coffee often made from gyp or brackish water. There was little comfort in the coach under normal conditions, but rain, dust storms, hail, blue northers, and extremely torrid temperatures added to the passengers' displeasure. Supposedly, a full load for a Concord coach was nine people; but occasionally as many as twelve sweating, swearing, and ill-tempered passengers were crammed inside a coach with several others riding on top. Seldom was any prospective passenger, who might want to ride only as far as the next town, turned away because of the number of travelers already aboard. Needless to say, sophisticated through passengers from the East found riding in the same coach with dirty, tobacco-chewing, sweaty Texans a most disagreeable experience.

The Butterfield overland stage enterprise in Texas was terminated in March 1861 with the coming of the Civil War. When Confederate guerrillas and Texas bandits found full-time employment looting stop stations and running off company stock, Congress moved the entire operation out of the Southwest.

Source: Albert D. Richardson, *Beyond the Mississippi* (Hartford, Conn.: American Publishing Co., 1867), pp. 224–234.

At Preston we crossed the Red River [from Indian Territory] into Texas. Light-draught steamers have sometimes ascended to Preston; but the river is really navigable only to Shreveport, Louisiana. Thirty miles above Shreveport begins the great "Raft" an immense collection of trees and drift-wood half imbedded in the earth and firmly wedged together. It extends for seventy miles up the channel, sometimes spreading out to a width of thirty miles, and dividing the stream into many branches which do not all reunite for a hundred miles. . . .

One authority derives "Texas" from *Teha* (happy hunting ground) applied by the Aztecs who fled thither after the subjugation of their country by Cortez. According to another tradition it is an Indian word signifying "friend."

Before daylight on the first morning [in Texas] we met the California mail, with six smoking horses on a swift run through the drenching rain, and the passengers lustily singing: "Down upon the Swanee river."

Every day thereafter we encountered a stage from San Francisco, always stopping a moment to exchange gossip and newspapers. . . .

Our first Texas town was Sherman, capital of Grayson county, on a high rolling site, with a population of five hundred. Five hours later we breakfasted at Gainesville, in Cook county, another pleasant village. Beyond stretched undulating prairies with soil as black and rich as that of Kansas a good stock region though liable to destructive drowths, which ruin grass and sometimes compel the farmers to fatten their cattle on wheat. During the day we passed but five or six farms; and night overtook us on a barren soil among thin groves of low scrubby oaks.

September 28 At one o'clock, A.M., found the West Trinity river too much swollen for fording. The little station was full; so we slept refreshingly upon cornhusks in the barn, or in the western vernacular, the "stable." After breakfast we crossed the stream on foot by a slippery log, while drivers and conductor brought over heavy mail bags and trunks on the same precarious bridge. On the west bank another waiting coach was soon rolling us forward among mesquite groves. The long narrow leaves of this shrub are indeed "tree-hair." The slender hanging pods contain beans which both raw and cooked are palatable and nutritious to man. Horses also thrive and fatten upon them. Indians convert them, pods and all, into bread. Mexicans extract sugar and beer from them. Short fine mesquite grass also abounds. Like buffalo grass it is eagerly devoured by stock, and does not lose its nutriment in winter.

Breakfasted in . . . [Jack] county where the Indians were so troublesome that settlers dared not enter their fields to cut their wheat. In one direction the nearest white neighbors were a mile distant; in another five; and in another eight, and to the north (toward Kansas), two hundred and fifty miles. Lumber for doors and floors of the log station had been hauled from the nearest saw-mill, a hundred and fifty miles.

All which I learned from our landlord who nervously paced his porch, ravenously chewing tobacco, and casting uneasy glances at the navy revolver by his side. Three weeks before, he had killed an employee of the stage company in a sudden quarrel upon the very spot where we now conversed. He was under three thousand dollars bail to appear for trial; but in this lawless region men are seldom convicted of homicide, and never punished. Within a month there had been three other fatal shootings affrays nearby; and our driver enjoined us:

"If you want to obtain distinction in *this* country, kill somebody!"

At dusk we passed old Fort Belknap, the last outpost of civilization. Thence to the Rio Grande stretches a lonely desert for six hundred miles. Our horses were now exchanged for little mexican mules. Four stout men were required to hold them while the driver mounted to his seat. Once loosed, after kicking, plunging and rearing, they ran wildly for two miles upon the road. They can never be fully tamed. When first used, the drivers lash the coach to a tree before harnessing them. When ready for starting, the ropes are cut and they sometimes run for a dozen miles. But on this smooth prairie they do not often overturn a coach.

Fording the Brazos, we passed a wretched log-cabin whose squatter, a frontier Monte Christo, had a hundred-acre cornfield, which here represented fabulous wealth.

We were soon on the plains, where Indians claim exclusive domain, and every traveler is a moving arsenal. We met a train of Mexican carts loaded with corn for the mail stations. A rude, primitive invention is this vehicular ox-killer, which must have come in vogue soon after the flood. The enormous wheels are of huge logs, clumsily framed together and loosely revolving upon a rude axle. The frame, of slats covered with hide or canvas, resembles a huge chicken-coop. No iron is used in its construction; and the lumbering cart creaks and rattles and sways along the road, apparently just tumbling to pieces. It is drawn by oxen, with a straight strip of wood across their shoulders and strapped to their horns, serving as a yoke. Ropes are substituted for chains and bows. The poor animals are driven with long sharp poles, by dirty Mexicans, blanketed and bare-headed.

All night our coach rolled noiseless over the soft road, while the wind trembling through the mesquite leaves swept after us a ceaseless lullaby.

September 29 Daylight found us at Phantom Hill, named from the white ghostly chimneys of a burned fort. Beyond were barren hills dotted with mesquite and cactus, and covered with cities of prairie-dogs which often live twenty miles from water. Some conjecture that they dig subterranean wells; others that they can live without drinking. In winter they remain torpid, closely shut in their holes, and when they reappear it is an unfailing indication that the weather is about to moderate.

All day upon the silent desert, stopping only to change mules at lonely little stations. Air delicious and exhilarating. In the evening passed Fort Chadbourne, sixteen hundred feet above sea level, a cluster of long low white barracks garrisoned by one company of infantry. But the Comanches regard our soldiers much as they would a company of children armed with popguns and penny whistles.

After dark, finding the Colorado impassable, we slept in the coach waiting for its waters to subside. The vehicle's roof was like a sieve, and cold pitiless rain deluged us all night.

September 30 Awoke cold and rheumatic; but holding with Sancho Panza that a fat sorrow is better than a lean, breakfasted heartily upon pork and mesquite beans; and dried our clothes before the fire of the adobe hut-station.

The Colorado, usually an insignificant stream a hundred feet wide but now a fierce torrent, compelled us to spend the day here in the favorite range of the Comanches. These fierce untamed savages roam over an immense region, eating the raw flesh of the buffalo, drinking its warm blood, and plundering Mexicans, Indians and whites with judical impartiality. Arabs and Tartars of the desert, they remove their villages (pitching their lodges in regular streets and squares) hundreds of miles at the shortest notice. The men are short and stout, with bright copper faces, and long hair which they ornament with glass beads and silver gew-gaws.

On foot slow and awkward, but on horseback graceful, they are the most expert and daring riders in the world. In battle they sweep down upon their enemies with terrific yells, and concealing the whole body, with the exception of one foot, behind their horses, discharge bullets or arrows over and under the animals' necks rapidly and accurately. Each has his favorite war horse which he regards with great affection, and only mounts when going into battle. With small arms they are familiar; but "gun-carts" or cannons, they hold in superstitious fear, from the effects of one fired among them long ago by a Government expedition which they attacked upon the Missouri. Even the women are daring riders and hunters, lassooing antelope and shooting buffalo. They wear the hair short, tattoo their bodies hideously, have stolid faces, and are ill-shapen and bow-legged. When a Comanche would show special fondness for an Indian or white man he holds him in a pair of dirty arms and rubs his greasy face against the suffering victim's.

These modern Spartans are most expert and skillful thieves. An old brave boasted to Marcy that his four sons were the noblest youths in the tribe, and the chief comfort of his age, for they could steal more horses than any of their companions!

They are patient and untiring; sometimes absent upon war expeditions two years, refusing to return until they can bring the spoils of battle. When organizing a war party, the chief decorates a long pole with eagle feathers and a flag, and then in fighting costume chants war songs through his village. He makes many raids upon white settlers, but his favorite victims are Mexicans. Like all barbarians he believes his tribe the most prosperous and terrible on earth; and whenever our Government supplies him with blankets, sugar or money, attributes the gifts solely to fear of Comanche prowess. He is terrible in revenge; the slightest injury or affront will have blood. An American writer saw one chief punish the infidelity of his wife by placing the muzzle of his gun over her crossed feet and firing a bullet through them both.

After death the warrior is buried on some high hill in sitting posture, with face to the east, his choicest buffalo robe about him and the rest of his wardobe deposited by his side. His relatives mourn by lacerating themselves with knives or cropping their hair; and if he was killed in disastrous battle, by clipping the tails and manes of their horses and mules.

On vast deserts the Comanches convey intelligence hundreds of miles in a few hours. By day, green pine, fir, or hemlock boughs piled upon burning wood produces a heavy black smoke which is seen far away; and at night they telegraph by bonfires. Their signals are as well defined and intelligible as those of civilized navies – smokes and fires with stated intervals between, indicating the approach of enemies or calling the roving bands together for any purpose whatever.

They are inveterate smokers, mingling sumach leaves with tobacco; and they drink whisky to excess. When needful they easily abstain from food for days altogether, but afterward eat fresh meat in incredible quantities.

Never tilling the soil, insensible alike to the comforts and wants of civilization, daring, treacherous, and bloodthirsty, they are destroying angels of our frontier, the mortal terror of weaker Indians and of Mexicans. According to tradition their ancestors came from a far country in the West, where they expect to join them after death.

October 1 This morning the river had so far subsided that we crossed, though the strong current swept our six little mules several yards down the stream, and compelled them to swim. Beyond, in ancient lake beds, our coach wheels crushed rattlesnakes, lying lazily in the road. They seldom bite except in August, when they are said to be blind and to snap indiscriminately at every living thing. Hogs do not fear them but kill and eat [them] voraciously. Their flesh is a favorite dish with old plainsmen.

Dined at the North Concho. Our spirited little landlady, reared in eastern Texas, gave a description of an attack made by a hundred and twenty Comanches three weeks before. A stock-tender, her husband and herself shut themselves in the house, and with their rifles kept the assailants at a respectful distance. The savages drove away all their mules and cattle, and a dozen of their iron-pointed feathertipped arrows were still sticking in the cottonwood logs. That very morning a party of Comanches had pursued the station-keeper when within two miles of his dwelling. One of their arrows passed through his hat, but his fleet horse saved him. He laughed heartily at this morning amusement, but his little wife was only angry, declaring vehemently that they would not be driven out of the country by worthless Red-skins.

Many species of cactus beside our road. One, the soap plant, has a large fibrous root said to possess saponaceous properties, and the Mexicans are reputed to use it in washing their persons and clothing; but generally they cherish strong antipathy to *all* soap. Most of them would be impoverished by spending half an hour under a pump spout, with a vigorous man at the handle. Scores of spotted antelopes in sight. The wolves are said to chase them in a circle, thus enabling a fresh pursuer to take the place of the weary one every time they pass the starting point. Fleetness falls a victim to cunning, and the poor antelope soon furnishes a feast for the hungry pack.

At dark, with fresh strong team and additional rifles and revolvers on board, we entered upon that old terror of immigrants, the Great Staked

Plain. In the cold dreary night this barren table land stretched afar an utter sand-waste with a few shrubs or cactus and greasewood. A few weeks before, travelers had narrowly escaped death from thirst. At one stage-station during four-fifths of the year, water for the mules was hauled in casks twenty-two miles. But now the ground was saturated. Again and again during the dark night our conductor left the stage with his lantern, searching for the track, which neither driver nor mules could see many yards ahead; there was danger of wandering off into the wilderness.

October 2 Daylight found us on a shoreless ocean of desolation. . . .

The ancient Mexicans marked the route with stakes over this vast desert, and hence its name. It is four hundred miles long by two hundred in width, and two thousand eight hundred feet above sea level. . . .

We journeyed for eighty miles across the corner of the desert, passing two or three mail stations, the most desolate and lonely of all human habitations. Then through a winding canyon we descended into the broad valley of [the] Pecos River.

1859

The Removal of
the Reservation Indians

On February 6, 1854, the Texas legislature set aside twelve leagues of land for Indian reservations in the state. These lands were selected, surveyed, and prepared for occupancy by the United States government. After consultation with various Indian tribes, sites were selected on the Brazos River below Fort Belknap, on the Clear Fork of the Brazos at Camp Cooper (see map 3), and on the Pecos River in the western part of the state. The last site was intended as a reservation for the Mescalero and Lipan Apaches, but these Indians refused to occupy the reserve. The other two reservations, under the supervision of the U.S. government, were in operation for only about five years.

Under the general direction of Major Robert S. Neighbors, the supervisor of all Indians in Texas, and Shapley P. Ross, the agent in charge of the Brazos reser-

Map 3. Some Counties of Civil War Texas.

vation, approximately two thousand Indians took up residence on the reserve near Fort Belknap. These included Caddo, Anadarko, Waco, and Tonkawa Indians, each of which erected a tribal village. The Indians put all available acreage into cultivation and produced corn, wheat, vegetables, and melons. The Federal government signed contracts with local ranchers to have thirty-four head of cattle delivered to the Indians each week, and additional supplies were also provided.

About forty-five miles west of this reservation, approximately 450 Comanches were placed on a reserve on the Clear Fork to begin a similar operation. The Comanches, however, were not farmers by nature and were not favorably disposed toward the sedentary life. Raids on frontier settlements by "wild" Comanches and other Indians who had escaped the reservation system lured young reservation Indians from the Clear Fork reserve. As Indian depredations increased during the 1850s, men of the frontier organized themselves into volunteer bands to stalk the red raiders. The very presence of Indians on the reservations increased the frontier residents' fear, distrust, and hatred of Indians. This typical pioneer attitude is apparent in the following excerpt written by James Buckner Barry, a noted Bosque County Indian fighter who played an active role in securing Indian removal. Once the Indians were escorted across the Red River, the last twelve leagues of land the state had provided for reservation purposes reverted to state ownership. The Texas Indian reservations were gone, but the Indian menace to Texas settlements, originating in the Indian Territory north of the Red River, continued until the late 1880s.

Source: James Buckner Barry, *A Texas Ranger and Frontiersman: The Days of Buck Barry in Texas,* ed. James K. Greer (Dallas: Southwest Press, 1932), pp. 111–117.

[The two Indian reservations in Texas during the late 1850's were] . . . the Comanche reservation on the Clear Fork and what was known as the Caddo reservation on the main Brazos. But there were other tribes on the Caddo reservation which included Anadarkoes, Keechies, Tonkawas, Wacoes, Tahwaccones, Delawares, and Shawnees. These latter tribes on the Caddo reservation were a great protection to the frontier settlers against the "wild" tribes of Indians. But the Comanche reservation was no protection. They had too many wild kinsfolk in the three tribes of Comanches that had made no treaty with the government. When the settlers would follow the raiding parties beyond all settlements and return by the Comanche reservation, they invariably found theirs or some of their neighbors' horses. At one time, I found thirty-two of my own and my neighbors'. After every raid that was made in this section, a number of horses would be later found on this reservation.

Even the conservative historians of the State have said that there were some Indians who could not resist the opportunity to plunder and steal, an old habit. Occasionally, these joined the "wild" Indians, and perhaps, certain white criminals, in forays against the settlers. I asked Colonel [M.] Leeper, the Indian agent, permission to talk to the chief, Long Tree. Then I questioned him as to how and why our horses were found on his reservation. Jim Shaw, a Delaware Indian, acted as my interpreter. The chief told me his wild brothers would come to see his people and that they would have a war dance and persuade his young men to depredate against their white brothers; and the horses that I found there were those of his stepson, which he received when they apportioned after the raid. . . .

The citizens asked the government, through their congressman, to move all the Indians out of Texas so that we might know that when we saw an Indian he was our enemy. As it was, they would pass themselves for friends and often take advantage of men under pretext of friendship. It sometimes happened that they would take a woman and kill her and her children after she fed them, thinking them friendly Indians. We went to the trouble and expense of getting up a petition to Congress to have the friendly Indians moved across the Red River, and we paid Colonel Nelson to take it to Congress with sworn evidence of the situation. . . .

When Colonel Nelson returned, he told those who had sent him with the petition that we would have to fight it out the best we could, as Congress thought more of an Indian, a foreigner, and a free negro than it did of American citizens. They had told our Texas Congressman on the floor of the Representatives Hall that they would never vote one dollar for appropriations to move the reservation Indians across Red River or to furnish any more protection to Texas until Texans freed her negroes; that the Indian and the negro were more preferable as citizens than the slaveholder. Such insults made me a secessionist.

We held meetings all along our frontier and determined that we would move the reservation Indians across the Red River ourselves, whether the government (Congress) wanted us to or not. It was agreed to drive only the Comanche Indians out of Texas, as we knew the Caddoes, Tonkawas, and other small tribes were our friends.

[In May 1859] . . . there came an alarming report about the reservation Indians. It was to the effect that many citizens were collecting to break up the reservations, some one hundred fifty miles up the Brazos from me. I made plans to start to that place. Several of a Minute Company, which had been organized a few weeks before in Meridian, with [John?] Hanna as captain and myself as lieutenant, had gone. I got others to agree to be ready to go with me. The harvest season was on and leaving meant sacrificing it and neglecting other affairs.

We started and rode beyond Stephenville where we stopped with Chandler Roberts. Next day we fell in with some men from Coryell County who were also on their way to the same destination. Another day's ride brought us to the camp of some four hundred men. Some of them had had a skirmish with the Indians on the Reserve in which three citizens and seven or eight Indians were killed.

Finally we decided to advance to the Comanche reservation and they fled to the Caddo reservation, forty miles distant. We pursued them. When we arrived, we sent a message, or rather started it, to the captain commanding the United States troops; Captain Palmer, I believe his name was. They were shot at and one of them wounded. This act opened the fight, which was bloody for a while. We lost several good citizens, and we soon saw that two hundred and fifty men could not hold out against a thousand or twelve hundred Indians, backed by United States troops. Colonel [John R.] Baylor, who was elected to command, ordered his command to fall back from the reservation lands in order to avoid fighting United States troops.

Baylor fell back into Palo Pinto valley, where he received recruits every day until his little enthusiastic band of citizens had grown to an army that felt itself invincible against the combined forces on the reservation, the United States troops included. We knew that if we should fail in the next fight that there were at least ten thousand as brave men as ever looked through the sights of a gun barrel, anxious and waiting to be notified that their services were needed. Some scattering recruits who had had their relatives and friends murdered by Indians, came two hundred miles to join us.

After recruiting had doubled our forces, it was thought best to reorganize. We reelected J. R. Baylor, Colonel, Allison Nelson, Lieutenant

Colonel, and Hood, Major. We knew that if we went on the reservation we would have to fight the United States troops, also. We kept a reconnoitering force around the reservation, cutting off their supplies and not even allowing the Indians to get out and kill buffaloes. At this time it was thought advisable to demand the surrender, or rather that the agents, Colonel Leeper, agent for the Comanches, and Captain [Shapley P.] Ross, father of ex-governor Sul Ross, who was agent for all the other tribes and the commanding officer of the United States troops, move all the Indians across Red River at once.

Baylor and Nelson put the hazardous duty on me to go into the reservation and make this demand. I was acquainted with both agents and many of the Indians. I call this a hazardous trip, for the agents and the Indians were angry to the point of desperation as were also our little army of frontier citizens, or "mob," as the agents called us. I took one man with me.

We bore no flag of introduction but our rifles and six-shooters. I carried no written communication to anyone, I was only instructed to demand of those who were in authority that all the Indians be moved across the Red River.

The agents and their employees were mad and sullen and would not talk with me, although one did inform me that the Indians were frenzied and that I was in danger. They did permit my companion and myself to sleep on our blankets spread on the floor of the council house, which was a log cabin. When the agents refused to talk business, I turned all my conversation to Captain Palmer (I believe that was his name). I told him we were now strong enough to cut off all supplies, which he knew to be a fact, as our scouts had already captured their meat, bread, beef, salt, etc., and that every man in Palo Pinto valley had friends and acquaintances who were swelling our ranks every day. As soon as the cold spell was over, our friends from the Rio Grande to Red River would make haste to join us. I also told him that Governor Houston could not check the excitement and determination of the people of Texas to move these Indians across her border. His reply was, "I am here under orders to protect these Indians as well as the frontier settlers. I can't afford to disobey orders. There is nothing I would hate more than to get into a deadly conflict with American citizens, but you tell your officials and the people that if they come on this reservation for the purpose of molesting these Indians that I am ordered to protect, I will have to fight them."

Everything looked dark and gloomy. Every person agents, soldiers, and Indians was all mad, and it seemed that blood had to be spilled. When I was ready to leave, the captain commanding met me out a distance from the agent's office and told me to tell Colonels Nelson and Baylor to hold their people off and keep them quiet for three days, and he would take the responsibility of seeing that the Indians were moved out of Texas, if it cost him a trial by court-martial and his position in the army, which he'd rather lose than shed the blood of American citizens. . . .

When I returned to the headquarters of the citizen soldiers and related (no one wrote a word) what the captain commanding had said, there was a mixed feeling in camps. The majority seemed to be vexed because they were swindled out of a fight, while others were well pleased that every Indian would soon be moved out of Texas.

After a day's rest in camp, I started with eleven men on a scout up the Clear Fork of the Brazos toward the upper agency and to look after the safety of several families living there. All night we rode through the woods and mountains and got to the settlements just at daybreak. Two days were used in getting the families together and preparing them for a march toward the more people[d] settlements. Several families and nine wagons were escorted to the Brazos.

Upon our return to camp, we found the citizen soldiers dispersed. They had gone home rather than have a conflict with the federal troops who were at the agency protecting the Indians while they depredated at the expense of the frontier settlers. The federal government was no doubt blind to the fraudulent conduct of some of its agents.

Three days were spent in getting home; forty miles was ridden on a tired pony the last day. My crops and stock were in poor condition due to neglect. Some of my wheat crop was lost, of course. But after a few days occupied with rounding up horses and branding calves, I was called to Meridian. A commission of five men from Governor Runnels wanted an interview into the difficulty of the frontier citizens and reserve Indians on the Brazos.

The Indians were assembled by the general government several weeks later, and escorted across the Red River to the vicinity of Fort Cobb in Indian Territory. Then they became bitter enemies to Texans, but when we saw an Indian we knew how to treat him. They depredated on our frontier so heavily that Governor Houston commissioned several of us to raise companies and patrol at intervals between the posts where the United States troops were stationed. We patrolled from the Rio Grande to the Red River and protected our frontier better than the United States soldiers had, with all the friendly Indians to help them.

ca. 1858–1860

Frontier Recreation in Central Texas

The following discussion of the various recreational activities of Texans during the late 1850s was written by James Buckner Barry, who moved from Corsicana to Bosque County in 1856. He and the members of his family experienced the tribulations as well as the joys of frontier living while working their farm on the East Bosque River north of the little settlement of Meridian. The following excerpt was taken from one of Barry's accounts written sometime after the period he describes. The sharpness of detail was made possible by a personal diary, kept during these years, which he used as a basis for the account. Barry died at his ranch near Walnut Springs in Bosque County on his eighty-fifth birthday, December 16, 1906.

Source: James Buckner Barry, A Texas Ranger and Frontiersman: The Days of Buck Barry in Texas, ed. James K. Greer (Dallas: Southwest Press, 1932), pp. 80–89.

There were multitudinous . . . jobs about a stock farm. Attention to crippled or sick stock, looking after stock water, repair of the fences about the houses, going to mill ten miles below Meridian on the Bosque, or a distance of twenty miles, getting of wood for cooking and fuel, and building neighborhood roads. I remember wanting to see a road toward Duffau, but there were not enough settlers to petition the county court for such a road, so I marked and cut out the road myself. A log and my oxen were used to drag the new road. And on rainy days, when we were not forced to go outside to look after stock, some time was devoted to repair of saddles, molding of bullets, cleaning of guns, and plaiting of hair ropes, or perhaps dressing bucksin for clothing. Pecans could be gathered when fields were muddy and other duties were not pressing. There were many other tasks such as making cloth sacks for wheat, digging wells for drinking water, building sugar cane mills for our limited supply of cane, cutting wood to fit the fireplaces, milking and churning, feeding the stock that were always around the house, and mending clothing and shoes.

But life for the pioneer settler was not all work and no play. The two were mixed. Frontier life was lonely, especially for the women, but there was some opportunity for fun and social contact. Logrolling, house raising, harvesting, weddings and deaths attracted all the neighbors. But as the population was sparse, the crowds were small after all. There was an occasional candy stew in the private homes back in the older settlements, well regulated balls, and socials at the masonic lodge temples. I remember attending with my wife a few of these functions at Corsicana. . . .

Of course one of our chief amusements was talking politics, particularly at the county seats where we gathered on court days or went to vote. Perhaps we were more interested than we had been before coming west as emigrants, as we felt keenly the need of strong government, particularly for the preservation of local order where it was frequently absent. Yet, no doubt, we all had spirit of personal independence in the absence of the law. I remember voting for Sam Houston as governor, Baylor for judge, and Jack Evans for our representative, and attending the Democratic convention at Corsicana, although a new citizen. . . . And one or two barbecues stand out in my memory as enjoyable events. One given by our community for Walker's Rangers, stationed in Bosque County for a while when the Indians had begun their raids, was a great success. As game was everywhere rather plentiful, we donated good beeves for the occasion.

Visiting or staying overnight was a welcome happening in the frontier household. Afternoon on Sundays was a favorite time for visiting because everyone worked during the week days. Preachers, newspaper editors, . . . relatives, friends from east of the Mississippi River, and neighbors were among these callers. Then there was the peddler, the infrequent traveler, and the surveyor or other officials. Sometimes one or two preachers . . . would stay with me and there would be preaching at my house at eleven o'clock. Again, several couples from the nearest town would drive to my house to have dinner with me. Perhaps Mrs. Barry and myself would visit some of our neighbors and take dinner with them. . . .

However, it was the church which provided a welcome social opportunity and an outlet for pent-up emotionalism. This was especially true for our women. Their life was hard, nerve-racking at times, and despite their hopes for a better day, something was needed to give them a chance to lift the restrictions of the daily existence. Not only was preaching held at private residences but in the absence of the preacher there was the infrequent prayer meeting.

But it was the camp meeting which was the change most thoroughly enjoyed. We attended Methodist, Presbyterian, etc., at Meridian. One of the best attended camp meetings in our section was held at Meridian in September, 1860, by a Methodist preacher, and we carried bedding, food, etc., to spend several days. . . . In the villages and towns, services were occasionally also held [during the] afternoon and were customary on Sunday nights. It was my good fortune to visit a session of the Baptist Association meeting at Waco, where I was visiting my brother. On another date at Waco, I attended a fair conducted by the ladies who were raising the means to buy a church bell. Weather was not allowed to handicap seriously our attendance on these welcomed services.

We had a few books, some of which I bought in Corsicana. I bought a two-volume history of Texas and some books on hunting in Africa. When any of the preachers happened to remark that they were going to Houston or Galveston, I sent by them for newspapers. I subscribed for the *Christian Advocate* at $3.50 per annum. Then we could secure copies of the *Texas Almanac*.

Such a means of relief (in the above mentioned church worship) from the daily struggle was not all that the church did for the settlers. The religion of the frontier settler gave him consolation at times when sorely needed. Injuries, deaths, and murders were to be expected by the frontiersman but, nevertheless, they always came as a shock. I had the experience of narrow escapes from death but received only serious injuries, and had my smaller son, Willie, seriously gored by a wild cow. Medicine and surgery were crude. It was my lot to help hold some patients for the doctor when he was amputating limbs without anesthetic. Both men and women had falls from horses, accidents at the hands of stock, tame and wild, and other injuries too numerous to record.

But it was death in the frontier home from other accidents or the hostile Indians that banished any youthful romantic ideas of the frontier that we once had. I helped husbands bury their wives and wives their husbands and saw the one that survived the other struggle to continue the plans that both had labored to complete. And I returned home one cold day in February, after an Indian hunt, in time to be present at the burial of our baby, Cora. Six months later we laid our little girl, Mary, by her. But the neighbors all came and were so kind, and next day the sun shone, and those of us who lived were well, and there was work that had to be done. So despite the loneliness we had to go ahead and no doubt it was better that we were so busy. Then my brother at Marlin passed away. But his going was not so sad as that of my nephew's little girl, Mary Bryant, who killed herself while at play by climbing to the top of the fence and pulling the top rail off on her when she slipped and fell. She and her mother was visiting us. We made her a coffin and buried her beside little Cora and Mary. And I was not through with sorrow, but I was more fortunate than so many people of my section that I could not complain.

. . . .

One of the most diverting forms of recreation open to the frontier settler was hunting. I enjoyed hunting and did a lot of it for the sport and for the meat to be had. Game was plentiful and of numerous kinds. We had bear, panthers, deer, otter, wolves, cats, some buffalo, turkeys, prairie chickens, ducks, geese, and birds too numerous to mention. We seldom wanted for game to eat during several years when the population remained sparse. One had plenty of chances to practice marksmanship with both rifle and pistol while hunting, and there was enough hunting to obviate "buck fever." It was my privilege to hunt over much of the country of central, north, and northwest Texas as well as some in other portions of the state. . . .

. . . .

Once, when it seemed that we were consuming our pork too fast and no fresh meat had been encountered while doing the regular work outdoors, I secured seven deer in two days while on the prairie after stock. It was in a cold November. Deer, coons, and hogs frequently damaged our crops despite the fences. Of course the coons could climb through or over, the deer jump, but the hogs would find a weak spot in the fence and break in. When we went to the fields inspecting them for such intrusion, we took our dogs. One July day the wild hogs found in a field were not disposed to run from the dogs but bunched for a fight. The result was a wicked fight, some dead hogs, and some slashed dogs. It was an interesting contest for a few minutes, but the dogs were outnumbered and I did not want them seriously injured, so I took a hand with my pistol.

. . . .

Up in the Rocky community, between Iredell and Stephenville, several of us staged a turkey hunt one January, and killed twentyseven. I brought four home. The weather was cold and in this same month hundreds of cattle on the range were frozen. So as bread had been scarce and now beef was apparently going to be, turkey would taste very well and was needed. Other game, including a couple of antelope I managed to get, supplemented the fare of much turkey during the weeks following. Fortunately, crops were very good the coming season.

The other outstanding sport we enjoyed, but which we also made yield some substance, was fishing. Our fishing was a real lark, although it was expected to yield something to take home with us or prepare on the grounds for the "fish fry." So our method of catching the fish was generally to use a sein. Seining was usually done in the summer and in the Bosques or the Brazos.

I went on one fishing spree in the North Bosque and caught over one hundred by seining with wagon sheets sewn together. We could not "round up" in the water as with regular seins, but "drug out" on the banks. Most of the fish would thus escape us, but we caught plenty of good-sized ones. Fish frys were held at intervals during the summer, and we always had one on the Fourth of July as a part of a holiday festival and celebration.

. . . .

At home . . . certain types of domestic work, such as spinning, which might have been a blessing, at times, was denied . . . [a frontier wife] because of a lack of materials such as raw cotton, and too much other work, with responsibility for the safety of the children in the absence of her man, and the worry over the absent and those present. . . . Even where there was some help from a new negro woman, the duties of the household were trying on the women's physical strength. But very few families in our section owned any negroes and during hard times these were frequently hired out. Keeping the home clean, food prepared, washing done, quilts made, rendering the lard when her husband killed hogs, and in the absence of the men, perhaps cutting wood and carrying water as well as looking after the stock about the house, was only a portion of the work of the women along the frontier of central Texas.

1860

The Alabama-Coushatta Community

Before the Civil War a few scattered bands of Indians were placed on reservations located on the Brazos and the Clear Fork; but the Indians hated the arrangement and so did white residents so the reservation system was abandoned. When the Texas Indians were forcibly moved across the Red River, a few Texans were aware of a peaceful group of eastern Indians living in the Trinity River valley not far from Houston. They had migrated into Texas during the late Spanish era, and both the Spanish and Mexican governments had adopted peaceful policies toward them. The government of the Republic of Texas had allowed them to remain in their encampments even during the Indian wars of the M. B. Lamar administration. These Indians eventually received land from the state of Texas and from the U.S. government and were allowed to establish permanent homes in the region they occupied. This reservation, occupied by the peaceful Alabama-Coushatta Indians, is the only one in Texas today.

Living in semi-isolation during the late 1850s and early 1860s, they avoided contact with whites as much as possible. They were a peace-loving and self-sufficient people, evidently held in high esteem by most of those who knew them. The following description of these Indians was written just before the outbreak of the Civil War.

Source: The Texas Almanac for 1861, with Statistics, Historical and Biblio-

graphical Sketches, etc., Relating to Texas (New Orleans: Thomas L. White, 1860), pp. 126–128.

It is . . . not generally known that in the very heart of Texas, surrounded by our settlements, there are some four hundred Indians, cultivating the arts of peace, sustaining themselves and their families in comfort and happiness by their own labors, and enjoying the friendship and confidence of the whites around them. They are branches of the Creek nation, who, early in the present century, withdrew from the contest with our race as hopeless, and sought a home on or near the Trinity river in Texas, then under the Mexican government[.] [W]hen immigration into Texas brought the Americans again around them, they persisted in their peaceful policy, receiving their former foes with kindness and hospitality, sharing provisions with them, and doing all in their power to alleviate the sufferings of settlers in a new country. In the war with Mexico, they adhered to the cause of Texas, remaining quietly in their villages, ready to take up arms with the rest of the population, if the Mexican army should reach the Trinity. Since our revolution, they have pursued the same steadfast policy of peace, abstaining from all offense, doing everything in their power to conciliate the whites, appealing trustfully when oppressed to the friends whom they have made by their own good conduct, thankful for justice when they could obtain it, and submitting patiently to wrong when told that there was no redress.

They are principally Coushattas and Alabamas, with some few Muscogees. They speak three different languages, all evidently dialects of the Creek, and most of them understand the Mobile tongue, or servile Choctaw, which, like the French in Europe, was the universal language among the different tribes, and their usual means of communication with the whites.

Their loyalty to our race, and their peaceful resolutions, have sometimes been severely tried. The base and unprincipled have plundered them of their crops and stock, because they were Indians, and it was supposed that therefore they could be robbed with impunity. . . .

The Legislature of Texas has taken them under its protection, extending to them a liberal and judicious assistance. An agency has usually been kept up for their benefit, and appropriations have been made at different times to purchase a tract of land for the Alabamas, and another for the Coushattas. The tract for the Alabamas has been bought, and they are settled on it, have made good clearings and improvements, and are doing extremely well, having abundant stocks of hogs, horses, and cattle, and making crops sufficient for their support. The tract for the Coushattas has not yet been bought. They are living partly with the Alabamas, and partly on land which is private property, the owner of which does not intend to disturb them. They too have good stocks, excellent fields well-inclosed, and are making fine crops. The Muscogees mostly reside with the last-named Coushattas.

. . . .

Their crops are cultivated for their own use, rather than for sale. Indian corn is the principal, though many of them plant sweet potatoes, and all of them vegetables, and they usually fill their villages with fruit trees. During the season of cultivation they remain closely at home, working industriously, and hunting only at such leisure times as their crops allow them. The interval between the working and gathering their crops is usually spent in rest and social intercourse, and occasional hunting. But when every thing is gathered and housed . . . then comes the return to Indian life and Indian enjoyment. They break up into hunting parties, after the Arab fashion, taking with them their wives and children, their horses and tents, and household utensils. They seek the wild pine forests, which our settlements have not yet reached, and work their way into the dense cane-brakes on the rivers, which the white men have not yet penetrated. They soon fill their camps with game, and, alone with themselves and nature, and safe from the intrusion of a superior and conquering race, they enjoy the realization of Indian life, as it was before the white man discovered their country. . . . When weary of the chase, or satisfied with its results, they return to their villages, their horses loaded with dried meat, deer skins to be dressed for market, and bears' oil in skins, after the patriarchal fashion, for their own use or for sale. These excursions occupy their time till the season comes for repairing their fences, and making other preparations for their crops, when they all return home cheerful and contented, to begin the routine of another year.

R. E. Lee's
Last Christmas in Texas

Fort Mason, situated on Post Hill above the little town of Mason in the north-western corner of present-day Kimble County, was one of the fortifications in the cordon of frontier forts garrisoned by U.S. troops in the war against the Indians. One of the fort's commanders, before it was surrendered to the Confederates in March 1861, was Colonel Robert E. Lee. Lee, who had served at the fort before, arrived in November 1860 from San Antonio to take command and reestablish a regimental headquarters for the Second Texas Cavalry. The Virginia colonel's stay at Fort Mason lasted only three months. On February 13, 1861, General Winfield Scott ordered him back to Washington to offer him command of the Union army. Shortly after Lee's departure, General David Twiggs, in command of U.S. troops in Texas, surrendered all Federal forts in the state, and the entire U.S. garrison at Fort Mason evacuated the fort on March 29. Although Lee disliked slavery and opposed secession, he declined Scott's offer and resigned his commission in the U.S. Army to join his fellow Virginians in secession and the creation of a separate Southern nation.

During his last three months in Texas, Lee experienced few moments of happiness. Grieving over the gathering clouds of secession and civil war, he spent long, dreary hours staring out a window in his regimental quarters. His presence at a Christmas party in 1860, attended by practically all military and civilian personnel in the Mason settlement, was necessary because it was held in his lodgings. The music, dancing, and laughter evidently held his interest, but he was not an active participant in the gala affair. The excerpt that follows contains an early Mason resident's recollections of the Christmas party and her impressions of R. E. Lee.

Source: Mrs. Wilson Hey, "Account of a Christmas Ball at Fort Mason," in Stella Gipson Polk, *Mason and Mason County: A History* (Austin: Pemberton Press, 1966), p. 26. Reprinted by permission.

The first dance I ever attended was there at the fort, in the regimental quarters of Robert E. Lee. The soldiers wanted to give a dance, but having no room for such an event in the fort, Commander Lee let the boys use his regimental quarters.

I was fifteen years of age and lived in Mason with Mrs. George Bowser. Having no suitable clothes for a ball room . . . Mrs. Bowser managed to dress me in some of her clothes. I wore a hooped skirt of white silk and a black waist. For jewelry, Mrs. Bowser gave me her gold broach, gold ear rings, watch and chain. As was the custom in those days, I placed the chain around my neck and the watch inside my belt. I was surely dressed up that night and could scarcely wait for the dance to begin.

The first man who asked me to dance was a soldier by the name of Crosby. I told him I had never danced before, and I requested that he wait a while until I could see how others went through the square dance. Finally I danced with young Crosby and he told me I was the best dancer on the floor. But I suspect in passing the compliment he just wanted to be nice to me because I was a beginner.

No, I didn't dance with Commander Lee. He didn't dance with anyone; just sat and watched the rest of us, although he seemed to enjoy the fun we were having.

1860–1861

Three Counties in the Red River Valley

The following excerpts were taken from the 1861 *Texas Almanac* to focus special attention on three counties in North Texas which were bounded on the north by the Red River. All three counties, Clay, Montague, and Cooke (see map 3), were sparsely settled when the Civil War began. Cooke County was the only one that could boast any appreciable growth, primarily because the Butterfield Overland Mail route between Missouri and California entered the county just west of Diamond's Station (the home of John R. Diamond, one mile west of present-day Whitesboro, Grayson County) with Gainesville (in Cooke County) serving as the third stop station in Texas. The inhabitants of isolated communities in Clay and Montague counties, dangerously exposed to Indian attacks, lived in constant terror of the red men. Many pioneer families deserted their farms in the

Devil's Backbone region of Montague County during the early 1860s, and provisional county organization in Clay County was suspended in 1862 because of the rash of Indian raids. Earl Van Dorn's expeditions against the Comanches before the war simply served to intensify Indian attacks after Texas seceded from the Union. Cooke County was created from Fannin County and organized in 1848. Clay and Montague counties were created from Cooke County in 1857.

Source: *The Texas Almanac for 1861, with Statistics, Historical and Biographical Sketches, etc., Relating to Texas* (New Orleans: Thomas L. White, 1860), pp. 187–190.

Clay County: Henrietta.

. . . Corn is principally raised, though there will be a considerable quantity of wheat put in this fall. The Chinese sugar-cane does remarkably well, as also all kinds of vegetables. . . . We have so far had no droughts, nor been troubled with grasshoppers. Our country is just settling up, the emigration being mostly from Illinois, Missouri, and Arkansas. White labor *makes the truck;* but it is only because we are too poor to buy the darkies at the present high prices *we want them bad enough.* There is only one village started, Hubert P.O., lying between Red river and the Little Wichita, but a few miles from the mouth of the latter. There is no military post in this county. Van Dorn's Station is beyond us; his supplies of corn, etc., are hauled through this county. . . . We expect a post-route to this place, via Gainesville, to supply also Montague and Catlett's Springs, and from them to Belknap, Young county, connecting again with the overland mail to California.

Montague County: Montague.

This county was created in 1858, and organized in the Spring of 1859. The Indian depredations have greatly retarded its settlement, but it is now settling with substantial farmers and stock-raisers. . . . It is destined to become a wealthy and prosperous country, as soon as its exposed condition to the inroads of the Indians can be overcome.

Cooke County: Gainesville.

Cooke was created, by Act of the Legislature, March 20th, 1848; but owing to its then extreme frontier position and remoteness from market, several years elapsed before extended settlements were made. . . . Its present population numbers 3,000, and its productive uplands and rich valleys are fast filling up with a respectable and industrial people; while the exceeding fertile bottom-lands of the Red river . . . are already opening their virgin bosoms to the cotton planter.

The Gainesville settlement . . . is the principal town in the country. It is beautifully situated on a prairie slope on the Elm fork. . . . It abounds with wells of superior water, the streets are clean, and the walks spread with white gravel drawn from the bed of the Elm. The great overland-mail route lies through the town, and passes centrally through the county.

1860–1861

Notes on Several Counties in the Central Hill Country

The Texas Almanac for 1861, which was published only during the early months of the war and then had to be discontinued, contained descriptions of several counties written either by prominent state residents or local officials. Though unnamed, these optimistic writers were gravely concerned with attracting new residents and therefore had much to say about rich and fertile soils, healthful climate, abundant rainfall, advantageous geographic location, beautiful scenery, safety from Indian attack, and rumors concerning railroad construction in the region. In spite of these glowing descriptions, the shadows of the "dark corner" were sometimes in evidence. Occasionally, writers could not hide their anxieties concerning recurring illnesses, grasshopper invasions, Indian depredations, and drought conditions.

The next excerpts from the *Almanac* focus attention on five counties in the rolling Hill Country of south central Texas: Coryell, Robertson, Milam, Hays, and Travis (see map 3). With the exception of Travis, these counties voted for secession from the Union in February 1861. Travis was the most densely populated of the group and was a trading center for the region, although many of the outlying settlements were largely self-sufficient. Coryell County, organized in 1854, originated from the nucleus of settlers situated in and around Fort Gates, which had been established in 1849. Milam County was trimmed down to its present size in 1856, although Cameron had been designated as the county seat as early as 1846. Robertson County was created from Milam County in 1837, but its present limits were established in 1846. During these early years the county seat of Robertson County was moved several times. First at Franklin, it was moved to Wheelock in 1850; in 1855 it was moved to Owensville on Walnut Creek. By the time the following excerpt was written, a change was under way that would locate the county seat at Calvert.

Most of the commercial activity of the region occurred in Hays and Travis counties. The stage and freight lines between Austin and San Antonio flourished, and the Old San Antonio Road was still a major artery for travel. Hays County was created and organized from Travis in 1848, and San Marcos was designated as county seat that same year. There were fewer than four hundred inhabitants in Hays County in 1850, but the area was alive with commercial enterprises. Sawmills, cotton gins, gristmills, and even a beef factory were among the county's business establishments. Travis County, containing the capital of the state, boasted a population of 8,080 in 1860. There were numerous small settlements around Austin which were of significance locally. By 1860 there were post offices at Bluff Springs, Webberville, Merrilltown, Gilliland, Gage's Mill, and Hornsby. Although a majority of the county's electorate voted against secession, there was considerable Confederate strength in the area, and the residents of Austin furnished Richmond with a full company of light infantry.

Source: The Texas Almanac for 1861, with Statistics, Historical and Bibliographical Sketches, etc., Relating to Texas (New Orleans: Thomas L. White, 1860), pp. 171–172, 177–180, 185–187.

Coryell County: Gatesville.
. . . The Leon River runs nearly central through this county, and constitutes nearly one half of the bottom-land of the county. [The remainder of the county is considered] . . . unsuited for cultivation. . . . Corn and wheat are the principal productions at present. . . . [There have been] . . . some severe droughts, in this portion of Texas for the last three years, until year before last; and my opinion is, the further west, the more severe the droughts are. [Livestock] . . . of all descriptions would do well here, if it were not for the Indian depredations. The Indians have been very troublesome here for the last two or three years; and if something is not soon done for our relief, we will have to give the county up to them, or all turn out in battle, and fight for our lives and property. Several of our citizens have been most cruelly butchered by them, and a

great many horses are stolen. The impression here is, that they are the Reserve Indians: the first reason assigned is, that all the children they take prisoners are dropped on the way, when they get a little out of the settlements; the second is, they speak English very well; and another is, that when they killed Mr. Riggs and family and others in this county, the old clothing they pulled off in exchange for better had stamped on the buttons, U.S. The people are at this time very much excited in this county [and] many have left the county. . . .

The grasshoppers are at times troublesome here. They have injured the wheat occasionally. This county has been settling five years; it now has four or five hundred voters. We have but little emigration here at this time, owing, doubtless, to the Indian depredations. This county is mostly settled by Tennesseeans, Missourians, and *Alabamians*. We have but one town, Gatesville. The population is small. There are two churches in Gatesville, two on Cowhouse Creek, one on Rainy's, one on Bluff Creek, one on Owl Creek, one at the head of Coryell Creek, one in Frankes' Neighborhood, one on Plum Creek, and one in Collard's neighborhood. We have not many slaves in this county, and no abolitionists: we are all constitutional men.

Robertson County: Owensville.

Robertson was created December 14, 1837, from Milam county, and comprised then, all the territory from its southern boundary the Old San Antonio road between the Brazos and Trinity rivers as far north as Red River. Like all mothers, this county has fed its numerous offspring by exhausting its own strength.

Owensville, the county-seat, is a pleasant village, of recent birth, situated upon a high, rolling prairie, over which are scattered a few trees affording good shade, and surrounded by a beautiful grove. There are few communities in which there is a more determined effort to preserve and enforce morality and order.

This village is on a direct line from the principal landing-points on the Red river to Austin City and San Antonio, and will, as it should, soon have the advantage of the greatest thoroughfare from eastern to western Texas. The bridging of the Navasota river which is now a fixed fact, will determine this matter. There are several other pleasant and prosperous towns, as Wheelock, which was formerly the county-seat, and Sterling, which is located immediately east of the Brazos river.

Milam County: Cameron.

The larger portion of . . . [the county] lies south of Little river, and is covered with dense forests of post-oaks, interspersed with small prairies of very productive land. Crossing Little river toward the north, you are ushered into large prairies, broken near the margin of streams, but become quite level as you advance toward the interior. . . . It is here that the stock-raiser realizes a handsome profit upon his capital invested. Thousands of beef cattle are annually driven from this part of the county to New Orleans.

. . . .

Cameron, the county-seat, is a beautiful little village, situated two miles north of Little river, in a beautiful grove, vies a lively trade with the interior, has a neat and handsome brick court-house, three dry goods stores, two family groceries, five or six lawyers' and doctors' offices, male and female academy, Baptist church, one silversmith, one gun-smith, three or four blacksmiths, one saddler, etc. A newspaper will be issued weekly in a short time. . . . According to the census of 1858, there were in this county 3476 souls, 1128 of which were slaves. There are about 550 voters.

Hays County: San Marcos.

Hays County is situated in one of the most delightful . . . regions of Texas embracing a large portion of mountainous, valley, and prairie land, including an area of eight hundred and twenty-five square miles. One third of the land in this county is adapted to the growth of cotton, corn, wheat, and barley. Barley has never been raised to any extent until this year, and the crop has been found to be very profitable, yielding upon some lands from fifty to sixty bushels per acre.

. . . .

The mountain region of this county is considered to be a very desirable section of county for the raising of sheep, and is rapidly filling up with shepherds, who have been very successful with their flocks, as they are much more healthy upon the mountains than they are upon the prairie.

. . . .

The town of San Marcos, situated near the head of the river by that name, . . . has a population of three hundred, and is the countyseat. The authorities of the county contemplate erecting the public buildings this year, such as a court-house, jail, clerks' offices, etc. We have religious service every sabbath, either at the Methodist, Baptist, Presbyterian or Christian Church.

Travis County: Austin.

The population of Austin is about 4,000, and, notwithstanding the hard times, dry weather, and grasshoppers, with which it had to contend for several years, it improves steadily. During the last twelve months many large, comfortable, substantial brick and stone buildings have been erected in Austin, and at present there are quite a number going up. These buildings are made of material that will last an age. The bricks made here are good and durable, and our stone quarries are inexhaustible. The Texas marble is chiefly used for building. There are seven churches in the city of Austin, namely, the Methodist, Baptist, Old School Presbyterian, Cumberland Presbyterian, Christian, Episcopalian, and Catholic; also Free Mason's Lodge, and Odd Fellows' Lodge, a Temple of Honor, two Good Samaritan Lodges, and seven American schools, and one German, three of them male, four female, and one mixed.

Webberville has a population of about two hundred, two churches, two schools, a Masonic Lodge, five stores, a hotel, and a debating society. It is fifteen miles below Austin on the Colorado. The road from Austin to Houston, Galveston, etc., runs through it. Merrilltown has a church, a school, a hotel, and a debating society: it is twelve miles north of Austin, on the road leading to Waco. Twelve miles east of Austin is Gilliland's Creek. At Parson's Seminary, there is a church, a Masonic Hall, and a fine female school. . . . There are other churches and schools scattered over the county.

Three Counties on the Sabine

During the early days of the Republic of Texas, the Sabine River furnished a means of transporting lumber, cotton, and livestock. Logs were cut from the pine forest and fashioned into rafts to be floated downstream. It soon became apparent, however, that the upper reaches of the river were not of sufficient size and depth to serve the transportation needs of the river settlements. Nevertheless, the East Texas lumber industry began to flourish because of increased demands for lumber all along the Texas coast and on the western frontier. The wagon freight industry boomed as the volume of lumber, grain, and cotton exports from East Texas mounted. On February 16, 1852, the Texas Western (Vicksburg and El Paso) Railroad was chartered to build a line from the eastern boundary of Texas to El Paso. Innumerable complications delayed construction until 1858, when twenty miles of track were completed east of Marshall. After the company had been rechartered and renamed the Southern Pacific, construction began westward from Marshall, which extended track into Upshur County, but the coming of the Civil War caused this work to end. In 1861 a scheme was devised to secure slave labor to work on the railroad, but this plan was soon abandoned.

The following excerpts focus on Wood and Upshur counties, situated upon the upper Sabine, and on Orange County, near the river's mouth (see map 3). According to the U.S. census in 1860, Wood County had a population of 4,986 and Upshur boasted 10,645. The two counties together had approximately 5,000 slaves. Upshur, created from Harrison and Nacogdoches counties in 1846, was organized shortly thereafter. Wood was created from Van Zandt County in 1850 and organized the same year. Quitman was selected as the county seat of Wood, and Gilmer became the county seat of Upshur. Orange County was created from Jefferson County in 1852 and was organized later in the same year with Madison, known as Orange by 1860, as the county seat. By the time the Civil War began, lumber and shipbuilding were the principal industries in Orange County, and some rice was produced. The great rice boom was not to arrive until the latter part of the century. The Texas and New Orleans Railroad reached the city of Orange on January 1, 1861.

Source: The Texas Almanac for 1861, with Statistics, Historical and Biblio-

graphical Sketches, etc., Relating to Texas (New Orleans: Thomas L. White, 1860), pp. 171–172, 177–180, and 186–187.

Wood County: Quitman.

Wood County was organized in 1850: its county-seat is Quitman: it has been improving ever since that time. Quitman is a thriving town situated very near the center of the county and is quite healthy. . . . The eastern part of Wood County is a forest of pine timber. There are some 12 saw-mills, mostly steam-power. From the 1st of April to December, there are from ten to thirty teams and wagons passing Quitman daily, going to and from the saw-mills, hauling timber to the counties west of Wood. This pine timber is the last pine to be met with going west. . . . The range of hogs, cows or sheep is good [and cotton, wheat, vegetables, potatoes, and corn are produced in abundance].

Society is good. There are good schools in every section of the county. A fine male and female institution in Quitman, has as many scholars as the teachers can attend to. Quitman has five large drygood houses, three family groceries, two retail stores, and one large and excellent hotel.

Upshur County: Gilmer.

Gilmer is the county-seat. It has three dry goods stores, two retail groceries, two provision stores, three blacksmith-shops, two wagonshops, one cabinet-shop, and a gunsmith-shop; one billiard-saloon, two bowling-alleys, two hotels, one livery-stable, a post office, and six law-offices, besides the usual public buildings, a Baptist church, a Methodist church, a male and female academy, a Masonic Lodge, and printing office, one tailor's shop, and one watch-maker. There are nine practicing attorneys, and seven practicing physicians. Coffeeville perhaps ranks next. It has two dry goods stores, two retail groceries, one drug-store, two black-smith-shops, one hotel, and three physicians; one Methodist and one Presbyterian Church, a Masonic Lodge, and one academy.

. . . .

There are no market-towns in the county. All the products of the county are sent to Jefferson, on Soda Lake, or to Shreveport, in ox or horse-wagons. The former place is about forty-five miles, the latter eighty miles. Wagoners charge seventy-five cents per bale cotton to Jefferson, and from one dollar to one dollar fifty cents to Shreveport. The Vicksburg and El Paso Railroad passes through the southern part of the county, and when completed will place the county in direct communication with the Mississippi river.

. . . .

Gilmer has eighteen mails weekly, on the following routes: three from Marshall, three from Quitman, three from Henderson, and three from Mount Pleasant, carried in two-horse stages; and three from Jefferson and three from Tyler, carried on horseback; also a mail from Jefferson to Quitman by way of Coffeeville and Simpsonville; also a mail from Marshall to Tyler via Earpville and Pine Tree. All these routes supply several intermediate post-offices. . . . The roads of the county are in good condition, all the streams that would cause delay by high water having been bridged, and the roads worked thoroughly, the road laws being generally enforced, thereby insuring good roads. The produce raised in the county will average as follows: 4600 bales of cotton, about 150,000 bushels of corn, and about 18,000 of wheat.

Orange County: Orange.
About half of the county is prairie, mostly low and level, with occasionally small ridges. It is generally well adapted to the growth of corn, cotton, and potatoes, and, on the lowlands, rice. . . . Some of our lands have been in cultivation upwards of thirty years, and where they have been cultivated and drained, they produce better than at first. . . . Orange is the principal town and county-seat, situated on the west bank of the Sabine. It has a Methodist church and several schools, etc. In the vicinity there are four or five saw-mills, and large quantities of timber and shingles are sent from here to Galveston or other more western seaports. Galveston and New Orleans are our markets, with transportation to both by water, though Galveston is much the nearest.

1861

The Texas Ordinance
of Secession

During the first three months of 1861, the Texas Secession Convention, in sessions extending from January 28 to February 4 and from March 2 to March 25, undertook several major projects that greatly altered the history of the Lone Star State. A resolution was passed declaring that Texas should secede from the Union, a declaration of causes for secession adopted, the 1845 ordinance of annexation repealed, a secession ordinance drafted, a Committee of Public Safety (to act for the convention during the recess from February 4 to March 2) appointed, and an election called to allow citizens of the state to vote on secession.

The actions of the Committee of Public Safety, chaired by an attorney from Tyler named John C. Robertson, were also noteworthy. The committee undertook to confer with General David Twiggs, commander of Federal forces in Texas, seeking possession of all arms, army stores, military posts, and other property in possession of the military forces of the United States. It appointed Ben McCulloch commander of state forces around San Antonio, Henry E. Mc-Culloch commander of Federal posts soon to be abandoned by Union garrisons on the northwestern frontier, and John S. "Rip" Ford commander of Brazos Santiago, Brownsville, and other posts along the lower Rio Grande. It also authorized O. M. Roberts, president of the convention, to attempt negotiation of a loan, not to exceed $95,000, which was to be used for military purposes under the direction of the Committee of Public Safety. The convention reassembled on March 2, canvassed the returns of the election held on February 23, announced popular sanction of secession, and on March 5 "approved, ratified, and accepted" the provisional government of the Confederate States of America then being erected in Montgomery, Alabama (see map 4).

One of the most dramatic and exciting moments in this tragic series of events occurred about noon on February 2, when the delegates to the first session of the convention voted on the ordinance of secession. The convention was assembled in the chamber of the House of Representatives in the capitol building, and the lobby and galleries were filled to overflowing. Governor Sam Houston, who opposed the secession movement, and Lieutenant Governor Edward Clark, who

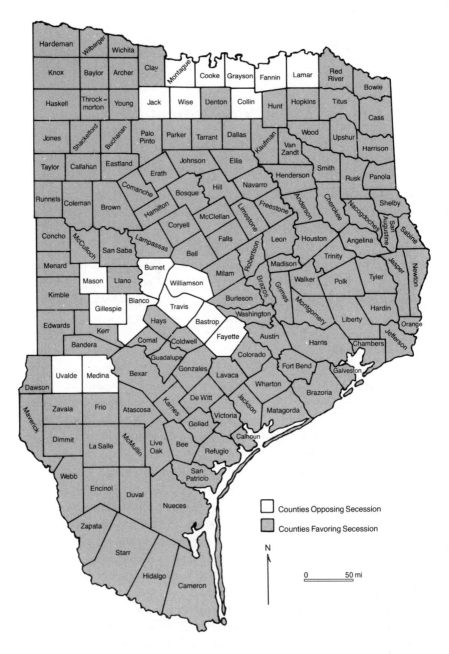

Map 4. Counties Voting for and against Secession. (From Ernest Wallace, *Texas in Turmoil* [Austin, 1965], p.70. Reprinted with the permission and assistance of Steck-Vaughn Company, publisher.)

would fill the governor's chair in the event Houston was deposed, were in attendance. Other important state officials and influential citizens were also present.
In spite of the crowded conditions, a degree of silence prevailed as a roll-call vote
of convention delegates began. As vote after vote was recorded in the affirmative, sporadic bursts of applause came from the galleries. Seventy delegates
voted in favor of the ordinance before Thomas P. Hughes, an attorney from
Georgetown, voted a resounding "no." Grumbling and cries of displeasure
poured from the galleries, but the roll call continued. Applause followed the affirmative votes of U.S. Congressman John Reagan and former governor H. R.
Runnels. The loudest and most threatening display of disapproval from the gallery came when James W. Throckmorton, an attorney from McKinney, proclaimed that he was "unawed by the wild spirit of revolution" and cast the second negative vote.

The final tally was 171 votes for the ordinance and 6 votes in opposition, although several of the affirmative votes came later when absentee delegates returned to affix their signatures to the document. William H. Johnson and George
W. Wright of Paris, A. P. Shuford of Quitman, and Joshua A. Johnson of Titus
County joined with Hughes and Throckmorton to make the six who voted
against secession.

When the roll call was completed, a boisterous demonstration began, and an
impromptu procession formed and snaked its way down the aisles. Many of the
demonstrators were female spectators from the galleries and lobby who joined
the wild march through the House chamber. The spirit of celebration permeated
the entire hall as Attorney General George M. Flournoy assumed the lead position carrying a huge Lone Star flag. Gradually the demonstration subsided, but
an overwhelming sentiment favoring secession had been registered. This sentiment was further demonstrated on February 23, when the voters of the state approved the ordinance by more than a thirty-thousand-vote margin.

The Texas ordinance of secession, as it appeared in its final version, is reproduced below.

Source: Dudley G. Wooten, *A Comprehensive History of Texas, 1685 to
1897*, 2 vols. (Dallas: William G. Scarff, 1898), 2:104–106.

AN ORDINANCE

TO DISSOLVE THE UNION BETWEEN THE STATE OF TEXAS AND THE
OTHER STATES, UNITED UNDER THE COMPACT STYLED "THE CONSTI-
TUTION OF THE UNITED STATES OF AMERICA." WHEREAS, the Federal
government has failed to accomplish the purposes of the compact of

union between these States, in giving protection either to the persons of our people upon an exposed frontier or to the property of our citizens; AND, WHEREAS, The action of the Northern States of the Union is violative of the compact between the States and the guarantees of the Constitution; AND, WHEREAS, The recent developments in Federal affairs make it evident that the power of the Federal government is sought to be made a weapon with which to strike down the interests and prosperity of the people of Texas and her sister slave-holding States, instead of permitting it to be, as was intended, our shield against outrage and aggression; *therefore,*

Section 1 – We, the people of the State of Texas by delegates in convention assembled, do declare and ordain that the ordinance adopted by our convention of delegates on the 4th day of July, A.D. 1845, and afterwards ratified by us, under which the republic of Texas was admitted into the Union with other States, and became a party to the compact styled "The Constitution of the United States of America," be and is hereby repealed and annulled; that all the powers which by the said compact were delegated by Texas to the Federal government are revoked and resumed; that Texas is of right absolved from all restraints and obligations incurred by said compact, and is a separate sovereign State; and that her citizens and people are absolved from all allegiance to the United States or the government thereof.

Section 2 – This ordinance shall be submitted to the people of Texas for their ratification or rejection by the qualified voters on the 23d day of February, 1861, and unless rejected by a majority of the votes cast, shall take effect and be in force on and after the 2d day of March, A.D. 1861. *Provided,* that in the representative district of El Paso said election may be held on the 18th day of February, 1861. Done by the people of the State of Texas, in convention assembled, at Austin, this 1st day of February, A.D. 1861.

[Including that of the president of the convention, O. M. Roberts, 171 Texans attached their signatures to the above document. A complete list of their names appears in Appendix I of this volume.]

David Twiggs's Surrender of U.S. Army Posts in Texas

Throughout his administration, President James Buchanan failed to take strong measures to defend Federal forts and outposts on Southern soil. He did refuse to evacuate Fort Sumter as South Carolina authorities demanded, but Fort Moultrie and Castle Pinckney were seized by Southern "fire-eaters" late in 1860, and Fort Pulaski and Fort Morgan at Mobile were taken early in 1861. In Texas, Georgian David E. Twiggs, commanding the Department of Texas, turned over nineteen U.S. posts to Texas troops while wearing the uniform of the United States Army. According to the *Official Records of the Union and Confederate Armies*, Ser. I, Vol. 53, p. 632, the estimated value of the grounds, buildings, and stores in San Antonio which Twiggs turned over to state forces was $781,808.39. All other posts in Texas with their properties, also surrendered by Twiggs, had an estimated value of $700,000.

Almost three weeks before the Texas ordinance of secession was ratified, Ben McCulloch, a noted Indian fighter, called upon citizens of southwestern Texas to collect their firearms and rendezvous with him a few miles north of San Antonio on Salado Creek (see map 3). Answering this call to arms, hundreds of Texans flocked to the designated rendezvous site, many riding all night to arrive in time to join the march on San Antonio the next day. McCulloch dispatched some of his men to surround the Alamo, which was being used as an arsenal for military supplies. McCulloch then placed his men, with rifles in hand, on the rooftops of surrounding buildings to be in position if U.S. soldiers attempted to use artillery against them. Twiggs's headquarters, located about a mile outside the city, was also quietly surrounded by armed Texans. The next day, February 16, Twiggs was escorted into the Grand Plaza, where McCulloch and several of his lieutenants had assembled. Within a few hours, Twiggs had agreed to surrender all U.S. forts in the state. A Lavaca County schoolteacher, J. K. P. Blackburn, who witnessed the scene, said that Twiggs "wept like a child" from the humiliation he suffered. Two weeks later Twiggs was cashiered out of the U.S. Army for "treachery to the flag."

The following account of the surrender was written by Caroline Baldwin

Darrow, the wife of one of Twiggs's confidential clerks. A strong Unionist, Mrs. Darrow was disgusted with the numerous manifestations of secessionism she saw in San Antonio, and her contempt for General Twiggs is unmistakable. She hid valuable government documents and official papers from the Texans until those materials were "no longer valuable." She and Colonel R. E. Lee, who arrived from Fort Mason on his way to Washington, felt much the same toward the Union; the latter, however, would soon make his painful decision to follow his "beloved Virginia" along the road of secession. Lee claimed to be neutral at this point, whereas Mrs. Darrow never wavered in her loyalty to the Union. She and her husband eventually returned to the North to be "under the protection of [their] own flag."

Source: Mrs. Caroline Baldwin Darrow, "Recollections of the Twiggs Surrender," in Clarence C. Buel and Robert U. Johnson, eds., Battles and Leaders of the Civil War, 4 vols. (New York: Century, 1884–1888), 1:33–38.

Early in December, 1860, a rumor reached San Antonio, Texas, that Captain John R. Baylor, well known throughout the State, was organizing a company of one thousand men for a buffalo-hunt. As Captain Baylor's secession sentiments were well known, this was believed to be a mere pretense, and his real design to be to surprise and seize the arsenal in San Antonio, in time to prevent any resistance on the part of the United States, should Texas go out of the Union. The Union citizens, alarmed lest the few soldiers stationed there should prove insufficient, appealed to General David E. Twiggs, then commanding the Department of Texas, to increase the force. He accordingly furnished several hundred men, consisting of Knights of the Golden Circle (a secret secession organization), the Alamo Rifles, two other citizen companies, and an Irish and a German company. This quieted apprehension for a time, but in January these troops were quietly withdrawn. At this time General Twiggs's loyalty to the United States Government began to be questioned, as he was known to be often in consultation with prominent secessionists, some of them ladies. Toward the end of January the Union men again appealed to General Twiggs, but nothing was accomplished whereupon they armed themselves, waiting with undefined dread for the next move. Meanwhile no one trusted his neighbor, since spies and informers abounded, and to add to the terror, there were fears of insurrection among the negroes, some of whom were arrested; while all of them were forbidden to walk or talk together on the streets, or to assemble as they had been accustomed to do.

Late in January was held the election for delegates to a State convention which should consider the question of secession. San Antonio was crowded. Women vied with each other in distributing the little yellow ballots, on which were printed in large type, "For Secession," or "Against Secession." Many an ignorant Mexican received instructions that the ballot "with the longest words" was the right one. The *carteros* from New Mexico, who were in town with their wagon-trains, were bought by the secessionists, and some were known to have voted three times. It was well known that the Federal civil officers were loyal; the French and German citizens were emphatically so; and yet against the will of the people, "by superior political diplomacy," secession triumphed in San Antonio by a small majority. Many Germans gave up their business and left town, taking refuge in New Braunfels, 31 miles away. Many of these men were political refugees of rare culture and scholarly attainments.

On the 1st of February, the ordinance of secession was adopted by the Texas Convention, and on the 4th commissioners were appointed "to confer with General Twiggs, with regard to the public arms, stores, munitions of war, etc., under his control, and belonging to the United States, with power to demand [these things] in the name of the State of Texas." To meet this commission, which consisted of Thomas J. Devine, P. N. Luckett, and Samuel A. Maverick, on the 9th of February General Twiggs appointed a commission consisting of Major David H. Vinton, Major Sackfield Maclin (secessionist), and Captain R. H. K. Whiteley. By this time the news of General Twiggs's disaffection had reached the Government, and Colonel C. A. Waite was sent to supersede him.

One day, accidentally overhearing parts of a conversation between General Twiggs and a prominent Southern lady, I felt no longer any doubt that he was about to betray his trust, and reported the matter to Major Vinton. He sought an interview with General Twiggs, and told me that he could find no suspicion of disloyalty, and that I was entirely mistaken. Getting information a few days later, which led me to believe that the day for the surrender was fixed, I again informed Major Vinton. He then decided to remove at once from his safe all papers that would give valuable information to the State authorities, and the moneys belonging to the Government, and he intrusted them to his confidential clerk, Charles Darrow. They were sent at midnight to his wife, who was waiting to receive them, and who buried part of them in a deserted garden; the rest, secreted in the ashes of an unused stove and in the tester of a bed, were guarded by her till the information was no longer valuable.

General Twiggs had succeeded in completely blinding his brother officers as to his plans; but he now had no time to lose before Colonel Waite's arrival.

On the 15th news came that some of the passengers on the mailcoach had alighted at the crossing of the Salado and joined a large company of Texas Rangers who, under the command of Ben McCulloch, had been encamped there for several days. Captain Baylor's buffalo-hunt had at last assumed a tangible shape.

To be prepared for any emergency, for many nights we had kept our firearms beside us. On the night of the 15th, worn out with anxious watching, we fell asleep, to be suddenly roused about 4 o'clock by the screams of the negroes, who were coming home from market, "We're all going to be killed!" I grasped my revolver, and springing to my feet, looked out upon the plaza. In the dim light I saw the revolutionists appearing, two by two, on muleback and horseback, mounted and on foot, a motley though quite orderly crowd, carrying the Lone Star flag before them, and surrounded and supported by armed men. The nights had been cold, and a week on the Salado without comforts had not added to their valorous appearance. Some had coats, but others were in their shirt-sleeves, and not a few were wrapped in old shawls and saddle-blankets. Their arms were of every description. By daylight more had appeared, perhaps a thousand in all, and so great was the enthusiasm of two women who had aided General Twiggs in his arrangements that they mounted their horses, in male attire, and with pistols in their belts rode out to meet their friends. Coffee and refreshments had been provided, and blankets and clothing were lavishly distributed. All the stores were closed; men, women, and children armed themselves, and the excitement was intense. Companies of Union citizens, well drilled and well armed, were marching and countermarching, presenting an imposing contrast to the other party, and a conflict seemed inevitable. The arsenal building had been opened and was swarming with Rangers. Early in the morning General Twiggs drove down to the main plaza, where he was instantly surrounded by secessionists demanding the Government property, whereupon he went through the form of refusing their request. He then held a conference with Major W. A. Nichols, his assistant adjutant-general, and Ben McCulloch, and was given six hours in which to reconsider. By noon he had surrendered all the United States posts and stores in Texas. When the result was known there was great indignation against him among the citizens. Two or three hours later he left for New Orleans, where he was received with public honors. Orders were sent to all the outposts to turn over the military property to the State. The officers and men were widely scattered, and many of them were taken completely by surprise. The Federal troops in town gave their parole "not to take up arms" against the Confederacy, and were ordered to leave the post in the afternoon. By this time the German company had refused to act against the United States, and the citizen companies had disbanded. The Irish company had twice torn down the Stars and Stripes from the Alamo, and had raised the Lone Star flag in its place. An attempt was made to disarm the troops, but they declared that they would kill any man who interfered, and marched away under Major Larkin Smith and Captain John H. King, with the stained and bullet-riddled old flag of the 8th Regiment flying over them, while the band played national airs. Strong men wept; the people cheered them along the streets, and many followed them to the head of the San Pedro, where they encamped. By 6 o'clock the Rangers had returned to their camp on the Salado, and the day ended without further excitement.

About 2 o'clock that afternoon, Colonel Robert E. Lee arrived in his ambulance from Fort Mason, Texas, on his way to Washington, whither he had been ordered by General [Winfield] Scott. As he approached the Read House I went out to meet him. At the same time some of the Rangers gathered around his wagons, and, attracted, no doubt, by their insignia of rank, the red flannel strips sewed on their shoulders, he asked, "Who are those men?" "They are McCulloch's," I answered. "General Twiggs surrendered everything to the State this morning, and we are all prisoners of war." I shall never forget his look of astonishment, as with his lips trembling and his eyes full of tears, he exclaimed, "Has it come so soon as this?" In a short time I saw him crossing the plaza on his way to headquarters, and noticed particularly that he was in citizen's dress. He returned at night and shut himself in his room, which was over mine, and I heard his footsteps through the night, and sometimes the murmur of his voice, as if he were praying. He remained at the hotel a week, and in conversations declared that the position he held was a neutral one. When he left it was my firm belief that no one could persuade or compel him to change his decision.

During the next two days the Rangers were drinking and shouting about the streets, recklessly shooting any one who happened to displease them. From this time on, Union men were in danger, and Northerners sent their families away. Some who were outspoken were imprisoned and barely escaped with their lives; among them, Charles Anderson, brother of Robert Anderson [who surrendered Fort Sumter to General P. G. T. Beauregard on April 13, 1861].

On the 26th of February a dozen men of the State troops were stationed on guard over the offices of the disbursing officers, and the occupants were ordered to leave, but forbidden to take away papers or effects, though allowed to keep the keys to their safes. Colonel Waite had now arrived and assumed command, and the secessionist commissioners made a second demand for "a statement of the amount of indebtedness and funds on hand" and "required a promise from each officer that he would pay outstanding debts with funds and turn the balance over to the State": it being very desirable to the enemy to possess the Government records, which exhibited the number of troops and the condition of the whole department. Imprisonment and death were to be the penalty in case of refusal; but Major Vinton of the quartermaster's department declared that he did not fear either, would do nothing dishonorable and would not comply. Major Daniel McClure of the pay department and Captain Whiteley of the ordinance department also refused, but several officers did comply and were returned to their offices. The larger responsibilities of the quartermaster's department detained Major Vinton after the above-named officers had left, and thus he fought his battle almost alone. His office was transferred to his own house, where with the aid of Mr. Darrow he transacted his business. He soon became so ill that it was impossible for him to leave his bed. Both were afterward arrested and given ten days in which to surrender the papers and funds or be shot. These threats were not executed, for on the morning of the tenth day we were gladdened by the news that United States troops from the different outposts were within a few miles of the town, having been three weeks on the way. They were met at the San Pedro and paroled not to take arms against the Confederacy or serve in any capacity during the war. These troops, representing the army in Texas, were loyal almost to a man, while all but forty of the officers went over to the Confederacy. The commissioners had promised to furnish facilities for the transportation of these troops to the coast, but so great had been the confusion and so many supplies had been carried off, that the soldiers were left almost destitute. I visited their camp and found them cursing the man who had placed them in this position.

Major Vinton and family, with my husband and myself, were the last to leave. On the morning of our departure, the 11th of May, as the ambulances and baggage wagons stood at the door, to add to the gloom, a storm broke over the city, enveloping us in midnight darkness. The thunder and lightning was so loud and incessant as to seem like the noise of battle. For two weeks we journeyed over the parklike prairies, fragrant and brilliant with flowers. We forded streams and rivers, crossed the Brazos by a rope ferry, and, taking the railroad train from Harrisburg to Galveston, caught the last steamer before the blockade of New Orleans. We went up the Mississippi in the steamer, *Hiawatha,* which was crowded with refugees, who made no sign until, in answer to a shot from shore at Cairo, the steamer rounded to and we found ourselves once more under the protection of our own flag.

1861

Reminiscences of a Common Soldier

A statue of a horse and rider, honoring one of the most famous fighting units Texas has ever produced, stands on the state capitol grounds in Austin. This unit was Terry's Texas Rangers. Soon after the close of the Secession Convention, Benjamin F. Terry left Austin in the company of Thomas S. Lubbock to serve in the Confederate military effort east of the Mississippi River. Terry, a planter from Fort Bend County, and Thomas Lubbock, brother of Francis Lubbock, who was elected governor the following November, served on the staff of General Pierre G. T. Beauregard during the first battle of Bull Run in Virginia. After their return to Texas they received permission from the Confederate War Department to recruit a regiment of cavalry in the Lone Star State for service in the eastern theater. After establishing a muster center for the proposed unit in Houston, they sent recruiting officers into counties in the southern part of the state with instructions to raise ten companies of mounted volunteers. This was accomplished in short order, and soon the companies began arriving in Houston. Captain John A. Wharton reported with a company from Matagorda and Harris counties; Captain James G. Walker brought a company from Montgomery and Harris counties; and Captain Louis N. Strobel, whose company is discussed in the excerpt below, arrived with over a hundred horsemen from Fayette County. Other counties represented by companies arriving in Houston were Gonzales, McLellan, Bexar, Goliad, and Fort Bend. On September 9, the regiment, consisting of ten companies numbering 1,170 men, was mustered into Confederate service as the Eighth Texas Cavalry.

This regiment averaged well over a hundred men per company, and all lined up on three sides of the square for the mustering-in ceremony. Lieutenant J. Sparks, a former officer in the United States Army, administered the oath of allegiance. After the ceremony, several men of the unit, eager to demonstrate their skill and daring, provided a show of horsemanship for residents of the city. They formed themselves into squads and rode through the crowded streets at breakneck speeds, swinging from their saddles to pick up pieces of cloth and sticks from the ground. Several Rangers forced townspeople to scurry in all directions to escape injury as they broke wild mustangs in the middle of a busy thoroughfare.

The unit left Houston the day following the mustering-in ceremony and, traveling in boxcars on the Texas and New Orleans Railroad, proceeded to Beaumont. Since only a few of the Rangers possessed mounts, most men of the regiment then marched on foot to New Orleans, where they secured passage on riverboats and were transported up the Mississippi to Bowling Green, Kentucky, to join the command of General Albert Sidney Johnston. Shortly thereafter the Rangers held an election and selected Benjamin F. Terry colonel of their regiment.

Although the following excerpt does not contain an account of the military operations of Terry's Rangers during the months that followed, the highlights of the unit's subsequent history are noteworthy. The regiment was involved in a bloody battle near Woodsonville, Kentucky, where Terry was killed and command of the unit passed to Thomas Lubbock. Lubbock, ill at the time, died before he could assume his duties, and Colonel Thomas Harrison of Houston became regimental commander. Thereafter, Terry's Texas Rangers fought at Shiloh, Bardstown, Perryville, Murfreesboro, Chickamauga, and Knoxville. The unit surrendered to General William T. Sherman at Greensboro, North Carolina, in April 1865. Almost two years later, surviving Rangers erected the statue in Austin honoring their fallen comrades.

The following excerpt was taken from an account written by one of the survivors. It deals only with the organization of the unit, the mustering-in ceremony in Houston, and the regiment's departure for Kentucky. It is of considerable value because it provides information concerning a young Texan's impressions of wartime Texas, life in an army camp, organizational procedures of the military, and the early composition of the famous cavalry regiment.

Source: J. K. P. Blackburn, "Reminiscences of the Terry Rangers," *Southwestern Historical Quarterly* 22 (July 1918): 38–42. Reprinted by permission.

When the Civil War commenced I was in school in Lavaca County, Texas, both as teacher and pupil, where I had been most of the time for four and a half years before. I was born in Tennessee in 1837 and in the fall of 1856, when I was about 19 years of age, my father emigrated to Texas with his family of wife and eight children. I taught a little primary school in Fayette County first for three months. Then I sold a horse my father gave me, got my money for teaching school, put these two funds together, and went to Alma Institute in Lavaca County for two years. I taught one year in Gonzales County, and after thus adding to my bank account, returned to my *alma mater* as pupil and assistant teacher and was there until hostilities commenced between North and South.

. . . .

[Daily routines and] . . . school work seemed tame [after Twiggs's surrender of U.S. military posts in the state] . . . and overshadowed by tragic events on every side. War was declared by Lincoln on the seceded States, calling for troops from the other Southern States to help put down the rebellion. The Confederate Government had been formed at Montgomery, Alabama. A blaze of enthusiasm and resentment sweeping over the southland prompted patriots on every hand to get ready to defend their homes and firesides against the ravages and destruction of an insolent foe who was then moving to invade the South. The seceded States established drill and instruction camps in different parts of their borders, training men on every hand for effectual fighting. The camps were provided with competent drill masters, mobilization went on day after day through the spring and the early summer and on through the year, and regiments were formed and sent forward towards the seat of war until thousands were mustered into service from every section that year, the year of 1861. I spent several weeks at Camp Clark on the San Marcos River, drilling and learning military tactics at that camp of instruction. All conversation on every side pertained to war and incidents and hopes and fears connected therewith. The question of, "Are you going to the war?" was rarely asked, but "Where will you go?"

I had a room-mate the last session in school named Foley, large hearted, intellectual and a poet, a Baptist preacher of ability, and a native of New York City. He and I discussed the question often and while we both preferred cavalry service, being good horsemen, he preferred to go west and northwest with the first regiment formed, I to go towards the east in order to be upon the main fields of battle even if I had to go with the infantry. We separated. He enlisted in [a cavalry unit and] . . . went to meet the enemy that was threatening Texas from the northwest. The next news I had from . . . [his unit was that] Foley had been killed in a charge on a battery at Valverda or Glorietta, New Mexico, (I have forgotten which) killed by the last shot fired from that battery before its capture. Thus passed from earth one of the noblest spirits I ever knew.

I considered a proposition from Captain Fly who was raising a company in our neighborhood for the 2nd Texas infantry and at one time told him I thought I might join his company when they got ready to start, but told him of my preference for the cavalry. Weeks passed. At last the opportunity came. A regiment of cavalry was to be raised in western and southern Texas for service in Virginia. Two Texans of wealth and leisure, B. F. Terry, a sugar planter, and Thomas S. Lubbock, a lawyer, who were traveling in the East whether for business, pleasure, or curiosity, I know not happened at or purposely were at the battle of first Manassas in Virginia, and rendered all the aid they could to the Southern cause. Terry acted as volunteer aid[e] to the commanding general, and Lubbock also exposed his life in bearing messages during the contest. About the middle of August commissions came to Terry and Lubbock from the war department at Richmond, Virginia, authorizing them to raise a regiment on certain conditions, viz.: each man to furnish his own arms (double-barrelled shotgun and two six shooters), his bridle, blanket, saddle, spurs, lariat, etc., the Government to mount the men on good horses. The men should always select their own officers from colonel down to fourth corporal and serve in the Virginia army as an independent command. This was the opportunity that many had wished for and in less than twenty days this call was answered by 1170 men assembling at

Houston to be enrolled in the regiment, afterwards called Terry's Texas Rangers. Colonel Terry immediately after securing the commission selected ten men in different sections and counties of the southern and western part of the State and asked them to raise a company of about a hundred men and bring them to Houston for enrollment in the army as soon as practical.

The company which I joined was made up from Fayette, Lavaca and Colorado counties, the majority being from Fayette. L. N. Strobel, having the authority, enrolled the names and set a day for meeting at Lagrange in Fayette County for organizing the company by electing officers from captain to corporal. At the called meeting Strobel was elected captain, W. R. Jarman first lieutenant, Phocian and William Tate (brothers) were selected second and third lieutenants, C. D. Barnett orderly sergeant, and J. T. J. Culpepper second sergeant. I cannot recall with any certainty the names of the other noncommissioned officers at this date. Our next meeting was called for Houston, Texas, where we were to be sworn in as soldiers of the Confederate States. Early in September the city of Houston was filled with volunteers anxious to enlist in the Terry Rangers. One thousand men were expected to constitute the regiment, but more and more were enlisted until the number reached 1170, an average of 117 to each company, and others, I don't recall how many, were denied the privilege of enlistment.

A Lieutenant Sparks, who had belonged to the United States army if I mistake not, came authorized to administer the oath of allegiance to the Confederate States and enroll us as her soldiers. A little incident happened at the time which showed the feelings and determination of the men. They were lined up on three sides of a hollow square (as I now remember). The enrolling officer in the center asked this question, "Do you men wish to be sworn into service for twelve months or for three years or for during the war?" With a unanimity never surpassed, a shout unheard of before, that whole body of men shouted, "For the war," "For the war!" not one expecting or caring to return until the war was over, long or short, and the invaders had been driven from our borders.

And now the regiment is ready for service, as fine a body as ever mustered for warfare. The majority of them were college boys, and cowboys, professional men, men with finished education, men just out of college, others still under-graduates, men raised in the saddles, as it were, experts with lariat and with six shooters, and not a few from the farm, from the counting houses and from shops. Just why the regiment did not elect field officers and become a fully organized body of soldiers at Houston I never knew. In the absence of this organization, the companies not being numbered or lettered, each company was called by its captain's name. Ours was Captain Strobel's company, and was sent forward as the vanguard of the regiment toward the seat of war by Colonel Terry who assumed command although he refused to be called Colonel until he should be elected to the position by his men. The election took place in Kentucky in December following.

The company was put in box freight cars and started eastward over what was afterwards to be called the Sunset Route, which at that time ran east from . . . Houston to New Iberia, Louisiana.

1861

A Young Recruit's Notes on the Organization of a Texas Unit

W. W. Heartsill was born on October 17, 1839, in a little village on the Holston River near Knoxville, Tennessee. He was twenty years old when he arrived in Marshall, Texas, to become a clerk in the mercantile store of Bradfield and Talley, where he was working when the Civil War began. His pro-Southern views are readily apparent in the opening comments of his journal, part of which is reproduced below. His disgust with Abraham Lincoln and the "aggressive" North is probably typical of a majority of Texans in the eastern part of the state during these months.

When Sheriff A. W. Crawford of Harrison County announced that a company of mounted infantry would be formed, Heartsill and several of his friends were among the first to enlist. The result was a company of 301 determined young men from Harrison and surrounding counties which was formally sworn into state service on April 19, 1861, as the W. P. Lane Rangers. After the company had elected officers, there followed the customary patriotic presentations and speeches, amid a mixture of happiness and grief. Some of the recruits became overzealous in their consumption of hard liquor, prompting Heartsill to remark that they were "half-seas-over." Lane's Rangers were commanded by Sam J. Richardson throughout the war.

One of the significant points revealed in the following excerpt is that most men of Confederate mounted units, unlike Union cavalrymen, furnished their own horses. Heartsill explained that, on April 19, the men of the W. P. Lane Rangers "spent much of the day undergoing valuation of [their] horses." Each horse was given a value by company appraisers with the understanding that the owner would be paid forty cents a day for the use of his mount. When a horse was killed in battle, the owner usually received its appraised value and a thirty-day furlough to find himself another horse. Some of a company's equipment and many personal items used by Confederate soldiers were supplied by patriotic citizens of the county in which the company was organized.

The editor has reworked the following excerpt far more extensively than most of the other excerpts in this volume. Young Heartsill, not a student of composition, was well educated for his time and wrote with considerable care, expecting his chronicles to be read by members of the unit and their "relatives and sympathizing friends." The editing of this excerpt has consisted largely of recasting the author's sentences and correcting punctuation in the hope of rendering the narrative more readable. For the most part, semicolons have been replaced with other punctuation marks because Heartsill tended to use semicolons almost to the exclusion of other forms of punctuation. The author's organization, phraseology, and spelling have been tampered with very little so that his warm and expressive style may remain intact. Great care was taken not to change the meaning of Heartsill's statements.

Source: W. W. Heartsill, *Fourteen Hundred and 91 Days in the Confederate Army; or Camp Life, Day by Day of the W. P. Lane rangers from April 19, 1861 to May 20, 1865.* Facsimile reprint, ed. Bell I. Wiley (Jackson, Tenn.: McCowat-Mercer Press, 1954), pp. 1–5 and 23–25. Reprinted by permission.

Marshall, Texas; April 19, 1861 – I do not propose to write this journal for the inspection or criticism of the public. Also, I do not expect it to be of interest to anyone outside of the relatives and sympathizing friends of the members of our unit. I shall occasionally express my own opinions which may prove ludicrous, but I shall endeavor to state the truth upon all passing events. In keeping my diary, I hope to write a history of our unit; but I expect to record many things of a personal nature which will be interspersed among descriptions of my unit's adventures. I ask only that my comrades bear with me if I do not get all things correct, for they will appreciate the many disadvantageous circumstances under which I have labored in producing this narrative.

It is useless for me to undertake to chronicle the causes that have brought on this great struggle. I believe that it will be short in duration, probably not lasting more than twelve months. Since our cause is just before Heaven, I further predict that we will succeed in our great undertaking. In later years, a person will be ignorant indeed who has not learned that in November, 1860, Abraham Lincoln was elected President of the United States, and that the people of the South construed this as an overt act. This, in turn, put into motion the mammoth wheel of secession. During the months of December, 1860, and January, 1861, mass meetings were convened in every county in the State, and delegates were appointed to attend a convention which was held in Austin in February. The convention was nearly unanimous for secession but referred the question back to the people for the final verdict. The results of the subsequent election supporting secession, held on March 2, 1861, is well known. The convention also authorized the governor to issue a call for two mounted regiments to occupy U.S. forts on the Texas frontier which are being abandoned by U.S. troops. The civilian inhabitants of our frontier are unprotected and subject to the murderous excursions of Indians and treacherous Mexicans.

Soon thereafter, Sheriff A. W. Crawford of Harrison County received authority from the Governor to raise one company of Rangers from the region around Marshall. Mr. Crawford immediately opened a book for the registration of names, and there was a great rush of young men to enlist. The impression was held by many that the newly formed company would be ordered immediately from Austin to Galveston. Luther Henderson, John Duke, James Curtis, and I joined the company on April 7th. By the 10th the list was full and overflowing; and Mr. Crawford designated April 19th the day my diary begins as the day for the formal organization of the company. I was prompted to enlist because of a strict sense of duty and because I feel that our cause is just. Certainly I have no desire for military fame even if I should have the ability to earn it. Duke and I, both being from Tennessee, have been clerking in the store of Bradfield and Talley; but we decided to embrace the first opportunity to enlist. We may not find so much fun and frolic as we anticipate.

April 19 – At a very early hour, the hitherto quiet of Marshall was disturbed by the "neigh of the war horse" and the assembling of cavalry.

The counties of Panola, Upshur, and Marion have sent forth some of their best material, and the town is full of soldiers, all finely mounted and prepared for military service. We are in need of arms, but we expect to receive these when we get to Austin. Over one hundred men made up our Company, most of whom were from Harrison and Upshur counties; but Marion and Panola counties were well represented, and we had a few men from Wood, Rusk, Hunt, Jefferson, and Smith counties. At 9 A.M., we fell into line on the north side of the courthouse, and spent much of the day undergoing valuation of our horses. This was conducted by Major William Bradfield, A. G. Scogin, and A. W. Crawford. Then at 3 o'clock in the afternoon we proceeded with the organization of the company.

The election of officers and members of the unit began, and upon the motion of Captain Sam J. Richardson, we adopted a name for our company: the "W. P. Lane Rangers." Our company was thus named in honor of a worthy citizen of Marshall who had distinguished himself during the Texas Revolution. About sunset the results of the election were announced and muster rolls were prepared. These results were received with great satisfaction and many of our boys began drinking and were soon "half-seas-over."

The citizens of Marshall provided lodgings for those of the Company who were great distances from home, and the entire town's activities were geared to servicing our unit. In the *Marshall Republican*, there was a request for Reverend Dunlap to preach a parting sermon to the Rangers; and when the request was met, the church house was densely crowded. The Marshall "Guards" turned out in full uniform, and attended the service which lasted more than an hour.

April 20 – The streets of Marshall resounded with the tread of spirited horses even before the golden streaks of dawn spread across the April sky. Increased commotion and excitement marked this day as no ordinary day. At 9 o'clock, Major Lane formed the Company in an old field east of town, and we marched four abreast into town. An orderly formation was lined up east of the Courthouse where we were presented with a splendid flag by the people of Marshall. Miss Sallie O. Smith, a prominent lady of Marshall, delivered a beautiful speech which filled us with pride and feelings of patriotism. The flag was accepted on the part of the Rangers by Lieutenant John T. Holcombe with a few appropriate remarks. This sentimental ceremony concluded, the remainder of the morning was spent saying goodbye to relatives and friends.

At noon we prepared to take our leave of the town, escorted by Captain F. S. Bass and the Marshall Guards. A hearty dinner was provided by the ladies prior to our departure, and "to horse" was sounded about 1 o'clock. Another address was delivered by Thomas J. Bell of the Guards, and we were off westward on "war's tempestious sea."

1861

Across Texas with the W. P. Lane Rangers

The following excerpt was taken from W. W. Heartsill's diary of his military service with the W. P. Lane Rangers. The unit was organized in Marshall in April 1861 and immediately set out on a lengthy trek to Austin, San Antonio, and finally Camp Wood, a recently abandoned U.S. outpost on the Nueces River in far West Texas (see map 3). Heartsill's detailed and colorful account of this journey, in addition to his attempts at humor and descriptions of his own experiences and observations, provides revealing insights into army life in the Confederate Trans-Mississippi Department. His references to topography, wild animals, climate, vegetation, livestock, frontier settlements, and local inhabitants reveal much about the state, the times, and the undeveloped nature of the country. Comments on cavalry techniques, hazards of travel, and the inconveniences of living in the open disclose many of the problems of mounted dragoons during the Civil War.

Heartsill's description of the "messmate" system of cooking and eating in the field is of special interest. Many of the friendships soldiers formed in this unique relationship lasted the rest of their lives. A member of W. H. Parsons's regiment, who enjoyed the company of the same messmates throughout the war, wrote in his recollections that the members of his mess "were always friends" and even after the war remained "warmly attached to each other." Heartsill's ownership of the coffeepot used in his mess won him instant status among his messmates. Other items, such as frying pans and stewers, were also considered vital commodities, although some messes had to get along without them. Many cooking utensils became battered or broken beyond repair or were lost in transit. A short distance from Marshall, Heartsill had to dismount to retrieve his coffeepot, which he had dropped along the trail.

The excerpt below reveals that the Rangers were painfully aware of the troubled political climate in the counties around Austin, where Union sympathies were strong. The vote for and against secession in most of these counties was almost evenly divided, and the margins of the winning factions were extremely slim. Belton, in a county that had gone secessionist by a narrow margin, did not welcome Heartsill and his companions and was said to be Unionist. Georgetown, in a county where a slim majority had opposed secession, seemed devoted to the "glorious cause" and received the Lane Rangers graciously. The secessionists in Austin, although essentially Unionist, also made the Rangers feel welcome. The antislavery Germans in Comal County treated Heartsill and his friends splendidly, but this sprang more from inherent German hospitality than from any desire to support secession.

Other points of significance in Civil War history are also brought to light. The shortage of firearms and the difficulty in obtaining them created a serious problem for the commander of the unit. The dangers on the Indian frontier, especially in the wild and savage country around Uvalde, help explain the almost constant clamor by frontier families for military protection during the war. This is especially interesting because the alleged failure of the Federal government to protect the lives and property of the people of Texas against the Indian savages was given as a major reason for the state's secession. An almost unbelievably lax system of discipline governing Confederate troops patrolling the Texas frontier is also reflected by an event described by Heartsill. Evidently a corporal of the guard fell asleep while on duty and left Heartsill and several other guards on their posts all night. In later wars this violation was punishable by death before a firing squad, but the only retribution the delinquent corporal suffered, as far as Heartsill reveals, was the "ill feelings" of the victimized privates confined to their posts.

The congenial and jovial personality of young Heartsill is reflected on almost every page of his journal. Unlike many who wrote diaries and "outfit histories" during the war, Heartsill fully intended to have his work published. After the war he printed his journal himself on a small Octavo Novelty Press, laboriously turning out one page at a time. He began this task in December 1874 and finally produced the last page in June 1876, working largely during his spare time. Heartsill's sentence structure has been altered considerably by the editor, and changes have been made in punctuation and spelling. Some of Heartsill's original spelling has not been touched, however, in an effort to preserve the style and flavor of the author. Extreme care has been taken not to change the meaning of any of Heartsill's passages. The excerpt that follows was taken from a 1954 facsimile printing of Heartsill's original.

Source: W. W. Heartsill, *Fourteen Hundred and 91 Days in the Confederate Army; or Camp Life, Day by Day of the W. P. Lane Rangers from April 19, 1861 to May 20, 1865*. 1876. Facsimile reprint, ed. Bell I. Wiley (Jackson, Tenn.: McCowat-Mercer Press, 1954), pp. 11–20. Reprinted by permission.

[On the afternoon of April 20, the recently organized W. P. Lane Rangers] . . . set off westward [from Marshall toward Austin]. . . . Now our first lessons in military service begins. Each horse and rider is laden with enough cooking rations to last several days, clothing, blankets, and a tremendous store of other merchandise. An observer would more likely believe us a disorganized trading caravan crossing the desert than a regularly organized company going out west to hunt Indians. I sat aboard "Pet," a jet black which was as pretty an animal as was in the Company. Pet had a long wavy mane and tail and was as fat as a ginea pig. In addition to yours truly, Pet carried my saddle equipment, curry comb, horse brush, coffee pot, tin cup, 20 pounds of ham, 200 biscuits, 5 pounds of ground coffee, 5 pounds of sugar, a large pound cake presented to me by one of the ladies of Marshall, 6 shirts, 6 pairs of socks, 2 pairs of pants, 2 jackets, a pair of heavy mud boots, a Colt revolver, a small knife, 4 blankets, 60 feet of rope, and a host of other items, including little momentoes from friends. Five miles out of Marshall, trouble began when I dropped my coffee pot. With great difficulty I climbed down from my horse and retrieved it.

The men of the Company were marching in order, but since many were drinking, they were scattered for miles across the countryside so that I was riding virtually alone. Upon arriving at the Sabine River, I succeeded in getting the ferryman to transport Pet and me across the river to Rusk County. Numerous cooking groups or mess camps were strewn over a vast area behind the town of Camden as stragglers of the march arrived hourly. The camp sites had already been designated along the route of march by our captain, and he had seen that forage for our horses was supplied at each site. Each mess camp contained from five to twelve members of the Company who shared their camping equipment and food. I was a member of a seven-man group we called the "Marshall Mess" and which included Luther A. Henderson, Mica J. Harris, John M. Duke, 2nd Lieutenant Alfred W. Harwell, Hiram M. Crisenberry and Thomas Twitty. After the horses had been fed, there was nothing to do but set up our mess camp, make a pot of coffee, and prepare our evening meal. Darkness was approaching before our first camp supper was ready, and it was quickly served. As we clustered in groups in the twilight, each man was largely occupied with his own personal thoughts. If you have never been a soldier, it may be difficult for you to understand the many thoughts revolving in our minds. The countenance of each man was something of an index to the nature of his innermost thoughts. Some of the men were happy, jovial and satisfied, while others were sad and gloomy. Many were thinking of wives and sweethearts left behind, mindful of the possibility of never seeing them again in this life. Still others were suffering from that "meanest of spirits" and were either asleep or in a drunken stupor. One by one the camp fires flickered out, and at 10 P.M. the Marshall Mess passed a unanimous motion to turn in.

April 21 – Long before daylight, our bugler made the lonely forest around Camden echo with his revelle. By sunrise we were already in our saddles, forming a line for our first roll call. Some of our boys looked rather fatigued from yesterday, and many had just arrived and had not slept at all. One of our boys did not get to our encampment at all last night since his horse had gotten sick and died on the way. He had to return to Marshall to get another one. A march of eighteen miles brought us through the village of Bellview. A small brindle dog followed the company out of Bellview, and the pup's owner followed us to Canton to get his dog back. About twenty of the Rangers bought the Bellview citizen several drinks while the diminutive specimen of the Canine race was passed through the back window of the saloon. Some time later and about six miles farther down the road from Canton, the pup rode contentedly on a sorrel mare behind John B. Rees. We camped three miles farther along at Sam Irvin's farm in Smith County. We were all well supplied with good things from home and little cooking was necessary except for the making of coffee. Since we had no wagons, many had overloaded their horses, and every few miles along the route of march could be seen articles that had been abandoned by our forces.

April 22 – Into line and off westward. Eight miles down the road we passed through another little town. Here we sold Cush [the dog acquired at Bellview] twice, once for whiskey and once for tinware, but he was reacquired each time. We crossed the Neches River at Sanders' Mill and passed through Canip on the west bank. Our bugler had been so untiring in carrying out his orders that his lips were so swollen that he could not raise another note. For this reason he handed in his resignation with the proud satisfaction of duties faithfully and frequently performed.

April 23 – Four miles on we passed through Kickapoo and many of our number were disappointed that no "bust head" could be obtained from its temperant and peaceful citizens. Sixteen miles farther along we arrived at Palestine, the county seat of Anderson County, and were welcomed by the citizens in grand style. We established our encampment four miles from town, and our boys took good advantage of a free treat in town which lasted about two hours. This was the last encampment which was supplied with forage from Marshall.

April 24 – A good night's rest had a decidedly beneficial effect upon the boys. Breakfast over, we fell in, had roll call, and hit the road again. After about three miles we struck what is called "scrub prairie." This is the first prairie that many of us have ever seen. We spent about two hours crossing the Trinity River at Bonner's Ferry. Twenty-five miles down the road we camped one mile west of Fairfield, the county seat of Freestone County. Half of the Company did not arrive in our camps, for we had traveled much farther than we expected to travel this morning. Henderson, Duke, and I reached the town and put up in the hotel.

April 25 – Having traveled twenty-five miles, we arrived in the little town of Springfield in Limestone County. Confederate cannon boomed a welcome as we approached. We camped about six miles west of town. Our march the past two days has been across prairie, and a person who has never seen a prairie cannot for an instant conceive the grandure and beauty of such country. The air is laden with the rich fragrance of every variety of wild flower. Multiplied thousands of horses, sheep, and cattle were grazing under the warm April sun.

April 26 – We continued our travels. About 12 o'clock a very hard rain began to fall and a high wind drove the rain into our faces. The rain continued until nightfall when we camped at the Sheds' sheep ranch in McLellan County. This was our first taste of the bitter portion. Everything was wet and there was nothing to make fires out of except green mesquite. There were no rations, no forage for the animals, and no dry places to sleep. Several of us curled up in the corner of a stable and passed the night there.

April 27 – Since our good things brought from home had disappeared, we breakfasted on beef steak and ash cake. Fourteen miles down the road we crossed the Brazos River at Waco, the county seat of McLellan County. We were met by two military companies which escorted us through the city-like town, and we made preparations to camp west of the settlement where there was splendid grass for our animals. While making camp, someone scared up a very strange little animal which was a phenomena to most of us. It proved to be nothing more than a mule-eared rabbit.

April 28 – A march of twenty miles brought us to Belton in Bell County and we are pained to report that this was the only place that did not receive us with some demonstration of welcome. When we made inquiries about this, we were told that Belton is Union. We camped on Salado Creek ten miles farther on near the Salado settlement.

April 29 – Marched fifteen miles and entered Georgetown, the county seat of Williamson County. Here the citizens made up for their neighbors in Belton. Each and every one of the citizens appeared to use every exertion to make us feel at home. We camped six miles to the southwest.

April 30 – A march of eighteen miles brought us to a school house on the Big Walnut where we camped. Several men of our Company were riding "wing" near the camp and stopped to rest their horses. Five or six of the horses became frightened, broke loose, and disappeared across the prairie. The unfortunate "wing" riders had to walk back to camp. By sunset, there was fine prospects for more rain.

May 1 – Daylight this morning did not find me where I had gone to sleep last night. About 11 P.M. the members of our mess were aroused by a drenching rain. We had hoped to stick it out, but after about four inches of water had pooled up under us, we set out looking for a house we thought was nearby. After about two hours of searching, we located a dry stable where we spent the remainder of the night. After helping locate one of the horses that stampeded yesterday, Henderson, Duke, and I returned to the camp site only to find that the Company had already pulled out. We set out to overtake the Company and entered Austin just six miles down the road. The Company was encamped about one mile west of the city. Austin was the point at which we expected to receive orders to turn coastwise, or perhaps to report for active duty east of the

Mississippi. At least, it was generally agreed that we would not remain long at this encampment.

May 2 – Goode's Battery from Dallas arrived in the city today.

May 3 – Day spent in camp near Austin.

May 4 – Received orders to proceed to San Antonio, and were furnished with transportation. At 1 o'clock we marched into Austin and were given a complimentary dinner by the Austin Light Infantry at the Avenue Hotel. By 3 o'clock we were off again. We crossed the Colorado River, proceeded for about ten miles and camped.

May 5 – The Company passed through Manchac Springs after a two-mile march this morning, and arrived at San Marcos on the San Marcos River after traveling another 25 miles. This place is the county seat of Hays County and is in the center of the best farming country that I have seen thus far in Texas. We camped six miles south of San Marcos and then spent some time in town before turning in.

May 6 – We camped after a march of 16 miles. My horse had thrown a shoe and was beginning to pull up lame. I got permission to go on to the next town, New Braunfels, to seek out a blacksmith. New Braunfels, the county seat of Comal County, was situated on the Guadalupe River seven miles from our camp. The inhabitants of this town were exclusively German, and I have never been treated better in my life. While I was having Pet shod, I put up at the Guadalupe House, C. Schmidt being its proprietor. While there, Captain Richardson came into town and spent the night at the same hotel.

May 7 – The Company entered New Braunfels about 10 o'clock and I fell in. We marched eighteen miles and camped on the Rio Ciblo in Bexar County. These prairies are covered with mesquite, a low thorny bush with leaves like the locust. The buildings of this country are generally constructed of stone and have flat roofs. I also saw my first adobe house today. These are built of large dirt bricks dried in the sun and put up with cement. They would not last long in a country where there is much rain or freezing weather, but out here they will stand as long as our hard-burned brick houses of the East. The country generally has a wild, desolate appearance, but there is plenty of mesquite grass for our horses. We are within a few miles of the ancient and war-torn city of San Antonio.

May 8 – After a march of about eight miles, the Company entered San Antonio, a place situated on the San Antonio River, eight miles from its source. Upon arrival we learned that Colonel Earl Van Dorn, who is in command of this Department, mustered all of his forces this morning and departed to intercept a command of U.S. troops from New Mexico who are on their way to the Texas coast under the command of Colonel A. Reeves. Captain Richardson, our commander, used every possible means of procuring arms for us, but all the heads of the various departments were in the field and he accomplished nothing. We pitched our camps on Alamo Plaza in front of the old Alamo Church where Davy Crockett and his brave comrades were butchered by the Greasers. In looking around for a smooth place to locate for the night, I found an old breastworks erected by Santa Anna during the seige of the Alamo.

[The next two weeks were spent largely in gathering equipment and supplies. Several members of Lane's Rangers saw limited action with Colonel Van Dorn's forces in the battle of Adam's Hill, about sixteen miles west of San Antonio, where a Federal infantry unit was completely overwhelmed by the more numerous Confederates. The Rangers otherwise occupied themselves playing billiards, drinking lager beer, and "knocking around" San Antonio. Their encampment was eventually moved from Alamo Plaza to the San Antonio River outside the city, but Heartsill and his companions still had access to the "fast life" of the Alamo City.]

May 21 – On this day we were asked if we would consent to being transferred to Confederate service for frontier duty in West Texas. This most of the boys did not want to do, but we decided that since the frontier did need to be protected and since we were already here, we might as well do as requested.

May 22 – We made our final decision to enter Confederate service and remain on the frontier. However, we insisted that we be allowed to choose our own kind and place of service one year from the time we were sworn into state service at Marshall. This meant that we would pull frontier duty for about the next eleven months.

May 23 – At 12 o'clock Major Sayers, C.S.A., arrived in our camp. With the consent of each man, the W. P. Lane Rangers were transferred to the Confederate Provisional Army for the unexpired term of our enlistment. John E. Adkins, Benjamin A. Duncan, Nathan Williams, C. W. Sherrod, Dallas Hanley, and John Lee indicated that they wished to be dropped from the company and their request was granted. Major Sayers swore us into Confederate service, and we became Company F, 2nd Regiment, 1st Texas Mounted Rifles. This new arrangement placed us under command of Colonel John S. Ford and Lieutenant Colonel John R. Baylor. The other regiment of the Texas Mounted Rifles was the 1st Regiment, commanded by Colonel Henry E. McCulloch. These two regiments of the 1st Texas Mounted Rifles were the ones ordered raised by the Secession Convention last February. Our surgeon, Dr. W. J. McCain, was appointed Assistant Surgeon, C.S.A.

May 24 – The officers of our company asked Harwell, Henderson, Smith, and me to drill the men in infantry tactics. Since this was the first effort our boys had expended along these lines, they were extremely awkward.

May 25 – Dr. D. C. Miller, a private in our Company, was appointed an Assistant Surgeon, C.S.A., and was ordered to report to one of the forts on the frontier. He was therefore stricken from our company roll. Smith, Henderson, and I continued to drill the Company.

May 26 – We waited patiently for arms and camp equipment.

May 27 – We drilled the men twice during the course of the day.

May 28 – Since it rained all day, most of the boys went into San Antonio.

May 29 and 30 – These two days were spent in the regular routines of drilling, fishing, washing clothes, grazing our horses, etc.

June 1 – A train of wagons arrived from San Antonio loaded with arms, cooking utensils, and other equipment and was issued to men of the Company immediately. Each man by this time had a Mississippi rifle and a Colt army six.

June 2 – We learned that the Rangers were to be sent to El Paso. This was the place we were hoping we'd be stationed.

June 3 – Colonel Van Dorn reviewed four Companies of the 2nd Regiment, and there was a number of ladies present.

June 4 – We learned today that our destination is not to be El Paso since other companies are already on their way to that point. We were very disappointed. We know, however, that we will probably be assigned to one of the forts which forms our system of frontier defense. These forts extend in a line from the Gulf of Mexico up the Rio Grande to the region of the headwaters of the Red River. They are spaced at intervals of 25 to 60 miles apart, and each one is supported by a garrison of soldiers. Communication between the forts is carefully maintained so that assistance will be only a few hours away if it is needed.

June 5 – We learned our destination. We have received orders to prepare to move out June 6 and proceed to Camp Wood, some 200 miles west of here. The evening hours are being spent making preparations for our departure.

June 6 – At sunrise we were off scattering in all directions, and practically all roads were filled with Rangers. This time, we have nine wagons. Three are for Company use, and six are loaded with subsistance stores. J. R. Bonner and S. G. Fitzpatrick of our Company are sick and were left behind in the hospital in San Antonio. After we were under way, it was generally believed that our forces were too scattered to attempt an orderly formation. I was traveling with a group of about forty men along the San Julian Springs Road when we learned that we were on the wrong trail. We struck across the country to the upper road and located four or five of our wagons and some of our boys. The country through which we are passing is desolate looking. After we camped, we learned that this is the edge of Indian country. A rancher told us that a man had been killed by Indians just a few years ago near the site of our encampment.

June 7 – Last night I pulled my first guard duty. Those on guard slept around the wagons except while on post. It was the first time I ever used a rock for a pillow, and it became very hard before daylight. All of the wagons had not come up by morning, so we made plans to wait another night. The wagons rolled into the encampment about 3 o'clock in the afternoon, but since it was so late our officers decided not to break camp until morning. A good number of the boys reconnoitered the neighborhood around Castroville.

June 8 – We got off to an early start this morning with fair prospects of a good days march. We crossed the Medina River six miles down the road and passed through Castroville, the county seat of Medina County. About one mile from town we reached the summit of a very high hill which laid to our view the beautiful valley of the Medina which was dotted with small cottages and farms. Castroville and Medina County are both populated entirely with Germans. We camped at nightfall fifteen miles from Castroville on the Rio Hondo.

June 9 – A march of fifteen miles brought us to Dhanis, another German town which our boys renamed "Egg-and-beer-town" on account of the large quantity of eggs we purchased and the abundance of Lager beer we consumed. Additional guards were posted that night since we were getting into Indian country. Our camps were set up about three miles down the road. This is an excellent country for hunting and fishing.

June 10 – We crossed Ranchero Creek, Rio Sabinal, and Comanche Creek. A few months earlier, a man named Davenport had been killed by Indians near the point where we crossed the Sabinal. We marched thirty miles during the day and camped in the evening on the Frio in Uvalde County. Before darkness, we engaged in the lively sport of target-shooting. Captain Richardson and Benjamin Wallace won the match, knocking the black out of the target on every shot. Our camps were pleasantly situated in a bend on the Frio where there was plenty of fine grass for our horses and dead mesquite for our campfires.

June 11 – Our bugler blew us up very early and we were on the march by good daylight. We marched for miles and miles before reaching any sort of settlement, which has been the case to some extent ever since we left San Antonio. The inhabitants of this country huddle together in small villages for protection against Indians. About 2 o'clock we arrived in Uvalde, the county seat of Uvalde County. At this point we turned to the right to travel in a northwestern direction, taking our leave of the San Antonio and El Paso Road. We marched about three miles and camped by a stagnant pool of stock-water. Captain Richardson, Henderson, and Curtis set off for Uvalde and from there proceeded to Fort Inge, situated three miles farther south on the Leona River. The town of Uvalde is a rather desolate looking place containing a courthouse, blacksmith shop, a grocery store, and a half dozen very ordinary dwelling houses.

June 12 – We were off early since we were anxious to get to some good water. Captain Richardson and his escort arrived back in camp last night. After a ten mile march we arrived at the Nueces River and crossed it two miles above the Adams' Ranch. After this difficult crossing, we traveled one mile up the river and crossed it again and camped about a mile farther upstream. Our camp was set up along the banks of the Nueces between the river and a large chalk bluff. Only two weeks ago two men on their way from Uvalde to Camp Wood were surrounded by about twenty Indians and killed after what must have been a most desperate fight. I visited and closely examined a large pecan tree under which their mutilated bodies were found. One of the men had been scalped once, the other three times and his heart had been cut out and laid on his body. In an effort to rid my mind of these unpleasant thoughts, I determined to go downstream on a fishing excursion. Happy to get away from the dark shadow of the chalk bluff, I found many of our boys fishing along the river. Needless to say, we were careful to arrive back in camp long before sunset. Our horses were placed under a good guard and well tied in as small a circle as possible as a precaution against theft by Indians. About 10 o'clock there was a tremendous commotion among the mules and horses. Every man in the camp seized a weapon and ran toward the cavy yard. It was only a Mexican teamster who had returned to the encampment with a mule that had strayed from the herd earlier. Mules are easily frightened and will let us know instantly when Indians are near. It is a remarkable fact which I cannot explain, but for some reason the mules have a perfect terror of the red man. We got another scare later in the night when Sam Kennedy opened up on a pack of wolves that were after our rations, but otherwise the rest of the night passed quietly.

June 13 – Among the wolves shot by Kennedy last night, we found a large, fine, black dog which belonged to a ranch below here. We moved out and crossed the river three times during the next eight miles. In general, the mountains ran parallel to the river and this forced us to the opposite bank on occasion when canyons and bluffs made travel difficult or impossible. During the day, we passed a very interesting work of nature known as "Crown" or "Cap" Mountain. It stands alone in the valley, towering high up among the clouds. A man cannot look upon these mighty works of God without emotions of sincere reverance and adoration. We camped fifteen miles above Crown Mountain on Pecan Creek. There was considerable firing on the mountain to our right just a few minutes ago, as several of our Rangers encountered three bears while hunting. One of the bears was killed while the other two escaped wounded. Since they had no dogs, the wounded bears made good their escape. I preferred fishing more than hunting, and since our encampment is about three miles from the river, my sport has been somewhat hampered. Late in the evening, some of our boys came in with large quantities of honey which they had taken from a bluff down on the river.

June 14 – Last night I pulled picket duty with Henderson, Hawley, Hyde, and Hudson. We were supposed to be relieved at 10 o'clock by another shift, but Corporal Hart went to sleep and didn't wake up until daybreak when the bugler sounded his horn. That was a pretty lengthy tour of guard duty that we pulled, expecting to get a tomahawk in our skulls almost at any moment. This morning we entertained some ill feelings toward Corporal Hart.

This was our last day in what may be called civilization. We marched eight miles and crossed the Nueces again and entered Comanche country. This was as far out of this world as we could get. Two miles beyond the river we arrived at Camp Wood, our haven of rest. The post is situated on the north bank of the Nueces with the mountains in the rear. A fine spring rises near the post and runs by our camp into the river. There is a row of Sibley tents, a nice comfortable house for officers, and a good commisary building along the river and on the spring branch. Our Rangers prefer to camp farther from the river, so we have pitched our new tents in a grove nearby and made ourselves as comfortable as possible.

Two important frontier scouts operate from Camp Wood. The principal one is Mr. E. D. Westfall, but another is a man named Rowan who acts as army guide during emergencies or when Westfall is sick. Mr. Rowan lives here at the post with his family. Across the branch is a sheep ranch where a German lives in a humble cottage situated among numerous sheep enclosures. Each morning he arises early to drive his fleecy flock to the green valleys among the mountains, and then returns late each evening to put his sheep in their enclosures. What a happy life.

The Rangers, wearied by their long march, relax, or fish or hunt, or swim in the river. It is a merry crowd, splashing, diving, and swimming like so many puddle ducks in a barnyard stock pond. Needless to say, for most of our boys, a little washing is most beneficial. By late evening several deer have been brought into camp, and so have lots of turkey and fish. With rations aplenty, the Lane Rangers are beginning to live, laugh, and grow fat.

June 15 – The Rangers were off early rambling over the mountains collecting honey or shooting deer, turkies, bears or other wild game. I turned my attention to fishing, my favorite sport. The waters of this strange, beautiful river are so transparent that I can see the bottom. I can see the small pebbles on the bottom at a depth of thirty feet, and even select the fish I want to catch by letting my hook down quietly. In some places the river is thirty or forty feet deep and a hundred fifty yards wide, but farther downstream I can walk on dry sand and rocks all the way across the stream. The waters of the river and the spring branch are cold and pleasant to drink while their beauty adds to the grandeur of the country which surrounds the post. The valleys and plains are covered with luxurious grasses and pecan trees, while chapparal, Spanish persimons, and wild plums are scattered about the countryside. In addition to the fine scenery around Camp Wood, there are the ruins of an old Spanish mission within a quarter of a mile from our encampment. Perhaps a cathedral or nunnery, it was once a large building although little remains today except the foundation. About a mile up the river is what must have once been a huge irrigation ditch about ten feet wide and about a mile in length. There is no way of determining its former depth since it is almost completely filled in. However, it must have been in use about the time the old mission was in operation.

June 16 – About 4 o'clock, F. M. Marshall was violently attacked with an epileptic fit and died within thirty minutes in spite of medical aid. His death cast a gloom over our camp such as was never witnessed before. At 6 o'clock Marshall was buried with full military honors beneath the wide spread boughs of a large live oak tree not far from camp.

[The W. P. Rangers remained on patrol duty on the Texas frontier during the first year of the unit's existence, serving at Camp Wood, Fort Inge, Fort Clark, Camp Hudson, and Fort Lancaster. Toward the middle of 1862 the unit was returned to San Antonio, where most of the Rangers reenlisted. After the company had undergone considerable reorganization, it was dispatched to Arkansas, where it was overwhelmed by the Federals at Fort Hindman on the Arkansas River. Heartsill and many of his companions were captured and imprisoned at Camp Butler near Springfield, Illinois, until April 1863, when they were released through the prisoner-exchange program.]

1861–1862

Intoxicated with the "Pomp and Glory of War"

The following excerpt is taken from the reminiscences of an aged Confederate veteran long after the war ended. The bitterness and disillusionment reflected in his remarks are noteworthy.

Source: Ralph J. Smith, *Reminiscences of the Civil War and Other Sketches,* reproduced on bond paper with cloth binding by W. M. Morrison of Waco, Texas, 1962, pp. 1–2. Reprinted by permission.

In the year of 1861 the grim visaged god of war reigned supreme throughout Texas. In June of that year Ex-Governor Stockdale, a man of brilliant attainments as well as a fiery Southern patriot, spoke to a large audience of citizens of Jackson county in the court house of the town of Texana [the county seat was moved from Texana to Edna in 1883]. His eloquent pleadings of the Confederate cause, for he was mightier in words than deeds, created great excitement and enthusiasm throughout the surrounding country, inflaming the minds of his hearers, especially the young men, to fever heat, and they were eager to enter the fray and drive the cruel invader of their beloved land off the earth or surrender their lives in the attempt. So I lost no time in joining the company being organized by Clark Owen who up to this time was a strong Union man, opposing secession, who became our Captain. He was a man about fifty-five years old and a Christian gentleman.

I wish I were able to describe the glorious anticipation of the first few days of our military lives, when we each felt individually able to charge and annihilate a whole company of blue coats. What brilliant speeches we made and the dinners the good people spread for us, and oh the bewitching female eyes that pierced the breasts of our grey uniforms, stopping temporarily the heartbeats of many a fellow that the enemies bullets were destined soon to do forever.

On the 10th of October we were ordered to Houston where we were mobilized into the Second Texas Infantry, commanded by Colonel John C. Moore, our company designated Company K. Here again all was excitement and all felt that it was only a matter of a few months until we would return home covered with glory and renown. The possibility of such a thing as defeat never for a moment entered the mind of a member of our inexperienced corps. Day after day we were dined, wined and flattered. Night after night we floated upon a sea of glory. The ladies petted and lionized us; preachers prayed with and for us, declaring that the lord was on our side, so we need have no fears. Alas how soon we were to realize the truth of the epigram that the lord was on the side with the biggest guns.

While in this camp that brainy old war veteran, Ex-President of the Republic of Texas, General Sam Houston, made us a talk calculated to dampen the ardor of men less intoxicated than we poor boys with pomp and glory of war. He told us we knew not what we did; that the resources of the north were almost exhaustless. That time and money would wear us out and conquor us at last. However he might as well had been giving advice to the inmates of a lunatic asylum. We knew no such word as fail.

[The author and his unit were transported by train to Beaumont, then to Wise's Bluff on the Neches by ship. From there they marched to Alexandria, Louisiana, where they boarded transports and sailed down the Red River and up the Mississippi to Memphis, Tennessee. Then they boarded a train for the last leg of their journey to Corinth, Mississippi. The Texas unit received its baptism of fire a few weeks later at Shiloh. Casualties among the Texans were extremely heavy, and the author himself was wounded below the knee and captured. After he had been exchanged he returned to the front and was captured and exchanged again. The wound he received at Shiloh bothered him the rest of his life.]

1862

The Great Hanging in Gainesville

The "Bleeding Kansas" war, culminating in the sacking of Lawrence and the Pottawatomie Creek massacre in 1856, increased the anxieties of frontier families living in the isolated North Texas region along the Red River. They were painfully aware that they were closer to the battleground of Kansas than they were to their own state capital. Many of the inhabitants of this region were free-soil immigrants from Illinois, Kentucky, Indiana, Tennessee, Missouri, and other border states, and the ideological conflict over slavery and secession in this area was especially bitter and vicious. All political affiliations, all levels of society, and all facets of North Texas life were affected by this struggle. Many of the heated discussions and fiery verbal harangues that characterized the controversy took place in houses of worship, and since prominent preachers and religious leaders lined up on both sides, interdenominational disputes and intracongregational divisions became commonplace.

Crisis conditions in North Texas counties rapidly worsened. When a large majority of the state's electorate sanctioned the Texas ordinance of secession early in 1861, slim majorities in eight counties in the Red River region voted in opposition (see map 4). Tension mounted when secessionist law enforcement officials, delighted that Texas was joining the Confederacy, took stern measures against Unionists accused of undermining the war effort. Rumors began to circulate of an underground Unionist conspiracy, said to have the support of Jayhawkers and cutthroats in Kansas, which was aimed at overthrowing Confederate authority in North Texas. Emotions in North Texas, induced by these rumors of subversive plotting, were further stimulated in the spring and summer of 1862 by a rumor of an impending slave insurrection in several counties to the southeast. When popular hysteria was at its peak, a Cooke County vigilance committee unearthed an underground Unionist plot to seize Gainesville and Sherman.

News of this conspiracy spread quickly through Cooke, Grayson, Fannin, Wise, and Denton counties. Martial law was declared in Cooke County, all suspected Unionists around Gainesville rounded up, and a "Citizens' Court" of questionable legality formed. Within a few weeks, thirty-nine alleged plotters were tried, convicted of conspiracy, and sentenced to hang. In addition, three suspects wearing the uniform of the Confederate army appeared before a military tribunal, promptly were declared guilty, and sentenced to death. In all, forty-two helpless men died in agony at the end of a hangman's rope.

Most of the executions took place under a large, wide-spreading elm tree about half a mile east of Gainesville. The condemned men, their hands tied behind them and described by an eyewitness as "pale and trembling," were herded into a wagon and transported to the place of execution. Not all of the convicted conspirators were hanged on the same day so that a public hanging became almost a daily spectacle during the month of October. Each condemned man was forced to stand in the wagon while a noose was adjusted around his neck. Then he was left hanging by his neck to strangle to death as the wagon was quickly driven from under him. A "sad and gloomy silence" descended over the crowd of spectators as "the branches of the . . . elm trembled . . . under the weight and shuddering motion" of each dying man. "After life became extinct," an observer wrote, "the body was taken down and placed in possession of the weeping family and friends, who . . . gave it decent sepulture."

Accounts of the Great Hanging in Gainesville were written by two North Texas residents who were in some way associated with the tragic event. The first, and perhaps the most detailed and accurate version, was written by George Washington Diamond, a Henderson newspaper editor, who had access to the "Citizens' Court" records. Although the account was written sometime between

1874 and 1876, and the author died in 1911, it was privately held by the author's descendants for almost a century. It was finally published as a feature article in the January 1963 issue of the *Southwestern Historical Quarterly*. In writing his account of the hanging, Diamond sought to depict the court as a legally constituted body and to legitimize its actions. The other account, a pemphlet titled *The Great Hanging at Gainesville, Cooke County, Texas,* published about ten years after the Diamond version, denounced the court as an extralegal vigilante group or mob. Thomas Barrett, the author of this later version, was actually a member of the court and wrote his account primarily to support his claim that he sat in honest judgment but actively opposed the hanging "from the beginning to the end."

Other versions of the awesome event, no longer extant, were set forth during the years following the Civil War, and these helped keep bitterness and animosity alive. The Barrett version, however, was perhaps the most disturbing because it raised the question of the legality of the court and reawakened bitterness among the descendants of those executed just as memories of the event were beginning to fade. It seems to have been one of the causes of a new wave of violence and bloodshed which swept through the Red River counties during the last two decades of the nineteenth century. Folklore has it that the mere possession of a copy of Barrett's narrative was dangerous. In fact, this version almost disappeared. A prominent rare book collector named Earl Vandale ran advertisements in North Texas newspapers for years before he finally located a copy. The University of Texas at Austin acquired this copy as a part of the Earl Vandale Collection, which was donated to the Barker Texas History Library. As a result, the Library of Congress finally secured a copy in 1936. In 1961 H. Bailey Carroll, director of the Texas State Historical Association, reproduced Barrett's account in the program of the association's Sixty-Fifth Annual Meeting. For the first time since its original publication in 1885, it became readily accessible to Texana collectors and Texas history buffs. The excerpt below was taken from this 1961 program.

Thomas Barrett was a physician and a Church of Christ minister who preached at Paris, Stewig's Mill (Lamar County), Mount Pleasant, Mount Vernon, and Sulphur Springs at various times during the Civil War era. R. L. Roberts, a librarian and church historian, called him one of "the best known pioneer preachers of North Texas." Barrett's name appears frequently in early religious publications and church literature. He was one of a committee of prominent preachers, for example, asked to investigate trouble involving two other preachers at Mantua, Collin County, in the spring of 1872. The *Apostolic*

Times, May 23, 1872, reported the committee's findings. Barrett's position on all questions discussed by the committee was included in the report.

Barrett was born in Anson County, North Carolina, on June 21, 1809. After spending several years in Missouri, he and his family moved to Hopkins County, Texas, about 1848. In 1860 they moved to Gainesville in Cooke County. After Barrett had served on the "Citizens' Court" under duress, he moved to Titus County because of threats on his life. Soon thereafter, he established residence in Tennessee until the end of 1866. Then he returned to Gainesville, where he and other members of the "Citizens' Court" were tried and acquitted in civil court of any crime committed through their participation in the Great Hanging. Although legally vindicated, Barrett grieved over his role in the dreadful affair the rest of his life. He died in Gainesville in 1892.

Source: Thomas Barrett, "The Great Hanging at Gainesville, Cooke Co., Texas," program of *The Texas Historical Association Sixty-Fifth Annual Meeting,* Driskill Hotel, Austin, Texas, April 28 and 29, 1961, pp. 7–38. Reprinted by permission.

The war between the states, north and south, having existed more than a year; the war fever having risen to boiling heat; the Confederate congress passed the conscript-law. This law was very offensive to many and particularly to those who were afterwards members of the organization for which they were hung.

. . . .

For some time after, there was strong and mysterious things which were not understood by the great mass of people. . . . We could hear war news frequently before it got into our newspapers. There was so much going on that I became convinced that there was some kind of [clandestine] organization in the country, and others came to the same conclusion. We afterwards learned that the members of the organization yet to be named had regular mails to and from Kansas jayhawkers.

. . . .

[When proof had been obtained that the organization existed] . . . the military sent out orders for all militia of Cooke county to report to Gainesville, armed and equipped for service at the earliest practical hour of the next day. Those over age were pressed into the service. I was exempt in three cases, and a special order was dispatched to me in the night to be in Gainesville early next morning. One company was ordered from

Wise, Denton, and Grayson counties each; one company was asked for sent from Fort Washita.

The night before these soldiers were to report in the morning, squads of men were sent out in different parts of the county, and directed to watch and not let the men whose names they had, leave in the night, and as soon as it was light enough in the morning, to close in and arrest the men. In this way, it was said, twenty were arrested the first grab. The arresting continued for about thirteen days and nights. How many were arrested, I have no means of knowing, having kept no account at the time, but I suppose there was not less than one hundred and fifty, and perhaps more.

There was a good many arrested who had no connection with the organization.

There were squads of men in every part of the country, and they arrested every man that they suspicioned, and in this way a good many innocent men were arrested. . . .

One of the squads came up with a man at his home, that they did not suspicion. They told him he must go with them and help arrest . . . [other] men. He very readily agreed to do so, for it was dangerous to refuse in this high state of excitement; for I never saw such a state of excitement before, nor since, and hope never to see its equal again. But the man fell in with them, but he had no gun, and all the men except the prisoners had guns. When the squads arrived at the prison, and put them in, this man failed to go in, and some of the men knowing he had been with them and seeing he had no gun, ordered him in, and being a green case, he went in, and stayed in one or two days if I recollect right. I had been acquainted with him in Titus county, so he sent me word in reference to his case. I had him brought before the jury and being no evidence against him he was set at liberty.

Although I was notified to report early in the morning at Gainesville, being exempt from military duty and having an urgent professional call before morning, I visited a patient that morning before going to town. My patient was in a neighborhood where there had been several men arrested, and I began to learn something of the matter, and dispatched my business as speedily as possible, and I got to Gainesville about eleven o'clock.

When I arrived near town, there were crowds in sight in every direction, armed, pressing forward prisoners under guard. The deepest and most intense excitement that I ever saw prevailed. Reason had left its throne. The mind of almost every man I saw seemed to be unhinged, and wild excitement reigned supreme. When I arrived on the square, there were perhaps three or four hundred men in town and in sight.

[The prisoners] . . . constituted a crowd whose words and actions seemed to indicate an upheaving of the most dangerous character, because it was known that the members of that clan were sworn to go to the assistance of any member who was arrested. [It was later evident] . . . that nothing but the overpowering numbers in arms prevented desperate fighting the next night.

The supposition at that time was, that the clan was strong enough to make a desperate fight.

Soon after I arrived on the square I heard hanging spoken of. I found the tree had been selected, that same old historic elm, with its long and bending limbs, which was afterwards used for that purpose.

The crowd seemed to be settling down on beginning to hang. I opposed it with all the power within me. Others also opposed it, and about the time we were in the heat of contention, the church bell rang for a meeting of the crowd for consultation. The ringing of this bell put an end to all plans, in order to see what would be the result of that meeting. This was a military move, sanctioned by soldiers and citizens.

The meeting was called to order and a chairman appointed. A motion was made and carried for the chair to appoint five men to select a jury to decide upon the course to be pursued with these men. This committee selected twelve men, and my name was reported as one of them. My first thought was, not to serve as one of them, when I took the situation under consideration; I at once saw that unless there was considerable influence in that jury against extreme violence, there was great danger of awful work, so I consented to serve, intending to oppose all extreme violence, which I did. And here I will state the excitement was so great that every man found it necessary to exercise much caution in reference to what he said or did. This condition of things had its influence with me in deciding this question.

The jury was instructed to go into a fair examination and bring accused and witnesses face to face and decide, and they would abide by their decision.

The meeting adjourned, and the jury met and organized, and night came on. The militia and others had been coming in all day, and after dark they continued to come.

Squads of men were sent to different parts of the country to ascertain what was going on, for an attack was expected, which would cause desperate fighting. A double line of sentinels were put around the town.

. . . .

About fifteen or twenty men had gone about half a mile from the square to stay all night; I was one of the men. We were ordered to the square. When we got there I walked around . . . to see how the thing was going on. The soldiers were in line of battle and some in the houses making cartridges, others moving to and fro as is always the case in times of great excitement, everyone expecting a desperate fight before morning, for the clan was supposed to be stronger than they were. In reference to their strength, I may as well state what I learned from a man whom I sent word to to leave the country . . . that the organization was about seventeen hundred strong, including Cooke, Wise, Denton, Grayson and Collin counties.

But I must return to the thread of my narrative. After seeing how everything was going on, and not having a gun and not having any desire to be in the fight, I went into a friend's house and asked the lady for a pillow and turning a chair down on the carpet slept till morning. There was no attack, consequently no fighting.

. . . .

It can be plainly seen from what has been stated, that nothing but the overpowering numbers at Gainesville prevented one of those bloody massacres which sometimes take place in war.

But the second morning came and no attack was made, but the intense excitement was almost universal.

There was some talk of taking the prisoners out and hanging or shooting all of them, but it was not done.

I have no language adequate to convey to the mind of the reader a full idea of the deep and dangerous condition of the excitement up to this time. Those opposed to extreme punishment found it necessary to be extremely cautious if they made a remark in favor of mercy.

While the multitude did not at this time know the full intention of the clan, enough was known to give the idea that if the clan carried out its designs, the country would be thrown into a bloody war, with neighbor against neighbor, and in some cases the brother against brother, and in some cases the father against the son and the son against the father, and a man's foes would be of his own household.

The second day dawned and no attack being made, the jury met. And now comes the tug of war. I would here remind the reader [that] . . . I shall not call names [but will] . . . tell what they said and did. . . .

I shall tell the course I pursued, inasmuch as my course has been misrepresented far and near, as far as I am known. I being a public man, a doctor and a preacher, some will object to the course I am pursuing in regard to myself. Let them object, I have weighed the consequences and am prepared to meet them. . . .

The jury met and passed an order that a majority should rule. I opposed this, and wanted it unanimous, or at any rate, two-thirds, but the majority rule was adopted. As far as could be done the leaders were tried first.

. . . .

One man, known to be a leader, was brought in and proven to be guilty, he being the man who initiated [into the organization] . . . two [of the informants who] . . . reported to the military. This man was condemned and hung; another was brought and was disposed of the same way, and this was continued till seven were doomed to die likewise. A number of others and I were opposing it with all our powers; I did all the speaking (nearly) but had as well tried to build a dam across Red River in a time of high water with straw, as to resist and control the excitement in the juryroom, and the crowd of soldiers on duty pushed on by influential men. There were eight hundred or a thousand armed men in town by the time the jury condemned seven men.

The crowd were threatening to take the prisoners out and kill all of them. There was a trial made to have me taken off of the jury, because I took the lead in opposing these violent measures. We who opposed hanging . . . [wanted] to turn the men over to the civil or military authorities instead of hanging, and those not very deep in the thing, to set them at liberty.

The eighth man was tried; he was only slightly in it, but the excitement was so great that he was condemned as readily as the others.

When this was done I concluded that I would stand it no longer; I was determined that I would have a change or leave the jury-room. I rose to my feet and addressed the jury as near as I can recollect as follows: Gentlemen: You are as reckless of human life as though it was a matter of little importance. I am not acquainted with this man, I never saw him till I saw him in the jury-room, consequently my course is not influenced by any particular feelings of partiality. But if you intend to hang all who are no further in this thing than this man is, it is not necessary to do more than bring a man before you and prove him to be slightly connected with this organization and hang him, so you had better pass sentence of death on every man in the prison, for if you continue to carry out the course you have pursued since you came into this jury-room, you will hang all, so you had better dispatch them at once and adjourn. Gentlemen, I have stood this thing as long as I intend to; if there is not a change I will leave. I see in the future the wives of these men in their widowhood, sitting by their fires in the long and lonesome winter nights; the little ones playing around them, the wife looking with a feeling of deep sadness, and casts her eyes on a chair by her side; it is vacant! her eyes are swimming with tears, she is thinking of the dead one, her beloved, the father of her children, and says to herself, where is he? Answer, gone, gone, sleeping the long, long sleep of death, to return to me and my children no more forever. She utters a heavy groan and the sobs of distress escape her lips, ruined, ruined forever, while a flood of tears pour down her cheeks.

And here the tears gushed from my eyes, my heart almost bled.

I took my seat. As soon as I was seated, one of the jurors who had stood shoulder to shoulder with me in opposing the hanging of these men, rose to his feet, took up his hat, and said, he was no longer a member of the jury, and said good bye, and started to the head of the stairs, (we were in an upper room). At this instant two men came rushing to me, one of them caught me by both arms and gave me one of those honest and friendly shakes, which is an indication of deep interest. When this took place the man who had bid the jury good bye, halted. The man who had me by the arms said, for God sake don't break this jury. I asked him why. He said if you break this jury, every man in that prison will be killed before the setting of the sun. The other man who came with him sanctioned what he said. He went on to state that the only chance to save these men, was for the jury to save them, and said he, you can save some. I told him that I knew that the outside proof was strong, but I was not apprised that it was so strong. They told me that I would find it as they had represented it.

I perhaps did as much thinking and planning in a few seconds as I ever did. I knew that if a general slaughter was gone into, unless I made good use of my legs I would go up with the rest, as my course in opposing this wholesale hanging had given great offense. The excitement in the jury room was of that still and deep character which some times takes place . . . [where everyone waits] in silence to see what would be done.

I said to the two men that approached me: Gentlemen, I yield to your judgment, I will try and arrange this thing.

I then went to the man who had told the jury good bye, and told him what these men had told me, and after a short consultation, we agreed to go back and if the jury would adopt the two-thirds rule, we would act with them, but unless the two-thirds was adopted we would leave. The jury readily adopted the two-thirds rule.

We then gave the man who had been condemned to hang, the benefit of the two-thirds rule and reversed the sentence of death, by deciding to turn him over to the military authority.

. . . .

After we adopted the two-thirds rule, we had some hot contentions in the jury-room, but we either set the men at liberty or decided to send them to the headquarters of the military authorities. Then the hanging ceased [temporarily], and the men were turned over to the military authorities, to be sent there after the jury had completed their work. The excitement increased outside, to give some idea of the excitement, I will state some things that occurred:

There was a man in jail who was charged with being a deserter from the southern army, and a horse thief. As the jury failed to furnish any men to hang, the bloodthirsty men outside took that man and hung him.

As the jury were furnishing none to hang, there was such a strong desire for blood, that the outsiders determined to take all the men in the prison and shoot them.

. . . .

That same night there were two attempts to take the men out of the prison and shoot them. The first attempt came very close to succeeding [but both failed].

. . . .

We must now go back to the jury after we adopted the two-thirds rule: Seven had been hung. When we commenced under the two-thirds rule, we had considerable contention till it was found that this rule would prevent hanging. After that was ascertained we got along quietly and speedily till we got through with all the prisoners on hand, and turned some of them over to the military authorities, the rest being set at liberty.

This brought Saturday evening, and the soldiers were beginning to leave. As the excitement had greatly moderated in the jury room, we thought it was moderating the same outside, and in order to give it time to moderate still more, we agreed to adjourn for a week and come together the next Saturday and let our decision be known, and I was to make a speech to the people to influence them to abide by our decision, for we were fearful of a mob. Our decision was to be kept secret till the next Saturday. Secrecy was enjoined on all, and we were ready to adjourn.

Some person betrayed us, and told the crowd outside of our decision, and a mob rose and sent two men into the jury room with word that if we did not give up twenty more to be hung, they would kill every man in the prison.

When this demand came, one of the jurors who acted with me, asked what will you do now? I said the Lord only knows what I ought to do; I have risked my life for six or eight days, and gone as far as I dared to go to prevent hanging. I could contend in the jury-room as I pleased, but cannot war against a regiment of men. I oppose it, but if they take them, they will have to do so, I am not going to say a word.

When I failed to oppose the taking of the men, there was no objection.

I thought when the military failed to protect us and suffered a mob to rise and take these men and hang them, contrary to the decision of the jury, I say, when I thought all this over, I concluded that it was in vain for me to raise my voice against it, so I remained silent. I knew my doom if wholesale killing commenced.

One of these men called for a list of the names of the prisoners. Our clerk handed it to him, and he went over it; took such men as he chose and wrote their names down, then handed the list back to the clerk, and called over the names he had and our clerk marked them out. He then counted his names and he had fourteen. He said as he rose from his seat: I reckon this will satisfy them.

These two men went into prison, called these fourteen men out, put them in a separate room, and notified them that they must hang next day, which was Sunday.

As soon as these men were gone, I said to the jury: Delay, breeds danger if we undertake to send these men to the headquarters of the military they will not get there, they will be killed. I propose that we meet next Saturday to set all the remaining prisoners at liberty. I told them I did not believe they would be molested, as we had set a good many at liberty, and none of them had been molested.

To this they readily agreed, and passed an order to that effect. I was to make a speech to influence the people to abide by our decision. The jury then adjourned, to meet the next Saturday morning.

I went home that evening, having been absent twelve days and nights. When I arrived at home my wife met me at the gate and asked the news. I attempted to tell her, but my feelings overcame me so, that I choked up and commenced crying. I said I would tell her after I became quiet. And here I will say that no tongue can tell or pen detail what I suffered during those twelve days and nights just closed; not that I had any sympathy for the plans and designs of the organization, for I abhorred and detested their designs. But I considered that it was war times, and as the organization was broken up, all that was necessary was to send them to the military, as the jury at Sherman did, and the county would be relieved.

But I must call the reader's attention back to that dreadful Sunday, the day of the hanging of the fourteen men which the mob took from the jury the evening before.

. . . .

The time for hanging arrived, and I left the prison. I took my seat in a porch at the northeast corner of the square, for I knew that the men would be hauled in a wagon down California street to that old historic tree, which is now dead and lies as still where it has been hauled as the bodies of the men who were hung on its long limbs. . . . . I had not been there long, till I saw the death wagon coming with two of the prisoners. I saw men with guns on each side of the wagon guarding, to prevent escape, and see that the hanging was done, and this was continued till late in the evening before the last one was hung.

. . . .

There was an order passed that women should not be permitted to be present at the hanging. The women were not noisy, but the signs of deep dispair was manifested by the heaving breast, the falling tears, the heavy groans as though the heart was breaking, and all the vitals of life were giving way. I believe all these men were the heads of families. The sun set that night on fourteen widowed families, and thirteen families of orphans, for if I recollect right, all these men had children but one.

Language is totally incompetent to express the deep sorrow of that night. Wailing, moaning, weeping and lamentation existed in these families on that dark and fatal night. Tears fell like the raindrop, as tears fall from my eyes at even this distant day, while penning these lines. When the little ones who were just beginning to talk would say: Ma where is Pa? Pa come home, O, Ma, go after him. How these words went like a dagger to the heart of that disconsolate wife. He was her husband, she loved him! Let the world say what they may.

I do thank God that I am not guilty of the death of any of those whose death I have just recorded. Neither is the jury, for as I have before stated, the jury had decided to send them to the headquarters of the military authorities in Texas, but that mob took them and hung them. As I have already stated the jury had decided to adjourn for a week, when they came together the next Saturday to set the remaining prisoners at liberty.

During . . . [the] week of adjournment, I went to town every day, and the excitement was moderating, and everything bidding fair for a favorable condition on the next Saturday, the day the jury was to meet.

About the middle of the week, when I got into town I was met with the startling news that . . . a citizen of Gainesville . . . had been killed in the brakes of Red River by a squad of men belonging to that organization. This revived the excitement to a flame.

. . . .

[When the clan was reported to have killed another man a few days later, the] . . . excitement was fearful. Men were swearing they would kill every man in the prison that night. I availed myself of every opportunity that presented itself to pursuade them not to murder the prisoners, but I was compelled to be very humble, in order to effect anything, and finally came down to hard begging.

Late that evening I went home, feeling the prisoners would be murdered that night, and I expected any minute to hear the horrifying report of the death warning guns, but that awful sound failed to reach my ears. When I arrived in town next morning, I learned to my great satisfaction, that the prisoners had not been molested.

. . . .

Saturday morning came, the day for the jury to meet, and when the roll was called, two of the jurors who had opposed the hanging were absent, and their places filled with men who failed to act on the moderate side.

The first thing the jury did, was to reconsider the decision of the jury to set these men at liberty when they met this moming. This decision was rejected, which placed the prisoners on trial the same as though they had not been tried.

The excitement had reached the juryroom. I and a few others saw the situation at once. The testimony against the men on which they had been tried was all written down, consequently there was nothing to be done but read it, and take the vote. One was put on trial the vote taken and he was condemned to hang; a second was disposed of in the same manner. I made a trial to stop the course of things, but I saw that it was useless to make any attempt to save the men by a vote. I then proposed a compromise: I proposed to allow them to select six of the worst ones and hang them, and set the rest at liberty. I saw they were going to hang a good many more than that, and I was striving to save as many as possible, but the jury rejected my proposition. When they rejected it, hope fled, and I took my seat to watch the course of events. I sat sad and silent till six were condemned and not one set at liberty, for it was hang or set at liberty.

The seventh one was put on trial, his was quite a moderate case, and some defended him. While they were talking on his case, they would look at me as though they wanted to say: help us. I thought now is the time to effect something.

I rose to my feet and addressed the jury about in these words: Gentlemen, I have remained silent, and suffered you to take your own course without interruption, but in this moderate case, I would with due respect, ask the question, if it would not be better to set these moderate cases at liberty, and if you must have blood, take the worst cases? We took the vote and set the man at liberty.

I saw that a reaction, to some extent, was taking place in the minds of some of the jury, and right here the day's fight commenced.

I did all I could to save the men, and those with whom I voted came up nobly to the work, and our side gained regularly. After we commenced setting some at liberty, we succeeded in saving about two-thirds.

This was the hardest day's work I ever did, or ever saw done. A portion of the men with whom I acted, contended manfully against all hanging, while the others sometimes voted against the men. This condition of things caused the fight to be fierce, each party striving to get those who sometimes voted for the men, who held the balance of power, and the party that got them, carried their point.

The present condition of things was well calculated to cause the contention to be of the fiercest character. Everything was done and said by each party that it was though[t] would cause them to succeed. As for myself, I know that I never exerted myself to the same extent as I did that day.

In speaking against the hanging, I said everything I could think of, that I thought would prevent hanging.

. . . I told the jury what I had often said to them before, that they were laboring under an excitement which had unhinged their minds. You think you are doing right, but said I, when the war closes and the excitement passes away, and you calmly look back on the course you are now pursuing, for you are bound to come to these sober hours of reflection, you will be astonished that you were so excited as to think that you were doing right. When you come to this, you will then say Barrett was right. All of those jurors that I talked with afterwards came to this sober conclusion.

Reader, the writer, who opposed the hanging, is the man whom you have so often heard was one of the leaders in this hanging. Most of the things I have written can be proven by living witnesses.

Now let us come to the result of this day's work.

There were nineteen men condemned to be hung; the balance, about fifty or sixty, were set at liberty.

These nineteen men were hung in consequence of the killing of . . . [the two men during the week of adjournment]. If they had not been killed, all of these men would have been set at liberty that Saturday morning.

The prisoners condemned, were notified that they were to hang next day.

. . . .

[When] . . . that dreadful Sunday dawned, and I went to Gainesville, not to see the men hung, for I would not see any of those men hung; but I went to see how the things which were going on would terminate. I took my seat in the same porch at the northeast corner of the square, where I sat when the fourteen men passed which the mob took from the jury and hung. The hanging did not commence very early, and when the last one was hung, the sun was low.

When I started home, my nearest way was to go so as to pass within twenty feet of the tree on which the men were hung, but I took the next street north, to keep from seeing any man hanging.

This day closed this thing, which had caused such an upheaving and excitement for the last twenty or twenty-five days.

There were forty hung, and two who broke from the guard were shot and killed, making forty-two deaths.

If I was to stop my history here, I am apprised that the reader would be disappointed, and desire to know what were the consequences resulting from this dreadful affair. This desire shall be gratified, as far as a statement of facts will do it.

This organization having been broken up, everything seemed to quiet down, but there was fears that the friends of those men might seek revenge, consequently every man connected with this thing was on the lookout day and night. But no revenge was taken.

I remained at my home, three miles east of Gainesville, about one year. I was in danger all the time from two sources, first, from a few persons who entertained a deadly hatred against me for assisting to set so many of these men at liberty. I dreaded them. Second, I dreaded the families and friends of those who were hung, being ignorant of my course, so I was between two axes. Some of the families of those who were hung treated me with a birth of friendship, surpassing what they had done before.

[When Federal troops came into Cooke County, many of those who had sat on the jury or had actively participated in the hanging took to the brush. Barrett moved to Mount Vernon, which was then located in Titus County. After civil courts were established under Governor Andrew J. Hamilton, a grand jury issued a bill against those who had sat on the jury. Fearful for his life, Barrett fled to Mississippi and Tennessee but soon returned to Cooke County, where he was tried and "honorably acquitted." He retired from his medical practice in 1878 but continued to preach until his death on July 24, 1892.]

The Hercules of
the Lone Star State

Sam Houston had a spectacular style of campaign oratory. Sometimes he wore frontier buckskins or the regalia of an Indian chief when he made speeches or went on speaking tours. He often appeared in the old military uniform he had worn in 1836 at San Jacinto, his pants tucked in the tops of his shabby boots, his old sword suspended at his side, and his dilapidated, weather-beaten hat perched on his head, the left side of the brim pinned up to the crown. The wound he had received at San Jacinto did not seem to bother him until election time, when he could be seen riding about the country in his buggy with his battle-scarred leg propped up on the dashboard. Among the charges leveled at him by his critics was that he was an egotist and wrote his name so that it read "I am Houston," scrawling his first name in such a way that the "S" in "Sam" looked like an "I."

From the very beginning the hero of San Jacinto was a determined opponent of secession. The fire of his opposition waxed hotter while he was a U.S. senator from Texas and after he was elected governor of the Lone Star State in 1859. No political gimmick was too ridiculous or any pressure tactic too compulsive if he thought it might be effective. Even threats on his life did not deter the old general from his continuing battle for the Union. His position produced bitter clashes with other important officials such as Judge O. M. Roberts, associate justice of the Texas Supreme Court, and Williamson S. Oldham, a member of the Confederate Congress. As governor, Houston obeyed the order of the legislature to submit the question of secession to popular vote, but he refused to take the oath of allegiance to the Confederacy and was deposed in March 1861. The story was told that the old man wept openly when the colors of the Confederacy replaced those of the United States at the top of the flagpole that stood at Hancock's Corner, at the intersection of Pecan and Congress streets in Austin.

Even after his removal from office, Houston continued to make speeches opposing secession for several months but made no effort to obstruct Confederate operations in the state. Opponents followed him, bitterly taking issue with his position, but Houston always seemed able to cope with the harassment. The following excerpt is a Yankee visitor's description of one of the old general's public orations denouncing disunion. Thomas North, the author, availed himself of a unique opportunity to hear Houston speak from a balcony of the old Tremont House in Galveston and obviously was impressed with what he saw and heard. Although North was prone to incorporate hearsay and rumor into his written observations, his analysis of Texans' views on secession and his discussion of political alignments are essentially correct.

Source: Thomas North, *Five Years in Texas* (Cincinnati: Elm Street Printing Company, 1871), pp. 86–95, 98.

The center of attraction to all political parties in the South was slavery; and no party could expect to exist with any respectable dimensions . . . that did not gravitate in that direction. . . . It is true, however, that there was a weak, maudlin, and mawkish anti-slaveryism here and there, through the South; but it had no bowels of effective demonstration . . . to stem the counter current, and throw off the shackles self-imposed. But when the South had drifted on the shoals of secession the issues were changed, and large and respectable masses of the people preferred the Union to slavery; but still the institution dominated everything in the shape of political action. The situation now was attended with schismatic sentiment and covert action against . . . secession.

There were different parties in Texas, representing many different views and measures, to meet the new monster now emerging from the deep waters of the nation's life.

First and foremost [there was] . . . the old original . . . John C. Calhoun . . . nullification party, which, though fewist in numbers, yet embraced in its ranks . . . most of the talent, wealth, and fashion of the South. This party believed in secession *per se* . . . and had been plotting and planning for long years to make it an accomplished fact. They thought the suitable occasion had now arrived for striking the effective blow in its behalf. They could now fire the public heart . . . through the medium of slavery . . . and win the prize of Southern independence.

There was another party, more numerous, who accepted the doctrine of secession . . . [as the only way in which] the rights of the South could be preserved. . . . They argued, "Wait till the commission of an overt act by the new [Lincoln] Administration . . . then [there] will be . . . [a] better excuse . . . for secession."

A third party believed in preserving the Union at almost all hazards;

even with the loss of the peculiar rights of the South. They argued and urged that Southern rights could be maintained by fighting for them, if need be "in the Union and under the old flag." This party was quite numerous.

A fourth party said . . . "Let slavery slide . . . [for] it is not worth shedding blood over, but let us have Union. Besides, the sentiment of all mankind is against our servile system, and history will dig its grave at last." This party was in the minority of all.

Still a fifth party opposed secession under any circumstances, on the ground of *bad policy* . . . and *inexpediency*. They said, secession is suicide, the very course to pursue by which to swap and lose our rights. Secession will be a stupendous failure, and we shall lose by it the very thing we propose . . . to defend and save. Prophetic words, which subsequent events literally fulfilled.

This was old General Sam Houston's position. He led this party in Texas. He spoke his mind freely anywhere, and in the face of threats, denunciations and mobs. We [of the North family] remember the interest and excitement manifest a few days before the vote on secession was taken in Texas. . . . [At this time] the "old man eloquent" of the "Lone Star State" came down to Galveston from Houston . . . to address the people on the exciting topic. The rumor spread through the city that Houston had come and would speak the next day at eleven o'clock A.M., from the second gallery of the Tremont House. It was evident there was a deep undercurrent of excitement . . . with a glassy calmness on the surface. . . . There was an unsearchable depth in each man's eye, like the shadowy stillness preceding the bursting storm. In the morning of the day when he was to speak a self-constituted committee of several leading citizens waited on the General at his quarters, and warned him not to attempt making a speech that day . . . as they feared serious disturbances and personal harm [might come] to him. . . .

The General replied with characteristic dignity: "Gentlemen, I thank you for your personal considerations, but I have seen stormy times in Texas before, and I have seen my personal friends tremble for my safety before; but, gentlemen, I shall make the speech to-day at eleven o'clock A.M., as already given out, from the upper gallery of the Tremont House. . . ."

One of the parties to the interview came into our office and reported what had passed. The writer had then never seen the General, and felt a strong desire to go and hear the "old warhorse," but concluded, . . . not wishing to be caught in the presence of a mob, not to go. Eleven o'clock came, and twelve, and some one came in and said: "Houston is speaking, and has been for an hour, and all is quiet." We went and heard the balance of his speech. After seeing and hearing him a few minutes we did not wonder he was not disturbed by a mob.

There he stood, an old man of seventy years, on the balcony ten feet above the heads of the thousands assembled to hear him, where every eye could scan his magnificent form, six feet and three inches high, straight as an arrow, with deep set and penetrating eyes, looking out from under heavy and thundering eyebrows, a high open forehead, with something of the infinite intellectual shadowed there, crowned with thin white locks, partly erect, seeming to give capillary condition to the electric fluid used by his massive brain, and a voice of the deep base tone, which shook and commanded the soul of the hearer. Adding to all this a powerful manner, made up of deliberation, self-possession and restrained majesty of action, leaving the hearer impressed with the feeling that more of his power was hidden than revealed. Thus appeared Sam Houston on this grand occasion, equal and superior to it, as he always was to every other. He paralyzed the mobocrat by his personal presence, and it was morally impossible for him to be mobbed in Texas, and if not there then not anywhere. . . .

The drift of Houston's speech was *the inexpediency and bad policy of secession*. He told them they could secure without secession what they proposed to secure by it, and would certainly lose through it. He gave the greater force to his declarations by appealing to them to know if he had not generally been right in the past history of Texas, when any great issue was at stake. Told them he made Texas and they knew it, and it was not immodest for him to say so; that the history of old Sam Houston was the history of Texas, and they knew it; that he fought and won the battle of annexation, and they knew it; that he originally organized and established the Republic of Texas, and they knew it; that he wrested Texas from the despotic sway of Santa Anna; that he commanded at San Jacinto, where the great Mexican leader was whipped and captured, and they knew it.

"Some of you," he continued, "opposed the annexation of Texas to the United States, and I suppose you have never forgiven me, even to this day, but I appeal to your sober judgments if, as it were, the very next day after annexation became history, Texas did not enter upon a career of fortune she had never realized before. I appeal to you for the frank confession that you have always prospered most when you have listened to my counsels. I am an old man now. I knew you in infancy, took you and dandled you on my knee, nursed you through all your baby ailments, and with great care and solicitude watched and aided your elevation to political and commercial manhood. Will you now reject these last counsels of your political father, and squander your political patrimony in riotous adventure, which I now tell you, and with something of prophetic ken, will land you in fire and rivers of blood.

"Some of you laugh to scorn the idea of bloodshed as a result of secession, and jocularly propose to drink all the blood that will ever flow in consequence of it! But let me tell you what is coming on the heels of secession. The time will come when your fathers and husbands, your sons and brothers, will be herded together like sheep and cattle at the point of the bayonet; and your mothers and wives, and sisters and daughters, will ask, Where are they? and echo will answer, where?

"You may," said he, "after the sacrifice of countless millions of treasure, and hundreds of thousands of precious lives, as a bare possibility, win Southern independence, if God be not against you; but I doubt it. I tell you that, while I believe with you in the doctrines of State rights, the North is determined to preserve this Union. They are not a fiery impulsive people as you are, for they live in cooler climates. But when they begin to move in a given direction, where great interests are involved, such as the present issues before the country, they move with the steady momentum and perseverance of a mighty avalanche, and what I fear is they will overwhelm the South with ignoble defeat, and I would say, amen, to the suffering and defeat I have pictured if the present difficulties could find no other solution, and that too by peaceable means. I believe they can. Otherwise I would say, 'Better die freemen than live slaves.'

"Whatever course my State shall determine to pursue my faith in State supremacy and State rights will carry my sympathies with her. And, as Henry Clay, my political opponent on annexation said, when asked why he allowed his son to go into the Mexican War, 'My country, right or wrong,' so I say, my State, right or wrong."

We noticed several times the very men applauding the speech who had opposed the speaker and the speaking in the morning. The power of

General Houston over a Texas audience was magical to the last degree, and doubtless well understood by himself; hence he feared no mobs.

. . . .

The old General died at Huntsville, Texas, a year or so before the war closed, but he lived long enough to see fulfilled what he had predicted in his speeches, and to receive the acknowledgment from some of his bitterest opponents that he was right. His lone widow followed him to the grave, by yellow fever, December 5, 1867. Thus ended the career of the Hercules of the Lone Star State, and she will never do herself honor, and the name of Houston justice, until she has a monument for him in granite or marble, surmounted with his statue, or an equestrian statue, in the metropolis of the State.

1862–1863

Facts and Fables in
the Battle of Galveston

The excerpts contained in this volume, written by persons contemporary with the events they describe, are examples of "history in the raw." Before most of the accounts from which they are taken can be accepted as factual, they need to be "processed"; that is, they must be scrutinized closely, analyzed carefully, and compared studiously with other contemporary accounts to determine their reliability. Failure adequately to "process raw history" is one of the most serious crimes in historical writing, and even seasoned historians occasionally stand convicted of this unscholarly practice. The result is the recording of fable as fact.

The excerpt below, from the writings of Thomas North, contains some erroneous historical reporting and is included in this volume primarily to point out the dangers in accepting contemporary accounts without thoroughly processing them. If these editorial comments and this excerpt cause a single student of history to become suspicious of unprocessed history, or even to question the facts with suspicion, then one of the goals behind the inclusion of this excerpt will have been accomplished.

North's account below provides a reasonably accurate description of the Confederate loss and recapture of Galveston. The author had many of the advantages of on-the-spot reporting and should have had access to most of the facts. As a talented writer of colorful and readable material, he fell victim to an inclination to tell a good story without seeking authentication for what he wrote. His dependence on rumor and hearsay to add interesting details, largely incidental to the history of the event, contribute to his failure as a "historical detective."

Perhaps the most glorious hour for Texans in their reconquest of Galveston was the sinking and capture of the *Harriet Lane*. A Federal vessel commanded by J. M. Wainwright, it was rammed by the *Bayou City*, an old wreck of a steamer converted into a ram. Confederate boarding parties swarmed over the vessel and much hand-to-hand combat resulted. Commander Wainwright was killed in the fighting and the *Harriet Lane*'s second officer, Lieutenant Commander Edward Lea, was mortally wounded. Neither Sidney Sherman, Sr., nor Sidney Sherman, Jr., was Wainwright's "first lieutenant" as North contends, and neither was even on board the *Harriet Lane* during the battle. It was Major Albert M. Lea, an engineer on General John Magruder's staff, who boarded the Federal vessel and found his dying son, Edward Lea, sprawled upon the bloody deck. Edward Lea died in his father's arms. Young Lea's last words, it has been generally believed, were simply, "My father has come." These words are inscribed on his tombstone in the Old Episcopal Cemetery in Galveston.

General Sidney Sherman, Sr., was a resident of Galveston and had been in command of Confederate coastal fortifications in the bay area until his resignation in 1861 because of ill health. As North correctly reported, his history "ran back to the stirring times of the Texas republic" when he had commanded the "left wing" of Sam Houston's little army in the battle of San Jacinto. His son, Lieutenant Sidney Sherman, Jr., was killed in the battle of Galveston but did not die in his father's arms and was not on board the *Harriet Lane*. His death occurred at his artillery position on Twentieth Street in downtown Galveston.

The next day, all of Galveston turned out for the funeral services of Confederate and Union soldiers who had fallen in the battle. Texas Masons took over the services of J. M. Wainwright because the Federal commander of the *Harriet Lane* was a high-ranking official in the Masonic order. Major Albert M. Lea read the Episcopal burial service for his son. Lieutenant Sidney Sherman, Jr., and other heroes wearing the blue and the gray were accorded impressive military funerals. General Magruder ordered the temporary parole of all Federal prisoners in Galveston to attend the services. X. B. DeBray's Twenty-sixth Texas Cavalry acted as military guard and kept an eye on the parolees.

One hundred years later, on January 1, 1963, special commemoration ceremonies were conducted in Galveston in honor of those who died in the great battle. Mrs. W. C. Cameron, representing the United Daughters of the Confederacy, helped place wreaths on the graves of Sidney Sherman, Jr., and Edward Lea. The excerpt below begins in May 1862 and extends through January 1, 1863, when the Confederates regained control of their Island City.

Source: Thomas North, *Five Years in Texas* (Cincinnati: Elm Street Printing Company, 1871), pp. 105–113.

[Although] . . . Texas was never invaded . . . she was pretty thoroughly blockaded on the coast; and artillery duels between land and sea frequently took place, but seldom to Confederate disadvantage. General [Paul Octave] Hébert was first in command of the Department of Texas, but he proved to be a man of no military force or practical genius, though a West Pointer, and had enjoyed the advantages of military associations in Europe, the reflex of which appeared rather to damage his usefulness than otherwise. He brought with him so much European red-tapeism, and being a constitutional ape, that he preferred red-top boots, and a greased rat-tail moustache, with a fine equippage, and a suite of waiters, to the use of good, practical common sense. Cannon, heavy siege guns, that had cost weeks of time, and thousands of money to transport from Virginia by rivers, through floods, storm and mud, lay on the wharves at Galveston, for months, waiting orders from the commandant to be placed in position on the fortifications erected at divers points on the island beach. Everybody became tired and disgusted with the General and his policy. He was too much of a military coxcomb to suit the ideas and ways of a pioneer country; besides, he was suspected of cowardice.

In May, 1862, the naval fleet outside made a demand for the surrender of the city, giving four days for a decision. The demand was refused. It was believed, of course, that Hébert would at least make a show of fight for the reputation of it, if for nothing more, and that a handsome artillery duel might be expected any hour. This expectation was strengthened by an order for all non-combatants to leave the island in a given time. The next few days witnessed a general stampede of people and valuables up country, the writer and his family with the multitude, to save them from the dangers of flying shot and shell. Every dray and available vehicle was brought into requisition to convey people and goods away from the city. Anything that could freight a thousand pounds or more, could easily command five dollars a load, four miles to the bridge, where the cars stopped. It was hurrying times.

On the fourth or fifth day a gun-boat ran in and opened fire on "Fort Point," near the entrance to the inside harbor. According to secret order, previously given, the fort responded with one gun, and then it was abandoned. Meanwhile the General and staff, with most of the troops, were making safe retreat to Virginia Point, four miles down the bay, on the main land side. Thus the city was left to be occupied by the Union forces. The naval fleet entered the bay in peaceful triumph, and no doubt they felt a contempt for the Confederate General in command, who had so ignominiously fled when they looked around and saw the facilities he had for defense.

The intervening space between city and railroad bridge was neutral ground, not occupied by either party. Non-combatants were freely allowed passes to and from the city. This cowardly flight so incensed the people against Hébert, that they petitioned for his removal, and it was granted. In the fall of 1862 he was replaced by General Magruder the gay, dashing, and festive Magruder; and this suited Texas. But Magruder soon saw that Texas expected him to retrieve the disgraceful loss of Galveston, the metropolis of the State.

So in a quiet and undemonstrative way, without giving to the expectant public either time or mode, he prepared to recapture the Island City and the fleet in her bay of which the celebrated and staunch "Harriet Lane" was the flagship, and stood at the wharf in central raking attitude to the city.

A few miles below the city of Houston, on Buffalo Bayou, at a point of narrows, where the huge forest trees on either bank locked arms across the waters, and the shade thereof made still deeper by the mustang vine, and the ever creeping old ivy, might have been seen three or four old steamer hulks being transformed into rams and gun-boats, whose sides were barricaded with compressed cotton bales. And this was the naval force with which to attack Uncle Sam's heavy iron-clads. Magruder had called to his side for consultation, upon the feasibility of his daring enterprise, his predecessor in command, who laughed him to scorn, as a dreaming fanatic, with more courage than brains. But not being disheartened by Hébert's wet blanket, he prosecuted his plans and purpose to completeness of preparation. Hébert left, and went to some private retreat up country, where he would not be considered by any implication, of word or circumstance, to be partaker in so wild and reckless a scheme.

Outside it was not yet known what time Magruder would make the attack. The secret was yet in his own breast, or, at most, was confined to himself and staff. But a few days prior to the event, it was rumored that Magruder intended making the State a new-year's present. So on the 31st day of December, A.D. 1862, the fleet weighed anchor, and proceeded, while yet daylight remained, down the bayou to Red Fish bar, within fifteen or twenty miles of the Federal fleet, and there anchored and waited till the dark hour of morning should come, named in "special orders." The ugly-looking crafts were manned by volunteers for the occasion, and though never yet in a fight, they had even more than the determined spirit of the "veterans." They were spoiling for the fray. One fear only served to dampen their ardor. The waters might be flowing at low tide when the hour came to pass it, and they could not pass it before, for fear of discovery by the Federal fleet, to whom they intended a complete surprise.

The land forces were at Virginia Point, ready to cross the two-mile bridge, and move up the island toward the city. Just at the dying of the old year, and the birth of the new, the two forces began to move; the one by water, the other by land, with flying artillery. The rolling wheels were muffled in the sand, and with silent roll and tread they moved on, and took well chosen positions. The two forces were to co-operate. They were to strike together at the moment when the moon should be gone to rest, which was at five o'clock in the morning. The land forces were there, and ready to open fire at the time, but waited till a few minutes after, hoping to hear the signal gun from the fleet first. But not so; the fleet then was hanging on Red Fish in low tide, as feared. Fatal detention, if not soon released, and taking part in the action now progressing. They could hear the booming cannon miles away, and in panting mood, and with desperate effort, they float once more, and steam to the scene of action, two hours late but "better late than never." Victory was trembling in the balance between the contending forces. One ram made direct for the "Harriet Lane," firing as she went, and struck her obliquely on the hind quarter. The rigging of the two vessels became tangled together so that they could not separate. The boarders rushed upon the deck of the "Harriet Lane" with cutlasses, knives, and navy shooters, and demanded her surrender. But her commander, Captain Wainwright, refused. And then they fought, bravely fought, hand to hand, on both sides, until Wainwright fell, shot through the heart, on his own deck, saying as he expired: "Tell mother I defended the 'Harriet' as long as I could." Sherman, his first lieutenant, was mortally wounded. By this time the deck was running with blood from the dead and dying, and the white flag was run up to the masthead, and the whole fleet in the bay thereby surrendered. Meanwhile one of the Confederate gun-boats had sunk, being struck by a cannon-ball below water mark. One of Magruder's couriers was at this moment carrying an order to the troops to cease fighting and retreat; and another courier rushed to headquarters with the news of the surrender, and the General ordered him placed under arrest for bringing a false report. But he was soon released, for, sure enough, it was 8 o'clock, the victory was won, and the "New-Year's gift was made."

Touching incidents sometimes occur on such occasions. There was one deeply so on this occasion. General Sherman, whose history ran back to the stirring times of the Texas republic, was in command of the Confederate ram that fought the "Harriet Lane." Lieutentant Sherman, just fallen on her deck, was his son. There they had met in deadly strife, father and son, the latter mortally hurt, and life fast ebbing away. But they did not recognize each other till the bloody contest was over, and then, at the moment of recognition, the son exclaims in feeble tones: "O, is that you father? and have we been fighting each other? The day is lost, and I am dying now father! Can I not have the holy sacrament to my comfort before I die?" We will not attempt to describe the agony of that father's heart, as he bent to embrace his dying boy, and to say, "Yes, my son; O, my darling son!" The sacrament was given and taken together by living father and dying son, who in one short hour afterward as each said "Forgive me, father," and "Forgive me, my son" breathed his life out sweetly, lying on his father's bosom. The next day a solemn military procession, with soft and reverent tread, passed to the cemetery, where the father himself read the sublime service of the Episcopal Church of which father and son were both members over his boy's grave. Solemn salutes were fired in honor of the noble dead. The victory and the defeat were alike forgotten, and regretted for the day, under the sublime touch of a human scene so tender, so grandly holy! We know the father well, a *good* man, though a rebel.

The news of the victory passed over the State with an electric thrill, and gave the people an elevation of spirits, from which they never fully came down, even at the close of the war. This, with an easy victory obtained at Sabine Pass, about the same time, by an Irish company of artillery in fortifications, by which a fleet was repulsed, and one or two of the largest vessels disabled and captured, gave Texas somewhat of a feeling of invincibility.

1863

Running the Union Blockade

By the middle of the summer of 1863, the Union blockade was beginning to seal off the Confederate states from the rest of the world. The shortage of vital supplies not only hampered the Confederacy's efforts to carry on the war but created privation and suffering among civilians. During the first eighteen months of warfare, Union blockaders had made little effort to watch all of the Texas coast, concentrating largely on Galveston, Sabine Pass, Brownsville, and the Matagorda Bay area. After the battles of Vicksburg and Gettysburg in July 1863, Federal efforts to make the blockade 100 percent effective were begun in earnest. Because of the boom in international cotton trade going on along the lower coast and Rio Grande, it was natural for the Federals to concentrate on Texas. Demands in the North for cotton were unparalleled in the history of the nation, and Texas Unionists in Washington and the Lone Star State stepped up their agitation for a "new front" west of the Sabine.

Blockade runners along the Texas coast were painfully aware of the greater pressures and increased dangers they had to face during these months. Their philosophy was to run the blockade as quickly and often as possible for each trip might be the last. Only the most astute blockade runners were still in business by this time, and the vessels they used were carefully designed to avoid detection by the blockaders. Most vessels were constructed with low silhouettes, painted as nearly as possible the color of the water, and streamlined for the greatest speed. Both steam-propelled ships and sailing sloops were used by the runners because each had unique advantages. The captains tried to plot their "shooting" of the blockade so that it could coincide with either dusk or dawn. Darkness, overcast weather, and foggy conditions also helped conceal their arrival and departure. These daring commanders employed every known skill in their efforts to achieve their destinations and reap the huge profits of this incredibly exciting and lucrative business. To get maximum benefit from their vessels' limited space, they often used screwjacks to pack bales of cotton in their cargo holds, and a few ships literally burst at the seams under the pressure. Most vessels also carried cargo lashed to their decks.

The excerpt below is from a blockade runner's account of a voyage from Havana to an inlet near Galveston in December 1863. Written by Captain William Watson, the commander of the *Rob Roy,* it reveals some of the hazards of a sail-propelled vessel seeking landfall on Texas soil. Sailing vessels were especially useful for hauling heavy freight because steamers were usually loaded down with their own coal and could not take much heavy cargo. The *Rob Roy*'s cargo on this voyage consisted of about twenty-five tons of bar iron, a large assortment of ironmongery, and several crates of earthenware. There were also on board several boxes of furnace bars for the transport steamers and about thirty bales of army blankets, tent cloth, and army clothing. In addition, the cargo contained large quantities of stationery, tea, coffee, and other groceries, and about forty barrels of seed potatoes.

Source: William Watson, *The Adventures of a Blockade Runner* (London: T. Fisher Unwin, 1892), pp. 249–258.

Having got everything on board including the mails, a full crew shipped . . . and ready for sea, I cleared for Matamoras, intending to strike straight across the Gulf. It was now the beginning of December, shorter daylight, and steady winds, and I aimed at making a quick run, and to be less time exposed to risk, and not have to bear such a long period of suspense as on last inward trip. I had also got more accustomed to the business and become more bold and reckless.

Two United States gunboats lay in the harbour, but it was seldom they got up steam and followed a blockade runner, so we took no heed of them, but with a strong south-easterly wind blowing steadily we stood down the harbour and passed the More about three o'clock in the afternoon, the officers on the gunboats watching us steadily with their glasses, but as neither vessel had steam up I knew they could not overhaul us before dark.

In case, however, that they might watch the course we took, we stood to the westward until dark, and then set the course for the old place, thirty miles east of Galveston. So far as I understood, no particular precautions had been taken to watch this entrance; in fact, this eastern channel was so shallow that few vessels could or would attempt to enter that way, and the *Rob Roy* was about the lightest draught which entered Galveston from Havana.

The wind continued to blow steadily and increased during the night, with considerable sea, and I soon began to observe that although we had all our cargo under deck, she did not sail so sweet and easy as when cotton-loaded. The iron was a dead weight, and she jerked quick and did not toll so steadily or rise over the seas so easily, as when she had a deck-load of cotton; however, she was spinning along rapidly, though taking a good deal of water over her decks, and I was unwilling to shorten sail, as I was very wishful to get over to the Texas coast before we should meet a norther, as that would have been hard upon us loaded as we were.

The wind increased almost to a gale, and we were at last compelled to shorten sail and run under single reefs. Last trip we had too little wind; this trip we had too much.

There was nothing worthy of note, and we sighted nothing from the time we left Havanna until the sixth day out, when we were nearing the coast of Texas. The weather was somewhat thick with rain squalls, wind about E.S.E., with a pretty high sea, when we sighted a vessel to the eastward upon our weather bow, about four miles distant. She seemed a schooner somewhat larger than ourselves, under a heavy press of canvas, and was running nearly before the wind, and as we were steering about N.W., we would cross her track.

The sight of another vessel is generally a pleasing incident at sea, in the ordinary course of things. It relieves the monotony, and sends forth a feeling of companionship; but it was not so on board of a blockade runner.

We desired no company and wished to see no vessel, and the sight of any vessel caused less or more uneasiness; and there was the usual conjecture as to what she might be and how we should act.

We were tolerably certain that the United States had now no sailing vessels acting as cruisers in the Gulf, but she might be a prize with an armed crew on board, which would make a prize of us if they could, and we had not this trip any arms on board to make a show of resistance.

Seeing that we would cross her track about a mile ahead of her we kept on our course.

As the two vessels neared each other we could see that she was carrying every stitch of canvas she could bear; rather too much for the gale that was blowing, and she was evidently straining to the utmost for some object.

We had single reefs in the mainsail and foresail, which we immediately proceeded to shake out. By the time this was done we were crossing her track, and we would soon see whether she altered her course to stand after us. She kept on her course, however, and we were relieved in mind thus far.

One of the men supposed her to be the *Emma* which had sailed from Havana about two days before us, destination unknown, but she was a new vessel and this was supposed to be her first trip in blockade running.

Wondering why she was carrying sail to such a reckless degree, the idea at once suggested itself that she might be chased, although we had seen nothing astern of her, but the weather was thick so that we could not see far.

A man was sent to the mast-head to look in the direction, but before he was half way up a slight clearing of the weather showed a gunboat in the distance.

"Get the topmast staysail on her," I said.

"I am afraid she won't bear it," said the mate.

"We must try it," I said. "It all depends upon our speed for a short time; and it is now past three o'clock. Yon gunboat is seven miles distant, it is near the shortest day, and it will be dark before six. If she can't gain more than two miles an hour upon us, we are all right."

"She bore the topmast staysail in a heavier gale than this," said Hagan, who was standing by; "the night we came out from the Brazos River on the first trip."

"All right," said the mate, "let us set it."

The sail was set and it sent her along faster, but she plunged heavily into the seas and quivered violently, and I was a little uneasy, for it now recurred to my recollections that on the time referred to by Hagan, she was cotton-loaded, with a high deckload, but now she had a dead weight of iron in her hold which made a disagreeable difference in a vessel of this kind.

In the meantime I watched the gunboat steadily to see whether she would continue her course after the other vessel, or take after us. She did not seem to be a very fast steamer, and I thought she was not gaining very much on the large schooner.

One of the new hands that we had shipped at Havanna, named Charlie, was an old hand at blockade running, and had also been in the U.S. navy, and served in the blockading fleet. He said that the other schooner had taken the gunboat before the sea. The object in doing this was because these gunboats were generally short vessels, and when going before a heavy sea they pitched heavily, throwing their propeller out of the water, causing the engines to race, and requiring constant throttling of the engines, which impeded their progress very much: and from the clouds of spray which even at this distance we could see at times, shot out from the stern of the gunboat, it was evident that she was at a great disadvantage by having to run before the wind and sea.

I began to fear that on this account she might leave off pursuit of the other schooner and follow us, and determined if she did, to run before the wind also.

She seemed to alter her course about a point towards us with the object, I thought, of keeping in the wake of both vessels, and taking after the one she thought she would be most likely to make sure of.

She was not, however, gaining rapidly on either, and in about an hour after we had sighted her, she seemed to be fully five miles distant, when a rain squall came up and hid her from view.

While looking at our pursuer, I had been neglecting my own vessel, and the rain squall struck us suddenly, and crack went the topmast, and the staysail was fluttering in the wind. It was, however, got in safe and the wreck cleared away. This was a misfortune, but if the wind continued we could get along very well without the staysail, and while we were hid from the view of the gunboat, I thought it a good opportunity to alter our course, and now that the staysail was off her, she would sail faster by bringing her on the wind a little.

I altered her course to N.N.W. This put her on her best leg and took us off at more of an angle from the track of the gunboat, without the latter observing it.

The weather continued thick, and the gunboat was still hid from view, but we could hear now and then the whirr of her propeller as it was thrown out of water by her pitching. This, and the direction of the sound, showed to us that the gunboat was still keeping on the same course.

Just as it was getting dark the weather cleared off a little, and we could just see the gunboat about seven miles distant, bearing about south by west. We thought it probable she might not see us; we had altered our course, and our topmast and staysail being gone, we were less easy to be seen, and it got dark almost immediately after we saw her.

Although it continued to blow pretty hard all night we did not reef down as usual, as I feared that if the gunboat had seen us after the squall had passed, and the other schooner had escaped her, she would likely during the night stand towards the place where we would be likely to be, so that she might chance sight us at daylight.

Having had no observation for two days owing to the thick weather, I was not very sure of our position, but I knew that we must be getting near to the coast of Texas. About midnight, however, it became beautifully clear, and I got the latitude by an altitude of the polar star, which showed us to be about thirty-five miles from the coast, but as we had altered our course I expected that we would be to the eastward of the place we wished to make. However, as we should have to wait until night before attempting to run into Galveston, I determined to continue on the same course, and get up close to the land by daylight, where we would be more out of the track of cruisers.

We were now just in the track most frequented by them and we kept a good look out. Although there was no moon, it was clear and starlight, and some of the men said that by this sudden clearing up after thick rainy weather, we might look out for a norther. As that would be off the land, it was another inducement to us to get close up and be under the lee of the land if it did come.

About two hours before daylight we took a cast of the lead, and found 14 fathoms. This was just as we wanted. The wind had somewhat moderated, but still blew steady. At the first appearance of daylight we were on the look out, but nothing was to be seen. The coast was low and the land could not be seen at a great distance, but when it became clear daylight, the land could be seen about eight miles distant.

This was all very well so far, but now came the time of danger. We would have to remain here for the whole day, liable to be seen by any passing cruiser. We would have been glad if the thick rainy weather of yesterday had continued, but it did not; it had cleared off and the sun came out bright and warm.

I now got an altitude of the sun, and got the longitude. I found we were, as I expected, about eight miles to the eastward of the landmark of the three sand-mounds. We now stood to the westward, keeping a sharp look out from the mast-head and keeping as close to the shore as possible, but owing to the rough weather of the past few days there was a very heavy surf rolling up on the beach, and we could not now venture so close as we had done last trip, if a cruiser happened to pass.

The wind now began to lessen, and it was near noon before we got to our old anchorage opposite the three mounds, and soon afterwards it died away altogether. This enabled us to go a little closer in shore, but I was a little anxious for fear we should not have a steady breeze to run into Galveston during the night.

"I am much mistaken," said one of the old hands, "if we don't have wind enough before long."

"A norther do you mean?" said I.

"Yes," said he, "a norther will be on before night, or I am mistaken."

"All the better," said I. "We are all right for a norther now, wind off the land with smooth water; I only wish it and night were together."

"But how about getting up the main channel after we get into it. There is very little room for tacking with the centre-board down?"

This required consideration, and I thought it best to be prepared if the norther did come. The only plan I knew of was to warp up if the warp would be strong enough. In the meantime a sharp look out was kept from the mast-head, but nothing appeared in sight, and not a breath of wind.

About 3 P.M. the sun was obscured, and the air got a smoky appearance, and some gusts of wind came off the land.

I had, while in Havanna this last time, bought a light kedge-anchor, and it was that which we had now down. The vessel was hove up to it, and the heavy anchor was let go, and in half an hour the norther was on us with full force.

This added a little to the danger from cruisers, because, if a cruiser had been passing, she would probably have hugged the land closer to be in smooth water; however, it was now only two hours till dark, and all the rest was in our favor.

We could run in under close reefs, and therefore be less easily seen, while the cruisers riding at anchor would swing out to sea and have to pay out chain, so they would be farther off, and, as the wind was a little east of north, it was possible that we would be able to lay up the main channel the greater part of the way. However, we got the long line ready, and doubled it to use as a warp, and had the large boat ready to take out the kedge if necessary.

We then close-reefed the main and foresail, and put one reef in the jib, and, as we knew that the norther would be always lessening the water in the small channel, we determined to start early. As soon as it was dark we raised anchor and stood along the coast. It was blowing pretty hard, but, as the wind was off the land, the water was smooth, and we kept well up to windward in rather less than the stipulated three fathoms, for although what little tide there was, was rising, still the strong wind off the land shoaled the water a little.

As we got near the entrance to the channel we could discover dimly in the distance the first of the blockading fleet. She was just about the same place as we had seen her on last trip, but riding to seaward of her anchor, which kept her a little farther off our course.

We must be careful and not get into the same *cul de sac* that we got into last trip, but I was reminded by Old Charlie that I need not be surprised if we got into six feet of water, or even less, as the water would be sure to be very low on the bar in this wind. We soon found the entrance to the channel, and altered the course to W.S.W. It now required all hands, and the cook. There was barely six feet of water, the channel was narrow, and it was blowing furiously. We required to have a man taking soundings on both sides, and a good man at the helm.

On the first deepening of the water it was luff, quick, haul in sheets, and down centre-board.

She lay up the channel for a good stretch, but she was getting jambed on the western side of it. We put about, but we had scarcely gathered headway when we had to put about again, and we found that, owing to the strong wind, there was a strong current down the channel. We kept tacking, and gained a little, but the channel was getting narrower. At last we saw the light of the guardboat, and, thinking we were safe from the blockading fleet, we dropped anchor. The noise of the chain running out was heard by those in the guardboat, and they hailed us.

Owing to the howling of the wind, it was difficult to hear at that distance, but we understood that we were to come up to the guardboat, as we were not safe where we lay.

To get up was no easy matter. The channel here was narrow, and a strong gale of wind was blowing right down. There was no room to tack, and, had we raised the anchor, we would have been blown out among the blockading fleet before we could have gathered headway on either tack. We must warp up; but the question was, would the warp-rope, doubled, be strong enough, and would the kedge hold? We must try it. We knew it was good holding ground, though soft.

We got up some of the furnance bars which we had as freight, and lashed them to the stock of the ledge to add it its weight; we then got out the large boat, and, having got everything prepared, we started to pull up towards the guard-boat.

The water was smooth, but the wind blew so strong that, with four stout oarsmen, it was all we could do to make headway against it.

After a hard pull the boat got up a little past the guard-boat where the kedge, loaded with its additional weight, was let down; then hanging on to the warp, the boat dropped back to the schooner.

We hove gently on the warp until the anchor chain got slack; this satisfied us that the kedge was holding. We then hove up the anchor, and hung it by a stopper from the davit, ready to let to in a moment if the warp should break. We then hove on the warp as often as the wind lulled a little, but stopped heaving during the violent gusts.

After a great deal of hard labour, we got the schooner close up to the guard-boat, when the captain of the latter hailed us and said we might anchor there. We were quite safe from any attack by boats from the blockading fleet.

We dropped anchor with right good will, congratulating ourselves that we were in safe once more, although every one at the same time avowed that blockade running was no child's play.

Having made sure that the anchor was holding, we let the warp remain out also, and, setting an anchor watch, we turned in.

We had little communication with those on the guard-boat that night. It was blowing too hard for us to hear each other.

By daylight the wind had gone down a little, the nib of the norther, as it was called, had blown off, but it still blew a pretty hard gale.

About eight o'clock the boarding officers came on board, and we passed through the usual ceremony. It being midwinter, we had a clear bill of health from Havanna. There had been several steamers got in within the last month or two, but we brought the latest news by ten days.

They took a list of our cargo, which was satisfactory, and much wanted, especially the army blankets, as the weather was now cold, and we were ordered to come up to the town and get discharged as soon as possible, as the Quarter-master's Department was much in want of goods. They took the mails, consisting of letters and newspapers, and having, as usual, taken a few samples of our stores, which they declared good, especially the liquors, they left, landing at the Forts.

We now got up anchor and stood up the bay, and anchored opposite the town about noon.

There were several steamers (blockade runners) lying at the wharf, and some of the Transport service steamers, so that we had to lay at anchor until we should be assigned a berth at the wharf.

1863

Victory at Sabine Pass

The cries of cotton manufacturers in the North, along with the political designs of determined Texas Unionists such as Andrew Jackson Hamilton, kept almost constant pressure on the Lincoln government for a campaign of conquest against Texas. Lincoln was largely concerned with securing absolute control of the Mississippi River during the first two years of the war; after this was accomplished during the summer of 1863, the president evidently felt more inclined to accede to those advocating an invasion of Texas.

Henry W. Halleck, Lincoln's general in chief and one of the promoters of the Texas invasion, insisted that the most feasible route into Texas was up the Red River. Nathaniel P. Banks, the commander of the Department of the Gulf with headquarters in Union-occupied New Orleans, differed with Halleck and argued that fewer logistical problems would be encountered in an amphibious landing on the Texas coast near Sabine Pass. Because Lincoln was known to lack confidence in Halleck, Banks decided in favor of an offensive against the Sabine Pass fortifications.

On the last day of August 1863, Banks ordered William B. Franklin, a veteran of the 1862 campaigns in Virginia, to take the Third Division and one brigade of the First Division of the Nineteenth Corps aboard transports and proceed to the Texas coast. Banks was convinced that the Texas defenses were weak at this point and instructed Franklin to reduce Fort Griffin, occupy Sabine City, and then strike into the interior along the Beaumont-Houston railway. If Lincoln would supply reinforcements, Banks hoped to launch a major offensive against Houston and Galveston from the interior as well as from the sea. The next year Banks was to lead another large force against Texas, this time following Halleck's proposed route, but in 1863 the attack on Sabine Pass was Banks's first serious effort to invade Texas. The Confederate government considered the Sabine Pass attack nothing more than a feint designed to take pressure off Union forces in Mississippi and Tennessee.

On Monday, September 7, four Federal gunboats inched into range of the guns of Fort Griffin, the Confederate citadel situated at the narrows below Sabine City. During a forty-five-minute battle the next day, two of Franklin's gunboats were disabled and compelled to surrender. Federal casualties included 19 killed, 9 wounded, 37 missing, and 315 taken prisoner. There were no casualties among the Texan defenders. The Federal flotilla hovered about the entrance to Sabine Pass for several days, finally making a feeble attempt to slip through the pass under cover of darkness. Repelled once again, Franklin abandoned the invasion and sailed back to report to Banks in New Orleans.

The excerpt that follows was taken from the memoirs of Francis R. Lubbock. It includes portions of the official report submitted by Lieutenant Richard W. Dowling, the heroic commander at Sabine Pass.

Source: Francis Richard Lubbock, *Six Decades in Texas: Memoirs of Francis Richard Lubbock,* ed. C. W. Raines (Austin: Ben C. Jones and Company, 1900), pp. 503–509.

On the 8th of September, 1863, there occurred at Fort Griffin, commanding Sabine Pass, one of the most remarkable engagements of the war, resulting in a victory for the Confederate arms that immortalized those who participated in it. It is best described in the language of First Lieut. R. W. Dowling, who with Company F, of Cook's artillery, manned the works, and who was the recognized hero of the affair:

"On Monday morning about 2 o'clock," says Lieutenant Dowling in his official report, "the sentinel informed me the enemy were signaling, and, fearing an attack, I ordered all the guns at the fort manned, and remained in that position until daylight, at which time there were two steamers evidently sounding for the channel on the bar, and a large frigate outside. They remained all day at work, but during the evening were reinforced to the number of twenty-two vessels of different classes.

"On the morning of the 8th the United States gunboat Clifton anchored opposite the lighthouse and fired twenty-six shells at the fort, most of which passed a little over or fell short; all, however, in excellent range, one shell being landed on the works and another striking the south angle of the fort, without doing any material damage. The firing commenced at 6:30 o'clock, and finished at 7:30 o'clock by the gunboat hauling off. During this time we had not replied by a single shot. All was then quiet until 11 o'clock, at which time the gunboat Uncle Ben steamed down near the fort. The United States gunboat Sachem opened on her with a thirty-pounder Parrott gun. She fired three shots, but without effect, the shots all passing over the fort and missing the Ben. The whole fleet then drew off, and remained out of range until 3:40 o'clock, when the Sachem and Arizona steamed into line up the Louisiana channel, the Clifton and one boat, name unknown, remaining at the junction of the two channels. I allowed the two former boats to approach within 1200 yards, when I opened fire with the whole of my battery on the foremost boat (the Sachem), which, after the third or fourth round, hoisted the white flag, one of the shots passing through her steam drum. The Clifton in the meantime had attempted to pass up through Texas channel; but, receiving a shot which carried away her tiller rope, she became unmanageable and grounded about 500 yards below the fort, which enabled me to concentrate all my guns on her, which were six in number, two thirty-two-pounder smooth-bores, two twenty-four-pounder smooth-bores, and two thirty-two-pounder howitzers. She withstood our fire some twenty-five or thirty minutes, when she also hoisted a white flag. During the time she was aground she used grape, and her sharpshooters poured an incessant shower of minie balls into the works.

"The fight lasted from the time I fired the first gun until the boats surrendered; that was about three-quarters of an hour.

"I immediately boarded the captured Clifton and proceeded to inspect her magazine, accompanied by one of the ship's officers, and discovered it safe and well stocked with ordnance stores. I did not visit the magazine of the Sachem, in consequence of not having any small boats to board her with. The Confederate States gunboat Uncle Ben steamed down to the Sachem and towed her in to the wharf. Her magazine was destroyed by the enemy flooding it.

"During the engagement I was nobly and gallantly assisted by Lieut. N. H. Smith, of the engineer corps, who by his coolness and bravery won the respect and admiration of the whole command. This officer deserves well of his country.

"To Assistant Surgeon George P. Bailey I am under many obligations, who, having nothing to do in his own line, nobly pulled off his coat and assisted in administering Magruder pills to the enemy, and behaved with great coolness.

"During the engagement the works were visited by Capt. F. H. Odlum, commanding the post, and Maj. (Col) Leon Smith, commanding marine department of Texas.

"Capt. W. S. Good, ordnance officer, and Dr. Murray, acting assistant surgeon, behaved with great coolness and gallantry, and by them I was enabled to send for reinforcements, as the men were becoming exhausted by the rapidity of our fire; but before they could accomplish their mission the enemy surrendered.

"Thus, it will be seen, we captured with forty-seven men two gunboats, mounting thirteen guns of the heaviest caliber, and about 350 prisoners. All my men behaved like heroes; not a man flinched from his post. Our motto was, 'Victory or death.'

"I beg leave to make particular mention of Private Michael McKeenan, who, from his well known capacity as a gunner, I assigned as gunner to one of the guns, and nobly did he do his duty. It was his shot that struck the Sachem in her steam drum.

"Too much praise can not be awarded to Maj. (Col.) Leon Smith for his activity and energy in saving and bringing the vessels into port."

. . . .

To properly appreciate the value of Dick Dowling's valiant achievement, we need only consider that, had the land forces of Franklin's fleet made a successful landing at Sabine, the victory would have served the purpose of the enemy even better than if he had first moved on Galveston and captured that city, for the reason that had a lodgment been effected at Fort Griffin, the enemy could have perfected organization and equipment and marched into the interior before we could have assembled and confronted him with an opposing force, a movement that he could not have executed from Galveston, as he could have been confined to the island until the whole strength of Texas could have been hurled against him. Sabine Pass was of further value to us from the fact that it was the most available port for running the blockade, and that it was saved to us, if nothing more had been accomplished, would have amply justified the congratulations and words of praise that were showered upon its defender by civil and military officials, press and people.

Had the Federal army landed there, it would have been between [Richard] Taylor, [John] Magruder, and Kirby Smith. "Had the landing been accomplished either at the Pass or below," says General [Nathaniel P.] Banks, in a letter to General [Henry W.] Halleck, "a movement would have been immediately made for Beaumont from the Pass, or for Liberty if the landing had been made below, and thence directly to Houston, where fortifications would have been thrown up, and our line of communication and supplies immediately established at the mouth of the Brazos River, west of Houston, until we could have gained possession of Galveston Island and city. I should have had in ten days from the landing 20,000 men at Houston, where, strongly fortified, they could have resisted the attack of any force that it was possible to concentrate at that time. Houston would have been nearly in the center of the forces in and about Louisiana and Texas, commanding all the principal communications, and would have given us ultimately the possession of the State."

*

1863

Lynch Law on the Lower Rio Grande

Lieutenant Colonel Arthur James Lyon Fremantle, a suave and sophisticated tourist from English military circles, arrived on the Mexican side of the Rio Grande on April 2, 1863. At the little Mexican village of Bagdad (see map 1), a Texas merchant made arrangements with a Mexican named Ituria to take them by buggy to Brownsville. The merchant was not ready to depart immediately so Fremantle and Ituria made the trip alone.

The excerpt that follows is the Englishman's account of his impressions and experiences during this short journey. Fremantle was privileged to speak with prominent Texans along the way such as Brigadier General Hamilton P. Bee, the commander of the Confederate garrison at Brownsville. General Hamilton Bee was the brother of Barnard E. Bee, the Confederate general who gave General Thomas Jackson his popular epithet, "Stonewall." Fremantle also spent some time with Colonel James Duff, the commander of the Fourteenth Texas Cavalry, whose encampments were scattered all along the Brownsville road. When he had been in Texas only a few hours, Fremantle was permitted to glimpse the grisly results of a swift system of extralegal justice, known in the Lone Star State as "lynch law." Gradually, he was able to piece together the fragments of a story of a kidnap-lynching that involved a hapless *renegado* named Mongomery ("Montgomery" in other accounts).

Source: A. J. L. Fremantle, *Three Months in the Southern States: April–June, 1863* (New York: John Bradburn, 1864), pp. 9–12.

The Rio Grande is very tortuous and shallow. The distance by river to Matamoros is sixty-five miles, and it is navigated by steamers, which sometimes perform the trip in twelve hours, but more often take twenty-four, so constantly do they get aground.

The distance from Bagdad to Matamoros by land is thirty-five miles; on the Texan side to Brownsville, twenty-six miles.

I crossed the river from Bagdad with Mr. Ituria, at 11 o'clock; and, as I had no pass, I was taken before half-a-dozen Confederate officers, who were seated round a fire contemplating a tin of potatoes. These officers belonged to Duff's cavalry (Duff being my Texan's partner). Their dress consisted simply of flannel shirts, very ancient trousers, jack boots with enormous spurs, and black felt hats ornamented with the "lone star of Texas." They looked rough and dirty, but were extremely civil to me.

The captain was rather a boaster, and kept on remarking, "We've given 'em h——ll on the Mississippi, h——ll on the Sabine . . . , and h——ll in various other places."

He explained to me that he couldn't cross the river . . . as he with some of his men had made a raid over there three weeks ago and carried away some *renegados,* one of whom, named Mongomery, they had *left* on the road to Brownsville. By the smiles of the other officers, I could easily guess that something very disagreeable must have happened to Mongomery. He introduced me to a skipper, who had just run his schooner, laden with cotton, from Galveston, and who was much elated in consequence. The cotton had cost 6 cents a pound in Galveston, and is worth 36 here.

Mr. Ituria and I left for Brownsville at noon. A buggy is a light gig on four high wheels.

The road is a natural one – the country quite flat, and much covered with mesquite trees, very like pepper trees. Every person we met carried a six-shooter, although it is very seldom necessary to use them.

After we had proceeded about nine miles we met General Bee, who commands the troops at Brownsville. He was traveling to Boca del Rio in an ambulance . . . with his quartermaster general, Major Russell. I gave him by letter of introduction . . . and told him who I was.

He thereupon descended from his ambulance and regaled me with beef and beer in the open. He is brother to the General Bee who was killed at Manassas. We talked politics and fraternized very amicably for more than an hour. He said the Mongomery affair was against his sanction, and he was sorry for it. He said that Davis, another *renegado,* would also have been put to death had it not been for the intercession of his wife. General Bee had restored Davis to the Mexicans.

Half an hour after parting company with General Bee we came to the spot where Mongomery had been *left;* and sure enough, about two hundred yards to the left of the road, we found him.

He had been slightly buried, but his head and arms were above the ground, his arms tied together, the rope still around his neck, but part of it still dangling from quite a small mesquite tree. Dogs or wolves had probably scraped the earth from the body, and there was no flesh on the bones. I obtained this my first experience of lynch law within three hours of landing in America.

I understand that this Mongomery was a man of very bad character, and that, confiding in the neutrality of the Mexican soil, he was in the habit of calling the Confederates all sorts of insulting epithets from the Bagdad bank of the river; and a party of his *renegados* had also crossed over and killed some unarmed cotton teamsters, which had roused the fury of the Confederates.

About three miles beyond this we came to Colonel Duff's encampment. He is a fine-looking, handsome Scotchman, and received me with much hospitality. His regiment consisted of newly raised volunteers – a very fine body of young men, who were drilling in squads. They were dressed in every variety of costume, many of them without coats, but all wore the high black felt hat.

Notwithstanding the peculiarity of their attire, there was nothing ridiculous or contemptible in the appearance of these men, who all looked thoroughly like "business." Colonel Duff told me that many of the privates owned vást tracts of country, with above a hundred slaves, and were extremely well off. They were all most civil to me. Their horses were rather rawboned animals, but hardy and fast. The saddles they used were nearly like the Mexican. Colonel Duff confessed that the Mongomery affair was wrong, but he added that his boys "*meant well.*"

We reached Brownsville at 5:30 P.M., and Mr. Ituria kindly insisted on my sleeping at his house instead of going to the crowded hotel.

1863

The Elysium of the Prairies

While on board the British vessel that transported Colonel Fremantle to America, the Englishman became acquainted with a Texas merchant named McCarthy, who agreed to guide him across "that part of the Texan deserts" between Brownsville and San Antonio. McCarthy and Fremantle left Brownsville on April 13, 1863, in a "roomy, but rather overloaded, four-wheel carriage, with a canvas roof, and four mules." In addition to the driver of the carriage, a foulmouthed Texan named Sargent, there was a young Jewish passenger who was deathly ill during most of the journey. The fourth member of the party joined the travelers during the afternoon of the first day and was known simply as "the Judge." Fremantle described the Judge as "an elderly, rough faced, dirty looking man . . . mounted on a sorry nag."

The party averaged about eighteen miles per day, camping each night near a water hole, if possible. Fremantle and McCarthy slept together on a large bullock rug near the camp fire. The trip to San Antonio was largely uneventful except for Fremantle's brief visit with General John Magruder, whom he encountered along the trail, and the party's stopover at the headquarters of Richard King's famous Santa Gertrudis ranch. "For several days," wrote Fremantle, "I had heard this [ranch] spoken of as a sort of Elysium."

The ranch headquarters was a key station on the long road by which Southern cotton was hauled in wagons to Bagdad, Mexico, and shipped to Europe in foreign vessels to avoid the Union blockade. Shortly after Fremantle's visit, Federal troops occupied the lower Rio Grande, and the ranch headquarters became an advance outpost for Confederate cavalry. Richard King, who had paid three hundred dollars for his first parcel of land just ten years previously, was regarded as a rebel agent, and Union soldiers were instructed to keep a constant vigil and arrest him if he could be located.

Toward the end of the war John Salmon "Rip" Ford and his Confederates recaptured the Rio Grande port of Brownsville. King, as a contractor in cotton, beef, and army supplies, soon made up for the financial losses he had suffered during the Union occupation. Following the battle of Palmito ranch house in 1865, he was granted amnesty and a presidential pardon after he took the loyalty oath to the United States. His family, who spent most of the war in San Antonio, rejoined him. King spent the next several years reorganizing his ranching enterprise, erecting a wooden fence around part of his ranch land, and fighting off rustlers and Mexican *renegadoes*. In 1869, he and Mifflin Kenedy dissolved their ranching partnership, and King became the sole owner of the Santa Gertrudis.

The following excerpt from Fremantle's diary contains the Englishman's account of his visit to the historic ranch headquarters. He observed that most of his journey thus far had been through dry, desolate, sandy wasteland but that just before his party's arrival at the ranch they encountered rain and blackland soils. Fremantle was introduced to Mrs. Hamilton P. Bee, the wife of the Confederate commander in Brownsville whom he had met earlier. His comments on Mrs. Bee and the ranch are colorful and completely in keeping with the "soldier-gentleman" image he obviously sought to generate.

Source: A. J. L. Fremantle, *Three Months in the Southern States: April–June, 1863* (New York: John Bradburn, 1864), pp. 43–45.

19th April (Sunday) At 1 A.M. this morning our slumbers on the bullock rug were disturbed by a sudden and most violent thunderstorm. M'Carthy and I had only just time to rush into the carriage, and hustle our traps underneath it, when the rain began to descend in torrents.

We got inside with the young Jew, whilst Mr. Sargent and the Judge crept underneath.

The rain lasted two hours; and at daylight we were able to refresh ourselves by drinking the water from the puddles, and effect a start.

But fate seemed adverse to our progress. No sooner had we escaped from the sand than we fell into the mud, which was still worse.

We toiled on till 11:30 A.M., at which hour we reached King's Ranch. For several days I had heard this spoken of as a sort of Elysium, marking as it does the termination of the sands, and the commencement of comparative civilization.

We halted in front of the house, and after cooking and eating, I walked up to the "ranch," which is a comfortable, well-furnished wooden building.

Mr. and Mrs. King had gone to Brownsville; but we were received by Mrs. Bee, the wife of the Brownsville general, who had heard I was on the road.

She is a nice lively little woman, a red-hot Southerner, glorying in the facts that she had no Northern relations or friends, and that she is a member of the Church of England.

Mr. King first came to Texas as a steamboat captain, but now owns an immense tract of country, with 16,000 head of cattle, situated, however, in a wild and almost uninhabited district. King's Ranch is distant from Brownsville only 125 miles, and we have been six days in reaching it.

After drying our clothes and our feed after the rain of last night, we started again at 2:30 P.M.

We now entered a boundless and most fertile prairie, upon which, as far as the eye could reach, cattle were feeding.

Bulls and cows, horses and mares came to stare at us as we passed.

They all seemed sleek and in good condition, yet they get nothing but what they pick up on the prairie.

I saw a man on horseback kill a rabbit with his revolver. I also saw a scorpion for the first time.

We halted at 5:30 P.M., and had to make our fire principally of cow-dung, as wood is very scarce on this prairie.

We gave up the Judge's horse at King's Ranch. The lawgiver now rides on the box with Mr. Sargent.

1863

Kate Stone's Arrival in Texas

Kate Stone, a twenty-two-year-old refugee from Louisiana, wrote the following letter to a friend back home shortly after her arrival in Lamar County, Texas (see map 3). She, her mother, two brothers, a sister, an aunt, and a cousin, although not traveling in the same party, had recently completed a journey of more than three hundred miles from Brokenburn, the Stone family's large plantation in eastern Louisiana. The plantation was located on the floodplain of the Mississippi just thirty miles northwest of Vicksburg, the Confederate citadel that fell to General Ulysses S. Grant on July 4, 1863. The first leg of the journey to Texas had been to Milden, Louisiana, where Kate and her party turned northward through Walnut Hill in southwestern Arkansas. From there they had entered Texas near present-day Texarkana, roughly following a tributary of the Red River. Kate was not overjoyed at the prospect of living in Texas, which she had called "the dark corner of the Confederacy" in an earlier entry in her diary. Her revulsion for the state and its people is made clear in the letter below, written on July 7, 1863, and copied in her diary.

Source: Kate Stone, *Brokenburn: The Journal of Kate Stone*, ed. John Q. Anderson (Baton Rouge: Louisiana State University Press, 1955), pp. 223–225. Reprinted by permission.

Here we are safely in a dark corner of the far off County of Lamar after a tiresome, monotonous trip of little less than three weeks, and I am already disgusted as I expected to be. This part of the land abounds in whiteheaded children and buttermilk, my two pet aversions. It is a place where the people are just learning that there is a war going on, where Union feeling is rife, and where the principal amusement of loyal citizens is hanging suspected Jayhawkers. Hoops are just coming in with full fashion. This is indeed the place where hoops "most do flourish and abide." Have not seen a hoopless lady since entering the state. Shoes are considered rather luxuries than necessaries and are carefully kept for state occasions. As for bowls and pitchers, "Oh no, they never mention them. Their name is never heard." One tin pan or a frying pan answers every purpose. Wash tubs seem obsolete and not to be bought at any price. The only way of killing time and one never feels more like killing him than on this desolate wind-swept prairie is to attend some of the protracted meetings that are being carried on all around us. And oh, the swarms of ugly, rough people, different only in degrees of ugliness. There must be something in the air of Texas fatal to beauty. We have not seen a good-looking or educated person since we entered the state. We are in the dark corner. We could not stand it here for a permanent stay, but Mamma has only stopped here for a breathing spell. . . .

We camped out except when it rained, which it did most of the last week, thereby ruining most of the clothes we had so laboriously amassed after fleeing from the Yankees. We would be so tired by night we welcomed the rudest shelter. The longer we traveled the more wearisome it grew, and I never turned over at night without expecting to feel the sting of a tarantula or centipede. But we really saw very few and reached here without an accident. I wrote to Sarah Wadley [daughter of a prominent Louisiana physician and Kate's friend] never to come to Texas for pleasure, but if forced to come to cover herself with a thin coat of tar to protect herself from the myriads of insects along the road. And here, we have settled at their headquarters ticks, redbugs, fleas by the millions, and snakes gliding through the grass by hundreds. But we rarely hear of anyone being snakebitten. Game, deer, and turkeys, are abundant about here but not eatable on account of the insects tormenting them until they are too tough to eat.

1863

The Second Texas Cavalry Moves Out

Fighting units in Texas were usually formed by three different, but often overlapping, methods. A prominent citizen could be commissioned as a colonel in the army of the Confederacy with instructions to "raise a regiment"; a respected resident of an area could be ordered by the governor to form a "volunteer militia" unit; or a local "fire-eater" could simply take it upon himself to issue a public announcement that he was forming a company of "fighting volunteers" and invite all willing to join to come on a certain morning to some hotel, saloon, or public hall. Training and operational procedures were extremely flexible, but steps were quickly taken to initiate the recruits into the mysteries of military organization, elementary tactics, and close-order drill. Companies held elections to choose officers, and those most active in raising companies were usually elected captains. The men brought from home whatever arms and equipment they could find, including Enfield rifles, long rifles, carbines, shotguns, flintlocks, navy revolvers, Colt six-shooters, squirrel muskets, Bowie knives, lances, pikes, and even swords used in the Mexican and revolutionary wars. Their uniforms were usually the civilian clothing they brought with them, but a few companies were initially decked out in colorful and elaborate costumes, the product of local patriotism combined with the enthusiastic endeavors of devoted seamstresses. When organized, equipped, and christened, the unit officially tendered its services to state authorities or Richmond officials. If accepted, it marched away to the mingled cheers and sobs of the women left behind.

By 1863 most of the flashy uniforms and more ornate equipment had disappeared, and the critical shortage of weapons was everywhere in evidence. Troops were ordered to battlefronts although they were poorly trained, inadequately supplied, and sometimes ridiculously equipped. When Nathaniel Banks advanced across Louisiana toward Port Hudson in 1863, several Texas regiments were shifted to the Louisiana front. One such regiment was the Second Texas Cavalry commanded by Charles Pyron. It had been formed as horse cavalry, but the inability to secure mounts had necessitated its becoming a dismounted unit. Pyron's regiment moved out of Galveston on May 3, 1863, bound for Louisiana via Niblett's Bluff on the Sabine. Colonel Fremantle stopped to watch as this motley unit marched past.

Source: A. J. L. Fremantle, *Three Months in the Southern States: April–June, 1863* (New York: John Bradburn, 1864), pp. 74–75.

At 1:30 [Sunday, May 3, 1863] I saw Pyron's regiment embark for Niblett's Bluff to meet Banks. This corps is now dismounted cavalry, and the procession was a droll one. First came eight or ten instruments braying discordantly, then an enormous Confederate flag, followed by about four hundred men moving by fours dressed in every variety of costume, and armed with every variety of weapon; about sixty had Enfield rifles; the remainder carried shot-guns (fowling-pieces), carbines, or long rifles of a peculiar and antiquated manufacture. None had swords or bayonets – all had six-shooters and bowie-knives. The men were a fine, determined-looking lot; and I saw among them a short stout boy of fourteen, who had served through the Arizona campaign. I saw many of the soldiers take off their hats to the French priests, who seemed much respected in Galveston. This regiment is considered down here to be a very good one, and its colonel is spoken of as one of the bravest officers in the army.

1863

Life on the North Texas Prairie

Kate Stone and her mother began adapting to their crude surroundings soon after their arrival in North Texas. They visited with new friends and neighbors, sat on the gallery in the evenings and discussed the weather and local disorders, took carriage rides into adjoining counties to see the sights, and attended periodic religious revivals conducted throughout the region. Tarrant, a little settlement visited by Kate and her mother, was abandoned soon after the Civil War, but in 1863 it was the thriving new county seat of Hopkins County. The following excerpts were taken from entries in Kate's diary dated July 12 and 16, 1863. At this time she and her mother were staying with a family named Smith in Lamar County.

Source: Kate Stone, *Brokenburn: The Journal of Kate Stone*, ed. John Q. Anderson (Baton Rouge: Louisiana State University Press, 1955), pp. 225–228. Reprinted by permission.

We made our first visit in Texas yesterday. We went to a protracted meeting being carried on nine miles from here at an old schoolhouse called – it must be in mockery – "Paradise." After the meeting we went by invitation to spend the evening and night with some real nice people, settlers from Virginia, the McGleasons. They are a pleasant family and exceedingly hospitable. We came back this morning after a ride of nearly eighteen miles, having missed our road three times. The prairie roads are so much alike it is impossible for strangers to distinguish the right from the wrong.

The congregation was much more presentable than the Gray Rock crowd. We saw several nice-looking families, but all were in the fashions of three years ago. If they would only leave off their tremendous hoops, but hoops seem in the very zenith of their popularity. Mamma and I were the only women folks without the awkward, ungraceful cages. No doubt the people thought us hopelessly out of date. We have not worn them for a long time. Nothing looks funnier than a woman walking around with an immense hoop – barefooted.

Mamma and I went several days ago to Tarrant in Hopkins County. The road ran part of the way over a lovely rolling prairie, dotted with clumps of trees covered with the brilliant, yellow coreopsis in full bloom and gemmed with countless little mounds of bright green, like emeralds set in gold. Tarrant is the hottest looking, new little town right out in the prairie not a tree. We tried to eat dinner at the roughest house and with the dirtiest people we have met yet. The table was set on a low, sunny gallery and half a dozen dirty, unshaven men took their seats in their shirt sleeves at the dirtiest tablecloth and coarsest ware. We saw the Negro girl wash the dishes at the *duck pond* right out in the yard. That was too much for me, but Mamma . . . managed to swallow down something.

. . . .

The prairie we are living on is called a thicket prairie. There are clumps of dwarf dogwood, spice trees, and plums, tangled together with wild grape and other vines and alive with snakes. The plums are just in season, a sour, red variety just like the swamp wild plums, and are nice for jelly. The prairie is a mass of flowers, one variety covering it at a time. Before you realize it, the color has faded away and another has taken its place, and this succession of flowers and colors goes on until frost comes and spreads a brown sheet over all. There are many familiar garden flowers: blue salvia, coreopsis, verbenas, larkspur, standing cypress, and now as far as the eye can reach the prairie is a mass of waving purple plumes, "French pinks," the natives call them.

Jimmy [one of Kate's brothers] has just brought in a beautiful little fawn and given it to me. I have always wanted one. They make such gentle, beautiful pets. This one's ears are solidly covered with ticks, and one of the Negroes is laboriously picking them off.

We hear no news now but accounts of murders done and suffered by the natives. Nothing seems more common or less condemned than assassination. There have been four or five men shot or hanged within a few miles of us within a week. No one that we have seen seems surprised or shocked, but take it as a matter of course that an obnoxious person should be put to death by some offended neighbor. A few evenings ago a captain in the army had just reached home on a furlough three hours before when he was shot at through his window. He was killed and his wife dangerously wounded. The authorities are trying to find the men who did it. It is supposed to be one of his company who had vowed vengeance against him. The other miscreants go unwhipped of justice.

. . . .

We spent yesterday with Mrs. Vaughn, Mrs. Smith's cousin and our nearest neighbor. She lives in a double log cabin with merely the necessaries of life, but it is a more comfortable home than most we have seen. Texas seems a hard land for women and children. They fly around and work like troopers while the men loll on the galleries and seemingly have nothing to do. Mamma cannot start on her search for a new home for a week yet, and it is disagreeable living here *en famille* with the Smiths, though Mrs. Smith is kind and we should appreciate it. But their ways are not our ways.

As we sat on the gallery tonight, gazing across the darkening prairie into the gleaming west, the very air was brilliant with fireflies. The fancy came that they were the eyes of the departed Indians, come to look again on their old hunting grounds, flashing through the night, looking with scowling, revengeful faces on the changes wrought by their old enemies, the palefaces. I fancy I can see the ghostly shapes one minute taking the form of an Indian brave with bended bow and flying arrow, the next fading into thin air leaving only the fiery eyes.

We all spoke of going to Paris, twenty-five miles, to attend a large Baptist meeting, returning the next day, but concluded it was too far.

1863

From San Antonio to Alleyton by Stagecoach

Colonel Fremantle, making a tour of the Southern Confederacy in 1863, traveled by stage from San Antonio to Alleyton, where he could board a train and continue his journey to Houston by rail (see map 1). He left San Antonio on April 27 and arrived in Alleyton late in the evening on April 29. Fremantle evidently got little rest and no sleep during the uncomfortable, bone-jarring, forty-six-hour journey, but he occupied himself by talking with the tobacco-chewing passengers. The following excerpt contains the observant Englishman's account of this journey. His descriptions of the countryside and of the inconveniences suffered by passengers on Texas stages enhance the value of the account. English sympathy for the Confederacy, the South's frantic desire for British intervention, and the English aversion to slavery can be detected in this extract from Fremantle's diary.

Source: A. J. L. Fremantle, *Three Months in the Southern States: April–June, 1863* (New York: John Bradburn, 1864), pp. 58–64.

I left San Antonio by stage for Alleyton at 9 P.M. The stage was an old coach, into the interior of which nine persons were crammed on three transverse seats, besides many others on the roof. I was placed on the center seat, which was extremely narrow, and I had nothing but a strap to support my back. An enormously fat German was my vis-a-vis, and a long-legged Confederate officer was in my rear. Our first team consisted of four mules; we . . . [changed to horses early the next morning after crossing the Guadalupe River]. My fellow travelers were all either military men, or connected with the government.

Only five out of nine chewed tobacco during the night; but they aimed at the windows with great accuracy, and didn't *splash* me.

. . . .

We got a very fair breakfast at Seguin, at 7 A.M. [April 28], which was beginning to be a well-to-do little place when the war dried it up. It commenced to rain at Seguin, which made the road very woolly, and annoyed the outsiders a good deal.

The conversation turned a good deal upon military subjects, and all agreed that the system of election of officers had proved to be a great mistake. According to their own accounts, discipline must have been extremely lax at first, but was now improving.

They were most anxious to hear what was thought of their cause in Europe; and none of them seemed aware of the great sympathy which their gallantry and determination had gained for them in England in spite of slavery. We dined at a little wooden hamlet called Belmont, and changed horses again there.

The country through which we had been traveling was a good deal cultivated, and there were numerous farms. I saw cotton fields for the first time.

We amused ourselves by taking shots with our revolvers at the enormous jack rabbits which came to stare at the coach.

In the afternoon tobacco-chewing became universal, and the spitting was sometimes a little wild.

It was the custom for the outsiders to sit around the top of the carriage, with their legs dangling over (like mutes on a hearse returning from a funeral). This practice rendered it dangerous to put one's head out of the window, for fear of a back kick from the heels, or of a shower of tobacco juice from the mouths of the Southern chivalry on the roof.

In spite of their peculiar habits of hanging, shooting, etc., which seemed to be natural to a people living in a wild and thinly populated country, there was much to like in my fellow travelers. They all had a sort of bon-hommie honesty and straight-forwardness, a natural courtesy and extreme good nature, which was very agreeable. Although they were all very anxious to talk to a European who, in these blockaded times, is a *rara avis* yet their inquisitiveness was never offensive or disagreeable.

Any doubts as to my personal safety, which may have been roused by my early insight into lynch law, was soon completely set at rest. I soon perceived that if any one were to annoy me the remainder would stand by me as a point of honor.

We supped at a little town called Gonzales at 6:30. We left it at 8 P.M. in another coach with six horses big, strong animals.

The roads, being all natural ones, were much injured by the rains.

. . . .

[Having breakfasted at Hallettsville on the morning of April 29] . . . we took in four more Confederate soldiers as outsiders, and we were now eighteen in all. Nowhere but in this country would such a thing be permitted.

Owing to the great top weight, the coach swayed about like a ship in a heavy sea, and the escapes of a capsize were almost miraculous. It is said that at the end of a Texan journey the question asked is not, "Have you been upset?" but, "How many times have you been upset?"

The value of the Negroes working in the fields was constantly appraised by my fellow travelers; and it appeared that, in Texas, an able-bodied male fetched $2500, whilst a well-skilled seamstress was worth $3500.

. . . .

We passed many cotton fields and beautiful Indian corn, but much of the latter had been damaged by the hail.

I was told that one third of the land formerly devoted to cotton is still sown with that article, the remainder being corn, etc. . . .

We also passed through some very pretty country, full of fine post-oak and cotton trees, and we met many Mexican cotton teams — some of the wagons with fourteen oxen or twelve mules, which were being cruelly ill-treated by their drivers.

We crossed several rivers with steep and difficult banks, and dined at a farmhouse at 2:30 P.M. I have already discovered that, directly the bell rings, it is necessary to rush at one's food and bolt it as quickly as possible, without any ceremony or delay. Otherwise it all disappears, so rapacious and so voracious are the natives at their meals whilst traveling. Dinner, on such occasions, in no case lasts more than seven minutes.

We reached Columbus at 6 P.M., and got rid of half our passengers there. These Texan towns generally consist of one large plaza, with a well-built courthouse on one side and a hotel opposite, the other two sides being filled up with wooden stores. All their budding prosperity has been completely checked by the war; but every one anticipates a great immigration into Texas after the peace.

We crossed the Colorado River, and reached Alleyton, our destination, at 7 P.M.

This little wooden village has sprung into existence during the last three years, owing to its being the present terminus to the railroad. It was crammed full of travelers and cotton speculators; but, as an especial favor, the fat German and I were given a bed *between us.* I threw myself on the bed with my clothes on (*bien entendu*), and was fast asleep in five minutes. In the same room there were three other beds, each with two occupants.

The distance from San Antonio to Alleyton is 140 miles time forty-six hours.

1863

A Ride on the Buffalo Bayou, Brazos, and Colorado Railroad

The Buffalo Bayou, Brazos, and Colorado was the first railroad in Texas. The capitalists who financed its construction intended to lay track from Harrisburg to Austin and beyond, but by the time the Civil War started, track had been laid only as far as Alleyton. The greatest engineering feat on the line was a quivering railroad bridge constructed across the Brazos River at Richmond. The bridge was about thirty yards long and about fifteen feet high. In the following excerpt, Colonel Fremantle describes his journey from Alleyton to Houston. According to the sophisticated Englishman, the crossing of shaky railroad bridges was only one of numerous dangers passengers faced when traveling by rail in Civil War Texas.

Source: A. J. L. Fremantle, *Three Months in the Southern States: April–June, 1863* (New York: John Bradburn, 1864), pp. 64–65.

30th April (Thursday) – I have today acquired my first experience of Texan railroads.

In this country, where every white man is as good as another (in theory), and every white female is by courtesy a lady, there is only one class. The train from Alleyton consisted of two long cars, each holding about fifty persons. Their interior is like the aisle of a church, twelve seats on either side, each for two persons. The seats are comfortably stuffed, and seemed luxurious after the stage [which Fremantle had ridden from San Antonio].

Before starting, the engine gives two preliminary snorts, which, with a yell from the official of "all aboard," warn the passengers to hold on; for they are closely followed by a tremendous jerk, which sets the cars in motion.

Every passenger is allowed to use his own discretion about breaking his arm, neck, or leg, without interference by the railway officials.

People are continually jumping on and off whilst the train is in motion, and larking from one car to the other. There is no sort of fence or other obstacle to prevent "humans" or cattle from getting on the line.

We left Alleyton at 8 A.M., and got a miserable meal at Richmond at 12:30.

. . . .

Richmond is on the Brazos River, which is crossed in a peculiar manner. A steep inclined plane leads to a low, rickety, trestle bridge, and a similar inclined plane is cut on the opposite bank. The engine cracks on all steam, and gets sufficient impetus in going down the first incline to shoot across the bridge and up the second incline. But even in Texas, this method of crossing a river is considered rather unsafe.

After crossing the river in this manner, the rail traverses some very fertile land, part of which forms the estate of the late Colonel [Benjamin F.] Terry. There are more than two hundred Negroes on the plantation. Some of the fields were planted with cotton and Indian corn mixed, three rows of the former between two of the latter. I saw also fields of cotton and sugar mixed.

We changed carriages at Harrisburg, and I completed my journey to Houston on a cotton truck.

1863

Some Celebrities of the Confederate Trans-Mississippi

While on his tour of the South in 1863, Colonel Fremantle met almost every leader of importance in the Confederate Trans-Mississippi Department. During the first weeks of travel, he was privileged to visit briefly with General John Magruder, Confederate commander of Texas; Sam Houston, the hero of San Jacinto; and E. Kirby Smith, the commander of the Trans-Mississippi Department. Fremantle encountered General Magruder during his journey from Brownsville to San Antonio and met General Houston on a train between Galveston and Houston. His visit with General Smith took place soon after he had completed his trip through Texas and had arrived in Shreveport, Louisiana. General Magruder had been transferred to Texas after his blunders at Malvern Hill during the Peninsular campaign, and E. Kirby Smith had taken command of the Trans-Mississippi Department the previous February. Sam Houston, having been deprived of the Texas governorship by the secessionists, was still a proud, fiery old soldier, but he died only two months later at his farm near Huntsville.

Source: A. J. L. Fremantle, *Three Months in the Southern States: April–June, 1863* (New York: John Bradburn, 1864), pp. 33–36, 68–69, and 77–85.

15th April (Wednesday) – I slept well last night in spite of the ticks and fleas, and we started at 5:30 P.M. [actually A.M.] After passing a dead rattlesnake eight feet long, we reached water at 7 A.M.

At 9 A.M. we espied the cavalcade of General Magruder passing us by a parallel track about half a mile distant. M'Carthy and I jumped out of the carriage, and I ran across the prairie to cut him off, which I just succeeded in doing by borrowing the spare horse of the last man in the train.

I galloped up to the front, and found the General riding with a lady who was introduced to me as Mrs. ———, an undeniably pretty woman, wife to an officer on Magruder's staff. She is naturally the object of intense attention to all the good-looking officers who accompany the General through this desert.

General Magruder, who commands in Texas, is a fine soldierlike man, of about fifty-five, with broad shoulders, a florid complexion, and bright eyes. He wears his whiskers and mustaches in the English fashion, and he was dressed in the Confederate grey uniform.

He was kind enough to beg that I would turn back [toward Brownsville] and accompany him in his tour through Texas. He had heard of my arrival, and was fully determined I should do this. He asked after several officers of my regiment [the Coldstream Guards] whom he had known when he was on the Canadian frontier. He is a Virginian, a great talker, and has always been a great ally of English officers.

He insisted that M'Carthy and I should turn and dine with him, promising to provide us with horses to catch up to Mr. Sargent.

After we had agreed to do this, I had a long and agreeable conversation with the General, who spoke of the Puritans with intense disgust, and of the first importation of them as "that pestiferous crew of the *Mayflower*"; but he is by no means rancorous against individual Yankees. He spoke very favorably of M'Clellan, whom he knew to be a gentleman, clever, and personally brave, though he might lack moral courage to face responsibility.

Magruder had commanded the Confederate troops at Yorktown which opposed M'Clellan's advance. He told me the different dodges he had resorted to, to blind and deceive the latter as to his (Magruder's) strength. He spoke of the intense relief and amusement with which he had at length seen M'Clellan with his magnificent army begin to break ground before miserable earthworks, defended only by 8000 men.

Hooker was in his regiment, and was "essentially a mean man and a liar." Of Lee and Longstreet he spoke in terms of the highest admiration.

Magruder was an artilleryman, and has been a good deal in Europe; and having been much stationed on the Canadian frontier, he became acquainted with many British officers, particularly those in the 7th Hussars and Guards.

He had gained much credit from his recent successes at Galveston and Sabine Pass, in which he had the temerity to attack heavily armed vessels of war with wretched river steamers manned by Texan cavalrymen.

His principal reason for visiting Brownsville was to settle about the cotton trade. He had issued an edict that half the value of cotton exported must be imported in goods for the benefit of the country (government stores). The President had condemned this order as illegal and despotic.

The officers of Magruder's staff are a very good-looking, gentlemanlike set of men. Their names are – Major Pendleton, Major Wray, Captain Ponte, Captain Alston, Captain Turner, Lieutenant Colonel M'Neil, Captain Dwyer, Dr. Benien, Lieutenant Stanard, Lieutenant Yancy, and Major Magruder. The latter is nephew to the General, and is a particularly good-looking young fellow. They all live with their chief on an extremely agreeable footing, and form a very pleasant society.

At dinner I was put in the post of honor, which is always fought for with much acrimony – viz., the right of Mrs. ———.

After dinner we had numerous songs. Both the General and his nephew sang. So also did Captain Alston, whose corpulent frame, however, was too much for the feeble camp stool, which caused his sudden disappearance in the midst of a song with a loud crash. Captain Dwyer played the fiddle very well, and an aged and slightly elevated militia general brewed the punch and made several "elegant" speeches. The latter was a rough-faced old hero, and gloried in the name of M'Guffin. On these festive occasions General Magruder wears a red woollen cap, and fills the president's chair with great aptitude.

It was 11:30 before I could tear myself away from this agreeable party; but at length I effected my exit amidst a profusion of kind expressions, and laden with heaps of letters of introduction. . . .

[The letters of introduction assured Fremantle of free access to the upper strata of the Confederate and state military hierarchy but particularly endeared him to General William R. Scurry, who lived in Houston. General Scurry had served under Magruder when the Confederates had reconquered Galveston in January 1863 and therefore held Magruder in the highest regard. When Fremantle presented his letters to Scurry a couple of weeks later, Scurry not only insisted that the Englishman live in his house while he was in Houston but also telegraphed to

Galveston for a steamer to transport him to Galveston Island. Fremantle, however, was eager to continue his Southern tour, and when the steamer did not arrive on the appointed morning, he left for Galveston by rail on May 2. It was while he was on the train that Fremantle met Sam Houston.]

In the cars [of the train] I was introduced to General Samuel Houston, the founder of Texan independence. He told me he was born in Virginia seventy years ago, that he was United States senator at thirty, and governor of Tennessee at thirty-six. He emigrated into Texas in 1832; he headed the revolt of Texas, and defeated the Mexicans at San Jacinto in 1836. He then became President of the Republic of Texas, which he annexed to the United States in 1845. As governor of the state in 1860, he had opposed the secession movement, and was *deposed*. Though evidently a remarkable and clever man, he is extremely egotistical and vain, and much disappointed at having to subside from his former grandeur. The town of Houston is named after him. In appearance he is a tall, handsome old man, much given to chewing tobacco, and blowing his nose with his fingers. . . .

[Fremantle spent a couple of days in Galveston and then returned to General Scurry's home in Houston, where he began making preparations for his trip to Shreveport. The journey from Houston to Shreveport was accomplished in four days, traveling by rail and stage. Fremantle arrived in Shreveport on May 8.]

We reached Marshall [Texas] at 3 A.M., and got four hours' sleep there. We then got into a railroad for sixteen miles, after which we were crammed into another stage.

Crossed the frontier into Louisiana at 11 A.M. I have therefore been nearly a month getting through the single state of Texas. Reached Shreveport at 3 P.M.; and, after washing for the first time in five days, I called on General Kirby Smith, who commands the whole country on this side of the Mississippi.

He is a Floridian by birth, was educated at West Point, and served in the United States Cavalry. He is only thirty-eight years old. He owes his rapid rise to a lieutenant general to the fortunate fact of his having fallen, just at the very nick of time, upon the Yankee flank at the first battle of Manassas. . . .

He is a remarkably active man, and of very agreeable manners. He wears big spectacles and a black beard.

His wife is an extremely pretty woman from Baltimore, but she had cut her hair quite short like a man's. In the evening she proposed that we should go down to the river and fish for crayfish. We did so, and were most successful, the General displaying much energy on the occasion.

He told me that M'Clellan might probably have destroyed the Southern army with the greatest ease during the first winter, and without running much risk to himself. The Southerners were so much overelated by their easy triumph at Manassas that their army had dwindled away.

[Fremantle took the stage to Monroe at 4:30 the following morning to continue his tour of the Confederacy.]

1861–1864

Drought, Indians, and Panthers on the North Texas Frontier

The recollections of early residents of North Texas seem to uphold Kate Stone's statement that Texas was a "dark corner" of Confederate civilization. Contributing to the unwholesome and unhealthy environment were devastating droughts, hostile Indians, and predatory beasts. The following excerpt, concerned primarily with these three perils of frontier living, was taken from a narrative that was related to J. R. Webb by Phin W. Reynolds during the months of May 1936, April 1938, and October 1944.

Source: Phin W. Reynolds, "Chapters from the Frontier Life of Phin W. Reynolds," comp. J. R. Webb, *West Texas Historical Association Year Book* 21 (1945): 110–143. Reprinted by permission.

Two years after my birth in Shelby County, Texas, on the 3rd day of August, 1859, my father, B. Watt Reynolds, loaded his wife and his six children and his belongings in wagons and headed for the western frontier. His first stop was at Golconda, the county seat of Palo Pinto County, and which afterwards was changed to the name of Palo Pinto. He stopped there only a short time and moved to the adjoining county on the west, then known as Buchannan, but afterward changed to Stephens County.

He settled at the old Cantrell ranch on Gonzales Creek near the site of Breckenridge.

. . . .

Although a small child I can recall the severe drought which began in 1862 and lasted into 1864. So severe it was that two-thirds of the post oak timber in that section died and its effect on the timber could be seen for more than thirty years thereafter. I remember that my brother, William, and I walked up the dry bed of the Clear Fork for more than a half mile hunting drinking water in 1863. We were then living on the [John ?] Dawson ranch above Eliasville. I have never since then seen such a drought. Speaking of droughts though, I remember that old Tonkawa White, an Indian I later knew while living near Fort Griffin and who looked to me to be almost a hundred years old, told me that a dry spell once drove the western Indians almost as far down the Brazos as Waco village for game and water. He was explaining to me the reason for what we early settlers called the Dead Mesquite Forest. This was a forest of dead mesquite trees which covered parts of Taylor, Jones, Haskell, Baylor, Scurry, Dickens and other counties nearly to the foot of the Plains. At the time I first saw it there were standing trunks of large trees, the limbs having rotted away, but the hearts of the trunks being well preserved. There was no evidence of their destruction by fire and there was no sprouting out from the roots, and the strange part of it was that there was hardly a living mesquite in all that section and there were few even in Stephens County. This dead forest was there when the earliest settlers arrived and it remained until fencing started in the early eighties. Much of it was then hauled away by the settlers for fence posts. The settlers in Shackelford and Throckmorton counties hauled their posts from the dead forests of Jones and Haskell counties. I tried to get more definite information from old "Tonkawa" as to the time this drought occurred but all he seemed to know was that it was "way back."

While we were living at the Dawson ranch shortly after we arrived in Stephens County, we had a little Indian scare. My two oldest brothers, George and William, and two cowboys who were working for us were out on the range working some horses and they had taken with them all the pistols and guns that would shoot. We three younger boys, Ben, Glen, and I, were at home and out in the yard. One of the older boys had killed a panther and had brought it in and we were busily engaged cutting into its tail to obtain some sinews to fix some arrows. A couple of our horses were hob-

bled out and grazing some fifty yards away. All at once we were startled by
two Indians who swooped down on our horses, cut their hobbles and
drove them away. Three other Indians could be seen on a nearby hill above
the house. We gave the alarm and our father rushed out of the house with
an old gun that would not shoot; but it had its effect for they made no effort
to harm any of us. Ben recognized one of the horses ridden by one of the
Indians as belonging to Riley St. John who had recently arrived from the
territory of Colorado. The horse had been stolen from him the previous
night.

Speaking of panthers, about the year 1863, William Veale was teaching a little school in Miller's Valley on the Clear Fork of the Brazos and
my brother, Ben, was attending the school. He brought a panther's foot
home from school one day and told me how it was killed. He said that
the school kids were down on the river eating their lunch and Ann Clark
was on a shoal leaning over washing her hands. Looking around she saw
a half grown panther crouching and ready to spring upon her. She
jumped out into the water but the panther made his spring and lit on her
back. Press Mauldin, a school boy, grabbed a rock and knocked the panther off and into the water, but it came out on the same bank with the
school children and promptly attacked another school boy, Tom Curtis,
who was leaning over washing his slate. Press Mauldin got him again
with a rock, knocking him off Curtis and then killing him. Ben said he
looked half starved and this condition probably caused him to attack the
school children. Ten years after this, another panther made an attack on
a child at the home of John Selman. A man by the name of Webb and Selman and his wife were sitting in a room and there was an open door to
the outside. The Selmans had their baby lying in a cradle opposite the
doorway. A panther sprang through the open doorway and on to the
cradle and seized the baby and carried it from the cradle. Webb grabbed
the panther by the tail and Mrs. Selman at the same time snatched the
baby. Webb flung the panther into the fire place from where it sprang
back into the room; but instead of making for the open door it ran under
a bed. Both Webb and Selman obtained loaded rifles from their racks
over the fire place and the panther was killed while crouching in fright
under the bed. I read an account of this in a magazine, which I recall was
the *Saturday Evening Post*. It was published in one of its issues in the
year 1872, according to my recollection. We knew all of the parties and
heard all of the details before it was published by the *Post*.

Confederate Military Operations
Along the Texas Coast

England, Spain, and France invaded Mexico in 1862, in violation of the Monroe Doctrine, to collect claims against the Mexican republic. England and Spain withdrew from Mexican soil after a few months of occupation. France remained, established a puppet government in Mexico City, and displayed disturbing intentions of staying. French activities south of the Rio Grande did not escape the critical notice of the U.S. Department of State, but because the American nation was torn by civil war, it was unable to take action to force the invaders out of Mexico. Secretary of State William Seward, perplexed by rumors that French and Mexican troops were increasing in number along the Texas border, urged Lincoln to order an attack on Texas. French intentions in Mexico, he explained to the chief executive, were not clear. The puppet government in Mexico City could easily secure favorable trading relations with the Confederates, which would seriously damage Union plans to deplete Southern resources. French recognition of the Confederacy could enable Richmond officials to secure large foreign loans, thus prolonging the war indefinitely. Combined French-Mexican armies could conceivably seize Texas in the name of Mexican territorial "restoration" or French-Mexican expansionism. Seward skillfully exploited such fears, with the able assistance of Secretary of the Treasury Salmon P. Chase and Postmaster General Montgomery Blair, and Lincoln conditionally granted permission to begin limited military operations against Texas in the winter of 1862. Disputes among government bureaucrats, bickering among Lincoln's generals, disruptive influences within the Republican party, growing popular opposition to the war, and Lincoln's lukewarm support of the project hampered and delayed effective efforts to invade and permanently occupy portions of the Lone Star State.

Several assaults on Texas, however, achieved a measure of success the following year. After unsuccessful invasion attempts at Galveston, Sabine Pass, and along Teche Bayou in Louisiana, Union troops seized Brazos Santiago and swarmed up the Rio Grande and the coast of southern Texas. Additional Union naval strength was evident in Texas waters during the fall and winter of 1863–

1864 as hit-and-run commando raids and periodic naval bombardments of towns along the Texas coast became commonplace. Lincoln and Seward evidently still gave some passing thought to the possibility of French-Confederate cooperation, but this became exceedingly remote after Federal victories the previous summer convinced officials in Mexico City that the South was losing the war. French support of the Emancipation Proclamation, which went into effect at the beginning of 1863, also favored French noninvolvement. Nevertheless, pressured by Yankee textile manufacturers, Texas Unionists in Washington, and influential New York bankers, Lincoln agreed "to prosecute the war with vigor" in Texas for the first time since the war began. To meet the new threat of invasion, the beleaguered Texas forces mustered their strength.

The following account, taken from the memoirs of an assistant adjutant general on General John Magruder's staff, describes Confederate military operations along the coast during the bitter winter of 1863–1864. The author, Francis Lubbock, had just spent twenty-five months as governor of the state, but he joined Magruder's staff in 1863 and thus was able to produce a reasonably complete picture of troop movements and battles. In 1864 Lubbock became aide-de-camp for President Jefferson Davis and was captured with the Confederate president in May 1865.

Source: Francis Richard Lubbock, *Six Decades in Texas: Memoirs of Francis Richard Lubbock,* ed. C. W. Raines (Austin: Ben C. Jones and Company, 1900), pp. 528–533.

The Yankees, driven from Galveston and foiled at Sabine Pass, fitted out an expedition . . . to proceed to the Rio Grande for the purpose of invading Texas from the west. After a stormy passage of a week's duration, the fleet, with the Thirteenth army corps, arrived off Brazos Santiago in bad plight.

On landing, General Banks, who accompanied the expedition, sent the following dispatch to General Halleck and the President of the United States: "The flag of the Union floated over Texas to-day (November 2, 1863) at meridian precisely." This declaration was intended to make known to the world that Union troops were on soil for the purpose of subjugating Texas, and was in the nature of a notice served on the French to keep hands off. Frank Gildart, a Texan refugee who deserted to us immediately after landing, reported that the Yankees had lost on the trip three steamboats, four schooners, all their artillery except two six-pounders, and all their horses except about 100, but had preserved and brought in with them all their ammunition. There was other and corroborative evidence that the voyage had been disastrous. Banks subsequently expressed the opinion that he could not have effected a landing if as determined resistance had been offered as that encountered at Sabine Pass. He met with no opposition at Brazos Santiago.

On the enemy's advance to Brownsville General Bee evacuated that post and fell back to the Confederate line of frontier defense, carrying with him an immense quantity of government stores.

With [Assistant Secretary of War Napoleon J. T.] Dana's expedition were the regiments of Colonels Haynes and E. J. Davis, about 750 men all told. Haynes' regiment was known as the "Mustangs." These officers expected to fill up their skeleton regiments to their maximum strength with Texan renegades, but in this anticipation were somewhat disappointed, as this class as a rule were in extremely destitute circumstances, or burdened with the care of families, and did not care to enlist in the army. A. J. Hamilton, who had remained in New Orleans till advised of the Federal occupation of Brownsville, repaired promptly to army headquarters on the Rio Grande. He had been, on the intercession of Governor Gilmore, of New Hampshire, reappointed by President Lincoln military governor of Texas, and he proposed at once to assume the functions of office. On this demand the Governor of the State of Tamaulipas extradited one of the Confederate Texans who had abducted from Mexican soil and executed one Captain Montgomery, claiming to belong to the United States army; but for want of civil tribunals to try the case the prisoner was turned over to the military authorities for final disposition. Hamilton's bull-headedness soon made trouble with the Mexican authorities on the Rio Grande, and the ridiculous farce of a government possessing no power outside the range of Federal guns came to an untimely (or rather timely) end, "unwept, unhonored, and unsung."

Banks' plan of campaign being now to invade Texas from the Rio Grande, his ships proceeded rapidly along the coast eastward, driving or capturing small Texan garrisons. Point Isabel and Corpus Christi were occupied, the works at Aransas Pass captured with about 100 prisoners, and Fort Esperanza, commanding Pass Cavallo, the entrance to Matagorda Bay, taken, the garrison escaping. Gen. C. C. Washburne commanded a division of 6000 veterans, operating in the country about Matagorda Bay.

On the advance of the Yankees, General Magruder moved his army westward to meet them. After making a tour of inspection of his lines with his staff as far westward as Victoria, he returned and established his temporary headquarters at Rugely's plantation, on the San Bernard. It was here, early in December, that I found General Magruder and took my place on his staff as assistant adjutant-general with the rank of lieutenant-colonel.

The general had already, by proclamation, disclaimed any intention of abandoning the western country, and boasted of his strong works near San Antonio and Austin, lately constructed by impressed slaves, and proposed to dispute every inch of ground with the invader. The enemy took Magruder at his word, and soon slowed up to a dead halt in his front. In apprehension of the worst, Col. Stephen H. Darden was ordered to destroy the railroad from Indianola to Victoria, and thus impede the advance of the enemy inland. The circumstance that constrained us in our operation more than any other was the lack of arms. To secure 16,000 Enfield rifles just released from seizure (by the French government) at Vera Cruz, General Magruder made an earnest appeal to the Cotton Bureau through Col. W. J. Hutchins, saying: "These arms from Vera Cruz, if we get them at all, will come in lots of about 1000. They may cost as high as $60 each; but cost what they may, we must have them. The State of Texas and the whole Trans-Mississippi Department are in the greatest peril.

"Every other interest must yield to this paramount necessity. . . . There must be no delay and no obstacle of any nature interposed to protract or endanger the accomplishment of this purpose. At the present price of cotton and present value of our currency, it will require an immense amount of cotton to pay for the arms. I presume the price of cotton in specie at Houston is about 4 cents per pound; in our currency, about 40 cents. . . . In strict confidence, all that portion of our troops which are armed at all are badly armed, and fully one-fourth of the army are entirely without arms."

To another agent of the Cotton Bureau, James Sorley, of Houston, he wrote, December 21st: "On the subject of arms, I must say that the safety of the country demands them at any sacrifice, and that no time is to be lost. I have thousands of men entirely unarmed. . . . So great is the need, that all the cotton in Texas should speedily be sold (if possible) by the government for 30,000 stand of arms and their appropriate ammunition. We can exist without other things, but can not without arms."

A few small lots of arms were procured at intervals, but nothing like enough to supply our needs, and what we did have were of inferior quality. The irremediable condition ultimately proved fatal to our cause. The Yankees in our front were well supplied with arms and everything else necessary for campaigning, and outnumbered us more than two to one.

Under these untoward circumstances demoralization spread rapidly in the Confederate ranks, followed by desertions; but a prompt check was put to desertions by the enforcement of measures adopted for that purpose.

General Magruder was very active in inspecting our lines and reconnoitering the movements of the enemy. With his staff, and sometimes a small escort, he was almost every day in the saddle, visiting our outposts to ascertain the strength of our positions and the spirit of the troops. In this way, early in December, we traversed the Old Caney country, stopping awhile at Hawkins' plantation and other hospitable places, and inspecting the works on the San Bernard. In returning we visited Velasco, everywhere finding along the front our gallant boys ready and eager for combat. The Yankees were quiet, perhaps awaiting reinforcements. Consequently there was little picket fighting. Notwithstanding this lull, we kept strictly on the qui vive, holding ourselves in readiness to move at the word of command.

Never, in the pressure of civil business, had I neglected, when unavoidably absent, to write to Mrs. Lubbock; nor did I now omit to do so amid the exacting duties of the camp. Our married life, extending over nearly thirty years, had been a happy one. Realizing her anxiety, I wrote quite frequently such letters of cheer and hope as I could under the circumstances of our enforced separation.

With their increasing numbers, the Yankees a few weeks later in January became more active, and from their ships shelled at various times our works at the mouths of the Caney, San Bernard, and Brazos rivers. We managed, however, to hold our own at these places, and to drive off their ships, with some damage, doubtless. Our river fleet, under Commodore Leon Smith, proved quite serviceable in this emergency, furnishing transportion, making short cruises along the coast, and giving quick notice of the movements of the enemy. The Yankees in our immediate front and down the coast were estimated at 25,000 men, while our army, including Tom Green's division, called in from Louisiana, and the State militia, did not exceed 10,000 men. But these Confederate troops were nearly all veterans, and second to none in fighting qualities; especially was this true of Green's command, comprising the old Sibley brigade, under Col. W. P. Hardeman, and the brigade of Gen. J. P. Major. Not daring to attack our lines in force, the Yankees contented themselves with occasional shelling of our exposed works and petty depredations along the coast.

Our service on the coast during the latter part of the winter of 1863–4 was at times very hard owing to the severely cold weather. E. P. Turner, A.A.G., in a letter to headquarters respecting a bridge at Hinkle's ferry that Captain Howe with his engineer troop was engaged in constructing, said in reference to the weather: "The health of the troops, considering the intensity of the cold, continues good; for example, Colonel De Bray informed me to-day that not 100 of his brigade were unfit for service on account of sickness. The animals, also, have stood the rigor of the weather better than we imagined."

We lost quite a number of our gallant young soldiers who were frozen to death in an attempt to make an attack upon a detachment of the enemy that had landed upon our coast from the blockading squadron. The same night I made a very narrow escape on a trip down Galveston beach. I was ordered to go down the island on a reconnoissance; the night became very cold for that section extremely cold. I was in my saddle until near daylight, when I rode up to Colonel Buchel's camp, almost in a lifeless condition. I was lifted from my horse and placed in the musicians' tent between the warm blankets of a bed just vacated, where I went to sleep. Awaking about noon, quite revived, I was supplied with good strong coffee and breakfast. I then proceeded to headquarters. Had I not reached this refuge as soon as I did I would have lost my life.

The only time I was under fire during this campaign was on an occasion when I had gone to the Confederate earthworks at the mouth of the San Bernard under orders from General Magruder, to learn the facts as to the reported appearance of Federal war vessels off that point. When near there I turned back a crowd of stragglers and went with them to the fort. Soon after our arrival a heavy fire was opened upon us from the ships, the shells bursting in and around the fort. I had just remarked to the men that there was no danger, when a shell exploded in our midst, knocking over one of them. Our men, however, replied with spirit, and the enemy, if he meditated a landing, thought better of it and finally drew off.

The Yankees busied themselves in making fortifications down the coast, especially on Matagorda peninsula and near Indianola. Their next form of activity was in getting out of Texas early in 1864, reducing their army here by degrees. The Federal government had not found the easy sailing expected in Texas, and a change of policy was now being effected, as soon became apparent to us.

Baffled in the west as he had been in the east, Banks was next to invade Texas by way of Red River, and his forces on our coast soon began to disappear. The Yankees excused their defeat by saying their occupation of our coast was not so much a military movement as it was a political measure to save Texas from being plucked away from the Confederacy by France. On the assurance from Minister Corwin, in Mexico, that the French authorities there disclaimed any intention of interfering in our war in behalf of Texas, President Lincoln removed his army from the Texan gulf region, leaving only a few garrisons on the Rio Grande.

1864

Texas Railroads in 1864

In 1850 Bexar County and the city of San Antonio attempted to encourage railroad building in Texas by issuing bonds totaling $100,000 to subsidize the San Antonio and Mexican Gulf railway companies. A further inducement to railroad construction was provided two years later by the state legislature when a law was passed granting railroad companies eight sections of land for each mile of track laid. Although some construction resulted, many local and foreign investors were hesitant to pour their capital into such an expensive enterprise even though the popular clamor for railroads continued to increase. "Railroad fever" struck almost every town of any size across the state, and by 1854 it had reached epidemic proportions. In that year the state legislature passed another, more generous public assistance law which awarded up to sixteen sections of land for each mile of track laid. This law specified that a railroad company was to survey one adjoining section, to be set aside for public education, for each "free" section received. Toward the end of the decade, a shaky railroad network began to take shape radiating from Houston and Galveston (see map 1).

By the time the Civil War began, eight railroad lines were in existence although some, such as the San Antonio and Texas Gulf, had only a few miles of track in place. The Texas and New Orleans, by contrast, had nearly three hundred miles of track in operation. One of the most successful and heavily traveled lines was the Houston and Texas Central, which extended from Houston to Navasota in Grimes County, a distance of about seventy-five miles. There was little additional railroad construction during the war because neither workers nor building materials were available, and the lack of proper maintenance caused track and operational equipment to deteriorate. Travelers in Texas and the Trans-Mississippi Department had to use several modes of transportation to reach their destinations. Colonel Fremantle crossed Texas in 1863 by traveling by carriage from Brownsville to San Antonio; by stage from San Antonio to Alleyton; by railroad from Alleyton to Houston, Galveston, and Navasota; and by stage from Navasota to Shreveport, Louisiana. When Terry's Rangers journeyed from Houston to New Brashear (present-day Morgan City), Louisiana, early in the war, they traveled by train over a "newly constructed railroad" to Beaumont, by steamboat down the Neches and up the Sabine to Niblett's Bluff, on foot a hundred miles into Louisiana "through water much of the way," by cart to New Iberia on Bayou Teche, then by boat to New Brashear. By 1864 the dearth of essential equipment and manpower resulted in great gaps in the Texas railroad network, and many lines still in operation were undependable, dilapidated, and hazardous.

The following excerpt was taken from a railroad report, compiled in 1864 from out-of-date information, published in the 1865 *Texas Almanac*. It is obvious that more information was available for some railroads than for others although several lines were not in operation at all. The San Antonio and Mexican Gulf, listed in the report, had been burned by the Confederates in 1863 to prevent its falling into the hands of the Federal invaders. Only part of the Texas and New Orleans line between Houston and Beaumont was in operation because most of its track had been ripped up for use in the construction of fortifications at Sabine Pass. A Texas railroad not listed in the report was the Vicksburg and El Paso, also known as the Southern Pacific, not to be confused with the later Southern Pacific. Most of its track had been torn up in 1863 and relaid eastward from Marshall to Jonesville in Harrison County to connect with a short railway that extended westward from Shreveport. The opening of the Marshall-to-

Jonesville line may have been unknown to the publishers of the *Almanac* because the first locomotive to travel the new route ran from Marshall to Shreveport about the time the railroad report was compiled.

Source: The Texas Almanac for 1865 (Galveston: Richardson and Co., 1864), p. 3.

Houston and Texas Central Railroad.
. . . Trains leave Houston every day, except Sundays, at 10 A.M., and reach Hempstead, 50 miles at 2 P.M., connecting with the Washington County Railroad and triweekly stages from Brenham to Austin. Leave Hempstead at 2 P.M., and reach Navasota, 20 miles, at 4 P.M., where the cars connect with triweekly stages to Shreveport. Leave Navasota at 4 P.M., and reach Millican at 5 P.M., where the cars connect with triweekly stages to Waco and Dallas. Returning, leave Millican at 7 A.M.; Hempstead at 10 A.M., and reach Houston at 2 P.M.

Washington County Railroad.
. . . Trains leave Brenham every day at 6 A.M., and reach Hempstead, 25 miles, at 9 A.M. Returning, leave Hempstead at 2 P.M., and reach Brenham at 4 P.M.

San Antonio and Mexican Gulf Railroad.
. . . This road was destroyed by order of Gen. Magruder in December 1863, the rails and ties having been burnt, as well as a portion of the cars, and the engines dismantled and rendered unfit for service. Since then the company has been unable to rebuild.

Buffalo Bayou, Brazos and Colorado Railroad.
. . . Trains leave Harrisburg for Alleyton Mondays, Wednesdays and Fridays, at 9 A.M. Returning leave Alleyton for Harrisburg, Tuesdays, Thursdays and Saturdays at 8 A.M., making connections at Houston Junction with the H.T. & B.R.R. from Houston and Columbia.

Houston Tap and Brazoria Railroad.
Trains run three times a week between Houston and Columbia, distance 50 miles, connecting at the Junction with the Harrisburg trains.

Galveston, Houston and Henderson Railroad.
Trains leave Galveston Mondays, Wednesdays and Fridays at 9 A.M.; arrive in Houston at 1:30 P.M.; Return alternate days.

Texas and New Orleans Railroad.
Trains leave Houston Mondays, Wednesdays and Fridays at 7 A.M. and arrive at Beaumont at 4 P.M.; Return alternate days.

1857–1865

Recollections of Life in Austin during the War

Lillie Barr Munroe was the daughter of Robert Barr, an accountant in the Texas Land Office in Austin, and Amelia Barr, one of America's most prolific writers. When she, her parents, and an older sister Mary moved to Austin in 1857, Lillie was only four years old, but her memories of the Civil War period were still vivid in 1926, when she wrote her recollections of her famous mother. The manuscript, "Memoirs of Amelia Barr by her Daughter Lillie Barr Munroe, 1851–1867," was deposited in the State Archives in Austin and remained there until April 1966, when an abridged version appeared in the *Southwestern Historical Quarterly.* Lillie's father was typically English in his attitude toward slavery and devoutly Unionist in his politics although not a U.S. citizen. Her mother, a strange and deeply religious woman with definite ideas about the supernatural, was a devout Confederate and an ardent supporter of the Southern cause.

The value of Lillie's "Memoirs of Amelia Barr" is in its splendid description of life in wartime Austin. Her love for the people of the city, her lucid memories of significant events, her knowledge of social and political affairs, and her record of personal impressions add immeasurably to the importance and readability of her account. Her priceless descriptions of Congress Avenue with its early landmarks – Smith's Hotel, the Sampson and Hendricks general store, and the flagpole at Hancock Corner – should arouse nostalgic memories for many residents of the old capital city.

The Smith House, which Lillie called "*the* hotel" in Austin, was situated on the northwest corner of Congress Avenue and Pecan (West Sixth) Street. It had been constructed about 1854 and was known as the Swisher House until 1860, when it was purchased by E. M. Smith. Although it changed hands again in 1861 and became Cook's Hotel, operated by A. H. Cook and A. T. Logan, it was still popularly known as the Smith House during the war years.

This hotel was located on one of the most famous corners in downtown Austin. By the flagpole, just across Pecan Street from the hotel, political rallies were held, military bands played regular concerts, and fiery orators such as Sam Houston delivered controversial speeches. The balcony on the second floor of the hotel, overlooking Congress Avenue and the stage stop below, was almost always overloaded with shabbily dressed males, who spent endless hours chewing tobacco, spitting juice into the street below, and discussing the crucial issues of the day. Perhaps the chief reason for the popularity of this location, called Hancock Corner by most residents, was that one of Austin's leading Unionists, George Hancock, ran a grocery and dry goods store on the southwest corner of Congress and Pecan, just across the street from the hotel. Hancock was one of Houston's close friends and supported the old general in his efforts to prevent Texas from leaving the Union. Hancock erected the flagpole in front of his store for the sole purpose of flying the flag of the United States. The Stars and Stripes graced the pole until after the fall of Fort Sumter, when Austin secessionists burned down his store and replaced Old Glory with a Confederate banner. Hancock Corner remained Austin's unofficial stage for debate throughout the war. After the battle of Palmito Ranch, Hancock quickly hoisted the Federal colors again, and the first U.S. troops to enter the city were halted at the flagpole while Hancock delivered a welcoming speech.

Just as "Smith's Hotel was *the* hotel" in Austin, according to Lillie, "Hendrickes dry goods store was *the* store." The three-story Sampson and Hendricks building, completed in 1860, was located at the southwest corner of Bois d'Arc (Seventh) Street and Congress Avenue in the same block with the Smith Hotel. Except for the capitol building, on Capitol Hill at the north end of Congress Avenue, and the Swenson Building, between Hickory (Eighth) and Ash (Ninth) streets, this structure was the most prominent building in wartime Austin. The two partners, Sampson and Hendricks, moved into the new building soon after it was completed, and their business immediately became the major general merchandising enterprise of the region. At first primarily interested in dealing in dry goods, Sampson and Hendricks gradually expanded their operation to include groceries, hardware, leather goods, firearms, and sundries. Because of their large inventory and "foreign connections" in Mexico, the partners were able to carry on a lucrative business for many months after most other stores had closed their doors because of the shortage of salable commodities.

In her recollections Lillie mentions several other prominent businesses such as C. Spaulding's dry goods and groceries, Francis T. Duffau Drug, A. Bahn's Jewelry, and John T. Miller's City Livery Stable, but certainly the most prominent and important building in the city was the new state capitol. Although it is not mentioned in the excerpt below, its significance warrants comment. It was a large, square building located near the center of a ten-acre plot of ground set aside for the capitol when surveyors laid out the city. Broad stone steps at the front of the structure reached from the ground to the main floor, and four Ionic columns extended from the top of the steps to the overhead roof of the portico. A small dome rose from the center of the main roof, and chimneys stood at all corners of the building. Governor Francis R. Lubbock estimated that the building, including its contents, cost Texas taxpayers in excess of $150,000. It was probably valued at something less than that amount when it was destroyed by fire on November 9, 1881.

The impressive buildings and famous trading establishments, however, did little to dispel the gloom and deprivation that settled over the city during the last twenty months of war. Soon everything was in short supply. The Barr family used dried "leaves of the Upon shrub" for tea and largely subsisted on "corn pone, jonney cake, and hoe cake." When General John Magruder visited Austin and a banquet was planned in his honor, municipal leaders went to great lengths to secure suitable fare for him. The search for meat for the table resulted in the death of Nellie, Lillie's highly prized pet turkey. Lillie held Magruder responsible for this tragedy and spent many hours dreaming up what she considered a suitable punishment for him. Just to be shot by Yankees was not horrible enough, she reasoned, so she prayed that the enemy might kill him "with a *bayonet*." Lillie's impressions of Magruder, her lack of heartfelt devotion for the Confederate war effort, and her account of the untimely death of Nellie not only add new dimensions to Civil War history but perhaps warrant the addition of Nellie's name to the list of "great heroines" who died for the Lone Star State.

Source: Lillie Barr Munroe, "Texas Memoirs of Amelia E. Barr," ed. Philip Graham, *Southwestern Historical Quarterly* 69 (April 1966): 473–498. Reprinted by permission. This issue of the *Quarterly* was the last done under the direction of H. Bailey Carroll. He died in Austin on May 13, 1966.

[In the early days] . . . no railroad bridge spanned the Colorado, and only the stage coach brought people from the Outside World into Austin, then a frontier city. . . . It boasted one long avenue that ran from the Capitol the whole length of the city, shaded for quite a part of the way by stately pecan trees. Smith's Hotel was where the coach drew up, a two story frame building with wide piazzas on which men, loosely garbed and wearing sombreros, panama, or straw hats, sat tilted back on raw hide bottom chairs, the soles of their boots taking the landscape from the top railing. From later memories of the men who loafed here, no doubt the same tobacco chewing crowd watched the stage draw up at Smith's Hotel . . . and dislodge its occupants, answering the stage driver's salutations with a wave of the hand, or a monosyllable.

Smith's Hotel was *the* hotel, as Hendrickes dry goods store was *the* store; lower down was Spaldings, the saloon, then Tonges Grocery store, in front of which Governor Sam Houston and men of his fine type . . . sat under the awning. I think the awning was of weed that reached out over the whole sidewalk. Sam Houston always wore a wide panama or palmeto hat, his shirt was usually open at the throat and a hand-kerchief knotted loosely about it. Tonges grocery was a place of delight, having real old time stick candy, that tempted Governor Houston to stand little girls on the counter and spend real money.

DeFees was *the* drug store, and Bands *the* Jeweler. There were other stores, but mostly saloons and these were frequented by cowboys, Mexicans, and occasionally an Indian. The Comanches at that time were far from friendly with the white people, and of course the Mexican was for the most part if not altogether an open or secret enemy. They were not allowed to live in the city limits, and if I remember rightly could not be in the city after a certain hour at night. Their cabins could usually be known by the game cock tied by one leg just outside the door. There was the Roman Catholic Church, a Methodist, and a Baptist Church, but the principal church was the Episcopal church, a pink adobe building set on a hill. . . .

Miller's Livery stable was also on the main street and it was usually surrounded with a lot of men telling stories, loafing, and taking life off of lazy day platters with calm indifference as to tomorrow or tomorrow's duties if they had any.

The most prominent houses were Judge Carrington's, a large white house set in a garden. . . . The gardens were lovely and full of perfume; then there was the Hendrick's home, General Tom Green's home, the Elgin's, Swenson's, Judge Pasc[h]al's, the Governor's mansion.

[We were living at] . . . the present site I am told of the railway depot . . . [when the] Civil War was declared, and I can recall many pictures in Harper's Weekly then of the rising of the War cloud. Father who never became a citizen . . . held his place in the Land Office because he was an expert accountant, and understood the duties perfectly, and had a fine memory for all Land holders, and their holdings. His heart was with the North so far as slavery was concerned, for he hated that, and the only negro he ever owned was a man taken in part or whole payment for a debt, who lived for the most part in the woods, and showed up at the house only when necessity for clothes or food arose. Mrs. Amelia Barr was a Confederate from a to z and wrote for the Austin paper. . . . Everyone was then working for the soldiers, and when General Tom Green went, answering the first call to arms, as did the flower of Austin's young men, the Confederate spirit flamed high. The great Comet seen in the early part of those days was to us children a magic worker, and in some way we believed it was accountable for all the trouble.

[The war] . . . took deep hold of our imagination. One picture of the early days of Civil War is still clear in my mind. The City flag pole stood I believe on Hendrick's corner, just by his store and from its tip floated the United States flag, that meant to one man in Austin more than sentiment, more than just Union. He must have recalled the Alamo, San Jacinto; the time when his men crowded about him demanding to know if they had done well. Yes, to Sam Houston, that United States flag meant *his honour,* his life work, really, and when it was pulled down and the Confederate flag flung to the breeze in its place, can any one wonder at or blame the old hero that his eyes were wet with tears. It was not that he loved Texas less, but that he loved honor and a United world better. I saw that Confederate flag raised and I saw it taken down and once more the flag of the United States flapped in the Texas breeze.

War times began their hard pinch here and one of the clearest memories I have of them is that mother had no tea, we gathered the leaves of the Upon shrub or little tree and dried them, they made a substitute, but only a substitute; then white flour was almost impossible to get, and no one had white bread but Mother and Mary because she was delicate. Mr. Barr and we children ate corn pone, jonney cake, and hoe cake. Personally this was no trial, even today I prefer good corn bread to poor white bread, but I remember when the war was over Father saying to Mother, "Milley, please do not make any more corn bread – *I hate it.*"

And all those years he had eaten it to let Mother and Mary have the white bread. Poverty now stalked through our home, and that Christmas, Father made all of our Christmas presents. I remember a horse on wheels, painted black, a set of doll's furniture, and a ball among them, such loving patience as those toys showed, bring tears to my eyes as I recall them. The Confederate money was of little value and even if it had been, cloth was almost impossible to get.

. . . .

I recall no fortification built by General Magruda [John B. Magruder]. I have but one memory of him. When he came to Austin they gave a big dinner for him and scoured the city for turkeys. I had a lovely turkey hen named Nellie, that I had raised from a weakly poult, and fed out of the best on my plate until she was grown. I loved that turkey as devotedly as a boy loves his dog. Well, they came to Mothers, and bought all of her turkeys, my Nellie among them. *I was away at the time*. When I came home, and found my Nellie gone, my grief was perhaps unreasonable, certainly unpatriotic. Mother thought I would be proud to contribute my pet for so brave a soldier. *Not I*. I promptly went into the cornfields and prayed God if that man ate my Nellie, to let a bone choke him, and if he went back to the war to let some Yankees kill him with a *bayonet*. Probably he never tasted my Nellie, but he was the cause of her being killed, and hateful to me. They said he had his horse shod with Brass shoes. I can believe it, for he strutted round the city worse than a turkey gobbler looking for a fight when he knew no other gobbler was around. He may have been a good soldier, but my Nellie stands between him and my faith in that respect. I do not remember the near riot when the Federal flag was raised after the surrender, but I do remember the real grief for a lost cause in many homes. And also the solemn salute of it by old Texans, who had put that flag there when Texas was taken into the Union.

. . . .

All mail came to Austin by Stage and pony express, and all war news by Pony post. When news was hoped for, or expected, most of the city sat up at night, waiting for the Pony post. I can remember father and mother sitting in the bright moonlight, father smoking. Mother usually knitting to add to the endless pile of stockings required by little feet in winter, listening, and talking softly to one another, then the clip clop of the Pony post's flying feet far up on Robinson's Hill, down past General Green's, on, on, clip, clop, to the post office, but now I can not recall where the post office was or what it was like but the men hurried to that point to hear the latest news, the women I have no doubt thought more of the casualty or death list, as they waited for the news brought by the Pony Post. When the news came of Lee's surrender, Austin was practically in mourning. The women could hardly believe their men had died, been wounded, mutilated to be beaten at last. Indeed it was hard to believe, until the proof came in the shape of United States troops marching into the city.

1863–1865

Reminiscences of Life on the Gulf Coast with the Second Texas Infantry

Ralph J. Smith, the author of the following excerpt, wrote his wartime reminiscences over forty-six years after he had been "emancipated . . . from the restraints of military life." A flair for the dramatic, a sense of humor, and an uncanny ability to depict the grotesque enabled Smith to produce an often exhilarating though sometimes depressing contribution to the list of Civil War chronicles. Before being captured, paroled, reorganized, and stationed on the Texas Gulf Coast, the Second Texas Infantry participated in the battles of Shiloh, Farmington, Corinth, Hatchie Bridge, and Vicksburg. While at Fort Caney in Matagorda County, the unit engaged in a rather insignificant skirmish with Federal gunboats on February 7, 1864. The increasing effectiveness of the blockade, the arrival of yellow fever in Galveston, and the fading of Confederate hopes filled the last months of the war with bitterness, death, and despair. Smith's humorous account of the salvaging of a Spanish sailing vessel, however, was one of the unit's last enjoyable moments before the Confederate collapse.

Source: Ralph J. Smith, *Reminiscences of the Civil War and Other Sketches,* reproduced on bond paper with cloth binding by W. M. Morrison of Waco, Texas, 1962, pp. 31–37. Reprinted by permission.

About the first of October 1863, we received notice that the Second Texas had been exchanged and was to be reorganized at Houston. Though there was some doubt as to our being regularly exchanged, all the old members fit for duty reported as soon as their order reached them. Our Colonel [Ashbel Smith] soon convinced us that our exchange was all right and that we were not going to fight with a rope around each of our necks, for hanging is the punishment meted out to captured soldiers who have broken their parole.

We organized at the same camp about two miles from Houston where two years before we had originally entered into [the] service of the Confederate States as a regiment. We were at that time volunteers, nearly everyone young and thoughtless, filled with exhuberant hopes and strong in the belief that our regiment could wipe [out] the best brigade of Yankees that ever entered the field . . . any morning before breakfast.

But now what a change had come over the spirit of our dreams. We had fought, starved and laid in prison for two years until our ranks were reduced to two hundred and fifty of the volunteers, who though resolved to stand by our country as long as life stood by us, were without enthusiasm and almost without hope. We had learned many things about war that tended to lessen our zeal for glory thereby, and though we still answered the bugle call promptly, there was no spontaneous hopes of each sounding of its notes that we were to march into battle immediately. Orders that met our approval we obeyed but others we evaded as all old soldiers know well how to do.

Having completed our reorganization we were conveyed by rail to Sandy Point and from there marched to Columbia on the Brazos river. Arriving at Columbia we boarded a transport and went down the Brazos to Velesco, for what purpose we never found out as there was no enemy in miles of this place. Some of the boys said that we had probably come down for sea bathing. It being the middle of winter and our camp being located on a bare beach where we had no protection from the bitter North wind that prevailed, we came near freezing on several occasions. Finally we had orders to move west of the Brazos river about four miles where the country was heavily timbered and we were protected from the wind.

In January 1864 we were removed to cedar Lake, six miles from the mouth of Caney river where a Fort of the same name was located. This we were to guard. Several gunboats of the blocading fleet were at this time occupying the coast off Texas and had appeared in sight of Fort Caney and it was supposed that the enemy was making preparations to land troops nearby in order to capture the garrison. We were accordingly there to support it. Not long after our arrival two of the Federal Gunboats drew near and began to shell the Fort. Our company was ordered inside but on our remonstrating we were allowed to deploy up and down the beach behind sand hills. The one gun in the Fort was soon silenced.

An unexpected treat fell to our lot soon after the firing ceased. The Federal gunboat ran a Spanish sailing vessel in near the fort where she grounded. The crew, all Cubans, being much frightened, abandoned her and took to the woods. Our officers took possession of the boat and cargo, consisting of coffee, Irish potatoes, salt fish, calico, wash bowls and pitchers, bar iron and some few barrels besides numbers of cases of various tonics, which we called soothing syrup, consigned to R & G Mills of Galveston.

We were ordered by companies to unload the vessel which had now become a wreck and we were promised the usual salvage, one third of the cargo. Attaching a cable and the whole regiment lending a hand we soon had a suitable position for unloading and in a few hours had taken everything out except the bar iron.

Meanwhile the boys had tested the various brands of soothing syrup which they found to be greatly exhilerating in its effects. However, after continual sampling they discovered it to be overpoweringly intoxicating. In fact by twelve o'clock at night the whole command was stretched on the sands of the beach helplessly drunk, except Major [George W. L.] Fly, Sargeant Bill and myself.

On speaking of the matter afterward I placed our Chaplin in the list of the sober but Bill swore that he was as drunk as the rest. However, Bill was prejudiced against this "parson," called him a "one-eyed John who could see only a single side to a question and that to his personal advantage." Bill swore that any man who was too good to associate with the rank and file on earth would desert them on the road to heaven. On the strength of these convictions he refused to hear him preach. Drunk or sober the Chaplin was able to depart the next morning in a cart which he had loaded down with goods from the wreck.

The sun arose at the usual hour after the night of debauch but the regiment failed to greet his returning rays. Many of them were all day getting on their feet. There was visable of the cargo next day after unloading, six or seven barrels of tonic, one-fourth of the coffee and crockery ware, the remainder having been buried in the sand by the boys who were so drunk at the time that very little of it was ever recovered they not being able to remember the hiding places after they became sober.

General [H. P.] Bee sent wagons down and hauled off the remaining barrels of coffee, kindly leaving us the bowls, pitchers, the proper use of which would no doubt have improved our appearances but as he failed to furnish clean towels and soap to go with them we failed to appreciate their value.

About this time two of our conscripts, no doubt recognizing their ignorance of . . . [explosives] and with praiseworthy zeal to rise in a chosen (by others) profession concluded to begin an individual investigation of these forces, each for himself. Procuring two charged shells from the Fort they proceeded to experiment. One of the shells was placed at the roots of a large tree, and reaching around from behind one of the "students" touched the fuse with a lighted torch. The shell went off and so did two of the investigator's fingers. The other daring seeker after knowledge of things military placed his shell under a rude board and stood on it while he applied the torch. The result was a rapid ascension skyward in which I fear the victim came nearer reaching heaven than he ever will again. Strange to say this fellow returned to earth intact and unhurt except for slight bruises. The explosion made a terrific noise and caused quite a commotion. This was the first conscript we had ever seen elevated from the ranks. I always thought this fellow was what Josh Billings [American humorist] would call a "dam phul."

We remained two or three months in this section when we marched to Houston where we took [a] railroad [train] for Galveston which place we reached about the middle of April 1864.

We were assigned to post duty upon our arrival at Galveston and remained there until the close of the war. General McGruder, commander of the forces on Galveston Island, had his headquarters in the city and our duties consisted in guarding these together with the quartermaster and commissarry stores. In the intervals of guard duty we occupied our time trying to drill something like soldierly bearing into our raw conscripts in order to make them fit for the next war. Most of us had then lost all hope of the present one, for seeing that the complete subjugation of the Confederacy was only a matter of a few months, we soon gave up trying to make any improvements in the awkward squads of conscripts when assigned to drill them. We were never molested by the enemy while on Galveston Island. Our nearest approach to battle was with our own men when we were called out one night to protect Col. Hawes quarters from the assault of a mob, composed of resident soldiers and their families. These soldiers demanded that the government issue rations to their starving wives and children, which being refused on account of the depleted condition of our commissaries, had come in a riotous mob to secure provisions by force if persuasion did not avail.

No one who has not seen a mob of this kind clamoring for bread can have any conception of the crazed and uncontrollable rage of the participants or appreciate the difficulty of quieting them without the shedding of blood. However by promising to see that the women and children would be fed and ordering a company to fire over the heads of the mob our officers finally quelled the riot with only one man injured who was accidentally killed by some one's awkwardness in firing.

Here I took part in the first and only military execution I witnessed during the war. A private of German parentage belonging to an artillery company of Col. Cook's regiment was shot for desertion. He had made two former attempts to desert and it was at last decided to make an example of him. Our regiment was assigned to guard the prisoner at the execution out three miles from town. On reaching the appointed place three regiments were drawn up forming three sides of a paralelogram facing inward. The deserter was marched along in front of the entire lines and when the open end was reached, halted and the firing squad marched forward and fired.

The squad consisted of twelve men, the half of whose guns were loaded with powder and ball, the remaining six guns being charged with blank cartridges. None of the squad knew whether he fired a blank or a ball.

After the execution we were marched by where the body lay dead upon the ground in order to impress upon our minds the penalty for desertion.

This was the last man whom I saw killed during the war. But we were attacked during the summer of 1864 by a silent and insidious enemy against which our heaviest guns availed nothing. The Yellow fever invaded our camp and soon being epidemic, carrying off numbers who had courted death on numerous battlefields and endured the hardships of many campaigns, only to succumb at last to this dreaded scourge. This was a time that tried men's souls beyond the test of battle shouts. No surging crowds of men to urge one on to victory or death yet now what heroic bravery it required to sit alone through the sad silent watches of the night beside a plague-striken-comrad's bed and minister to the dieing wants of one who's very breath exhaled death into the surrounding atmosphere. But men were found in camp and women too in the city whose thoughts of self were drowned in other's cup of trembling so that not one was left to suffer and die alone.

And here during this epidemic was displayed equally as much heroism if not more than is required to go into battle by both soldiers and also the good women of the city, true heroines indeed who so kindly cared for and ministered to the sick and dieing soldiers.

1865

Ten Weeks in Texas
as a Prisoner of War

Union prisoners captured by Confederate forces in the Trans-Mississippi Department and lower Mississippi Valley were usually paroled or exchanged, at least during the early months of the war, but several thousand were placed in prison camps in Arkansas and Texas. Many of the camps were temporary and never intended to be permanent prisons, but three in Texas, in operation for only short periods, were established with the intention that they function for the duration. They were located near Camp Verde in Kerr County; at Camp Groce near Hempstead; and at Camp Ford, four miles northeast of Tyler. Camp Ford was the largest, consisting of approximately ten acres enclosed by a log stockade about eighteen feet high. The size of the compound varied because it had to be enlarged at intervals to accommodate the growing number of prisoners. As many as fifty-three hundred men were confined in this camp at one time or another during the war. The population constantly fluctuated because of the rate of exchange, the numerous successful escapes, and the simple system of parole.

Only a few inmates died during confinement: only 206 graves were moved from the site after the war.

Camp Ford was established in August 1863 at the site of a flowing spring on the Gladewater road. Without doubt, if the Confederate prison at Andersonville, Georgia, had had such a spring rather than a water supply polluted by seepage from the camp latrine, the horrors of incarceration there would have been greatly reduced. The artesian spring at Camp Ford, outside the western wall of the enclosure, formed a creek of fresh, cool water that meandered under the stockade wall and across the prison compound. Food and medical supplies were far from plentiful, but they were by no means unknown. Inmates cared for themselves, treating each other when ill, building their own huts, and cooking their own meals. Periodically, prisoners were allowed to leave the stockade under guard to replenish the camp supply of firewood. The Confederate overseers did not provide any shelter so each succeeding group of residents spent much time improving the shelters and shanties constructed by previous inmates. Some of these structures could accommodate as many as thirty-five men during rainy weather.

Camp Ford was in operation only twenty-one months. The last group of men incarcerated there arrived in the late spring of 1865, just a few weeks before it was abandoned. The following excerpt is a nineteen-year-old Union soldier's day-to-day record of his prison life at Camp Ford and his description of his departure on May 15, 1865, when the camp was in the process of being closed down. He was Sergeant Arthur E. Gilligan, Third Rhode Island Volunteer Cavalry, captured near Bayou Goula, Louisiana, on January 24, 1865. The sergeant's health was not good, and he remained in bed much of the time, unable to participate in the more active sports, taking "quinine and sedlitz powder," and making daily entries in his diary. Scurvy seemed to be the chief health problem at Camp Ford, but Gilligan also suffered from a painful rash and recurring malaria. He was widely read and versatile, repaired clocks and various mechanical devices, played several musical instruments, and helped in the preparation of the camp newspaper. He referred to making rings and working with metals at least twice in his diary so he must have also had interests and perhaps skills along this line.

Many of Gilligan's comrades at Camp Ford were old friends from Louisiana and a few, such as Corporal Harry Arnetts, were members of his Rhode Island unit. Like most boys in their teens, Gilligan spent a lot of time thinking about his girl friends. His diary contains numerous references to Eliza Anderson, whom he had known in Louisiana; Ella, his girl friend back home in Massachusetts; Mary

Louisa, whom he eventually married; and Agnes, a cousin whose childhood companionship he deeply cherished. When Gilligan arrived home after the war, he wrote that he "set up the rest of the night" talking with Agnes.

Gilligan enlisted in the United States Army at the age of sixteen. He joined the Eighth Massachusetts Volunteer Infantry Regiment and participated in the pursuit of Lee's Army of Northern Virginia after the battle of Gettysburg. After his enlistment had expired, Gilligan wanted to serve with a mounted unit so he enlisted in the Third Rhode Island Cavalry. In January 1864, his unit was ordered to New Orleans to take part in Banks's Red River invasion of Texas. During the campaign that followed, Gilligan saw action at Mansfield and Pleasant Hill. After the Third Rhode Island returned to New Orleans in May 1864, Gilligan was assigned scout and patrol duties in the District of La Fourche. He was a courier at the time he was captured by a Confederate patrol near Bayou Goula.

After his release from Camp Ford, he was transported via Shreveport to Satterlee Hospital in Philadelphia, where he spent several weeks recuperating. He was mustered out of the service in New York City on July 31, 1865. After his marriage to Mary Louisa, he worked as a foreman in a textile plant for a few years, then became a car inspector for the New York, New Haven, and Hartford Railroad. Gilligan died on September 20, 1922. His wish that he might "never have occasion to cross [the state line of Texas] again" became a reality.

Source: Arthur E. Gilligan, "Yankee Prisoner in Texas, 1865," typescript of the diary of Arthur E. Gilligan, in the possession of Arthur E. Gilligan II, of Fort Worth, Texas. Used by permission.

March Wednesday 8 1865 – [Six weeks after my capture I] . . . have nothing to trouble me, but the itch which has broken out on me, but I fixed one sore. I pulled off the scab and scraped the corruption off and it has not troubled me since. Tom made some more white bread today. I think we are going to have a rainy night of it, but we don't care now we have a good house.

March Thursday 9 1865 – Today has been the coldest day we have had since I have been a prisoner. The fire place not being big enough for 3 of us all at once, we had to take turns at it while one remained in bed. I wish I could hear what the news is and know what is going on.

March Friday 10 1865 – Today I have done nothing but loaf around and take it easy. I made a trip to the gate but could not get out in the morning. I annointed myself with an ointment I got from the Doctor. I took three more sores and doctored them the way I did the other day.

The day has been very fine and it passed very pleasantly. I have had dreams 2 or 3 each night.

March Saturday 11 1865 – Today everything passed off as usual till the Patroling Officer came in and called the roll and took our names. Some think we are going to be exchanged, but I think we are going to Tyler, Texas, but I hope we are not, for it is a good way to walk and I can't wear my boots I guess. Fine day.

March Sunday 12 1865 – This morning the 3rd Texas Cav. came to take us to Tyler. I had just got out and brought in some firewood when the order came. We started about noon and went two miles and camped for the night. Some went to dancing to amuse the rebs. We have an old fiddle among the crowd.

March Monday 13 1865 – I got up at daylight. I ate breakfast. After the whole [camp?] got through we were counted and then proceeded about 6 miles. We rested for about an hour and took lunch then started again. Passed through the town of Greenwood. We camped in a suitable place with water handy. We have made about 14 miles today I should think.

March Tuesday 14 1865 – Last night we camped about a mile and a half from the Texas line. It being Tom's turn to cook I went to bed. We started early this morning and walked pretty fast. After going about 6 miles we had a rest. While we were resting a train of cars came and it looked quite normal. We went on and camped about 6 miles from Marshall and it was my turn to cook. The sky looks as if it was going to rain tonight. We came about 12 miles today.

March Wednesday 15 1865 – Rainy We started early as usual. Two boys dug holes and hid in them, covering themselves with leaves and got away unobserved and by this time are far away. We passed through Marshall at 10 am and camped 4 miles this side. This is beautiful country and a good deal like Virginia. The grass is commencing to look green and the peach trees are all in bloom. I can travel yet, though my feet are sore.

March Thursday 16 1865 – We started from camp as usual. Marched about a 100 yards then halted an hour. During this time the guards searched the camp and found 9 of our boys buried in holes with leaves over them. The way it was found out, one of them that would not go left his hole uncovered. Then they searched the ground. I feel pretty well today. The road is soft and sandy.

March Friday 17 1865 – We started as early as usual. The road being good we traveled pretty fast. The country looks fine. Over hills and through vales and bottoms till at last the days march was ended by our arriving on the bank of the river Sabine which we crossed in a ferry boat and camped on the opposite bank of the river. I cooked supper and we went to bed. We made a march of 21 miles today.

March Saturday 18 1865 – This morning we proceeded on our way the same as ever. Nothing worthy of remark happened till 4 PM when we got to the stockade. As our names were called we went in. The first man I met was Bill Crandell of Company D. Then he took me up to his Qr's and there I found Lon Fenner. We told all the news, talked a while, ate supper then went to bed.

March Sunday 19 1865 – We went to bed early last night being very tired. I got up early and washed up, answered roll call then had breakfast. Talked over old times with the boys. I have a new chum. He belongs to the 1st La. Cav. His name is Charles Johnson. We live as though we were somewhat at home now. We are in a house which doesn't leak.

March Monday 20 1865 – *Rainy* This morning Bill C. pulled me out of bed and told me it was roll call. After it I washed up and laid down in my bunk and read a book named *Denis Mount Joy*. In the evening I went down to a house and was introduced to a Mr. Sawyer a Guitarist and leader of the String Band in here. We played a few tunes.

March Tuesday 21 1865 – Today has passed off as usual. Nothing to do, but the Paroling Officer came in and kept us in line for about 3 hours calling the roll. In the evening I went down to the string band and from there we went to the officers Quarters where we gave quite a performance after which we retired to our respective Qr's.

March Wednesday 22 1865 – Today has passed as usual. I spent most of the day in learning airs for the flute but I can't play with the violin because it can't be tuned to concert pitch. The strings consist of Beef since no silk thread or anything that is suitable can be had. A bass string costs a $1.00 in specie or $3.00 in greenback.

March Thursday 23 1865 – Today I have felt quite unwell. I lay in bed reading a book, then I went down to Charlie Sawyer's house and stayed an hour or two talking on various subjects and playing on the flute. Last night we had a rehearsal but I did not succeed very well with my instrument. The day has been very fine and passed quickly.

March Friday 24 1865 – Every day passes as usual. We get up in the morning then we pass the time as best we can till supper then after that we loaf around till bed time. Last night we had a rehearsal and I played the guitar. Today I have been practising most of the day. We are going to rehearse tonight.

March Saturday 25 1865 – Loafing around as usual today. Nothing to do but read a book called *Thinks I to Myself*. Time hangs heavy on my hands now. I am so lonesome. I don't know what to do with myself. I went down to Charlie Sawyer's to rehearse but did not for one reason or another.

March 26 1865-*Rainy* I have been in bed all day since roll call because I had nothing else to do and because I was very sleepy. I have got the itch and that plagues me a great deal. I think a good deal of home and friends and the good times I used to have, but also now gone forever.

March Monday 27 1865 – Today I have done as usual. I practiced awhile on the guitar in the afternoon. I had my hair cut Saturday. A close fighting crop. We had a rehearsal in the evening and I played the guitar. Oh, how I wish I had my own guitar to play and amuse myself.

March Tuesday 28 1865 – Today has found me as usual. After break-fast I went to bed till dinner or supper whichever you like (for we only have two meals a day) and after dinner I went down to Sawyer's house and had my usual chat with him. Then I came up and went to bed. The day has been rather dull.

March Wednesday 29 1865 – Today it was my turn to go out for wood. I went out at 1/2 past 8 till 1/2 past 11 then went to bed until sup-per time. In the day time I lay and think of the good times coming when we will all be free once more and in our lines where we can get enough to eat.

March Thursday 30 1865 – Today has been cold and windy and I have laid in bed most all day telling stories and talking till after supper, then I went down to Charlie Sawyer's and talked a while with him. We have very little to amuse ourselves with here. Some play baseball, chess, checkers and all kind of games. I am going to get a fellow to teach me French.

March Friday 31 1865 – Everything passed as usual. I found nothing but an old cow horn to scrape to amuse myself with. I went up on the hill and watched them play baseball then got up and ate supper.

April Saturday 1 1865 – All Fools Day I got fooled the first thing. Crandell came up and said "Pick that louse off your shoulder." I went to do so but there was no louse there. I went down to Charlie Sawyers and had a clean shave, then went down to C.L.'s and spent the evening talking over old times.

April Sunday 2 1865 – Today I have done nothing but lay and sleep all day. I have been dreaming all day of home and friends, but I have got to wait my turn to get out of this. Today we marched Johnson out of this mess. We got tired of him smearing us to others.

April Monday 3 1865 – This morning we went to work and overhauled the roof of our house for last time it rained the roof leaked. We built a shade in front of our house to sit under on hot days. In the Evening I went down to Charlie's.

April Tuesday 4 1865-This morning after breakfast I practiced on my flute a little, then I washed my shirts out and dried them. In the evening I stopped in on Tom Von's about an hour. I hardly know how to pass my time. I am getting quite lazy and if I can't find something to do I shall die.

April Wednesday 5 1865 – Today it rained all morning and all last night rather heavily. No rations came in and I don't think there will be any today for the rain has made the roads very bad. I laid in bed part of the forenoon and then played on my flute. Then I took a stroll down town. The day turned off cold.

April 6 Thursday 1865 – Everything went off as usual. After breakfast I watched the boys play baseball for a while then went to playing chess, then played on my flute for a while. In the evening I went down to Charlies and we got out the guitar and spent the evening playing and singing. Fine day.

April Friday 7 1865 – It rained all last night and all day today. I have been in bed most all day today. I was down to Bill Pierce's for a while. In the evening I went down to Harry Williams' and stayed for a while. I am getting lonesome and tired waiting for an exchange. I can't get anything to read or do. Every hour is lost.

April 8 Saturday 1865 – Today has been just like yesterday, a dull and mean day, and I have been in bed, the same as ever. I wish I could be somewhere I could improve my time or to have tools to make rings or something of that kind to pass the time.

April Sunday 9 1865 [day that Lee surrendered at Appomattox] – Today is the anniversary of the Battle of Pleasant Hill, but a far different day it is. It was a fine day then, but today is a dull and dreary one. I had plenty to do last year at this time, but now I haven't anything to do. I was in bed most all day. I went down to Charlie's and copied a song. In the evening I went down again and stayed until bed time. There is great excitement about an exchange. Rumors of all kinds are afoot.

April Monday 10 1865 – Today has passed the same as yesterday. Spent the day in bed except in the evening which I spent with Bill Pierce. I am getting awfully lonesome. I hardly know how to spend my time and the weather is so dull and rainy. The only thing I can find to do is learning songs from Bill. If I had some guitar strings I might have something now.

April Tuesday 11 1865 – Today has been spent like most of the others. It rained all the forenoon and didn't let up until the afternoon but at about ten in the evening it commenced to rain again. In the afternoon I borrowed Harry Williams' guitar and practised until dark on it. We hear but very little about affairs at the front.

April Wednesday 12 1865 – Today has been as bad as ever. After breakfast I turned into bed again till dinner time. After dinner I went down to Bill's shantie and got him to teach me a song named "The Ballet Girl," then I came up to my house and turned in until supper time. I spent the evening with Bill as usual. Our rations came in about 5 PM, but no bacon, but we keep ahead one days rations.

April Thursday 13 1865 – Today one year and six months of my term has expired and the time has passed very quickly and some of it very pleasantly. This morning the sun came out warm and pleasant. Today has been spent about as usual down at Bill Pierce's and Sawyer's. Sawyer went to the hospital this afternoon with the scurvy. There are a good many sick. A little rain.

April Friday 14 1865 – I laid in bed all the forenoon and the afternoon. I went down to Bill's and stayed until ten in the evening. I am getting very lonesome and hardly know what to do with myself. I don't seem to have any life to do anything. If I could improve my time some way I should get along quite well. I wonder what the boys are doing in regiment today and where the regiment is this time.

April Saturday 15 1865 – This morning came my turn to go out for wood. At 8 o'clock we went out and stayed until 11. While we were out I enjoyed myself first rate. The day was so pleasant. While I was out I got a good supply of scurvy root to be chewing and keep off the scurvy. In the afternoon I borrowed a bible and read in that for a while. In the evening I went down to Bill's and stayed till bed time.

April 16 1865 – After breakfast I went to bed till dinner time. Then after dinner I went up on the hill and watched a game of baseball. In the evening I went down to Pierce's as usual. The day has been a fine one and the fields and trees look beautiful. Summer is appearing fast. Oh, how lonesome I feel in here wasting my time for nothing. To be sure I get paid for my time, but I don't like the employment. I would find other if I could.

April Monday 17 1865 – Today has been spent much the same as usual. I went up and had a talk with Bob Arnett a while. During the time I was there it commenced to rain very hard for some time. In the afternoon I laid down and read a while a book entitled *Irons in Georgia*. News came in today that an order from General Smith has come to have rations for 1000 men for 3 days and to have them ready by Saturday, but I don't believe it.

April Tuesday 18 1865 – Time passes off as usual. I was in bed all the afternoon. In the forenoon I went up the hill to see a game of ball, then went down to Bill's. The evening I spent at Bill's I copied off two songs named *Cloe in the Celler* and *Riding in a Railroad Car* both of which I am going to learn. We had a light shower in the morning. The day has been a very fine one.

April Wednesday 19 1865 – Today I find I have got the itch quite bad and the Doctor can't give me anything for it. In the evening I took a bath in salt and water; afterwards a good wash in lye water. The day looked rather gloomy as if it were going to rain. The news came in that Richmond has been taken, but I believe as much of it as I ever did. I have been laying in bed reading a book named *Fourth Kind*.

April Thursday 20 1865 – Today Bill Crandell got a pass for four of our mess to go out for greens. Lon Fenner, Star Grover, Jack Sheppard [and I] went out and got a good mess of greens which we ate in short measure. This has been the first change in food I have had since I have been in here.

April Friday 21 1865 – This morning I got a pass for 2 men and we all went out, but first we went into the woods and got some brush and poles also some grass. In the afternoon we went out and got some greens. In the evening we put a shade with brush we brought in.

April Saturday 22 1865 – Today Frank Chase got a pass for three men besides himself and they went out after greens. Lon Fenner and I stayed in today. I laid down and went to sleep. While I was asleep someone came in and stole my flute. When the boys came in they brought in an owl, a male one, and he is the drollest thing I ever saw. Some boys have pet squirrals.

April Sunday 23 1865 – Today has been passed mostly in bed. In the evening Bill Pierce and I went up to the hill and walked round a few times. We had three messes of greens today. The news came again that Richmond was taken, that Lee had surrendered with 45,000 men, also that Johnson [General Joseph E. Johnston at Durham Station, North Carolina] with 25,000 men had surrendered, but I don't believe a word of it.

April Monday 24 1865 – Three months ago today since I was captured. Today I have been in bed as usual. Chase traded off his blanket and bought some beans, tobacco, vinegar and eggs. We had boiled eggs, ham and corn bread for supper. In the afternoon I walked around the ring then went to Tom Von's and spent the evening.

April Tuesday 25 1865 – This morning Lon woke us up before roll call and we had breakfast of baked beans, bacon and cornbread. I passed the time off by walking round the camp. In the evening I went down to Tom Von's house and we had some music. My mind turns back to the good old times I was having while I was back at camp. A man in this world does not know when he is enjoying himself.

April Wednesday 26 1865 – Every day follows each other and passes off just the same. Today has been dull and rainy and I was in the usual place bed. I went down to Pierces as usual in the evening. In the latter part of the afternoon I went down to Bob Arnett's and talked of home and the prospect of getting a furlough when we got back. I think our chance is slim.

April Thursday 27 1865 – A pass came for us this morning and four of our boys went out and brought in a lot of wood, enough to last a week or two. In the evening Bob Arnett and I took a couple of turns around the ring on the hill. I have been thinking of the future and wondering if I will ever get out of this.

April Friday 28 1865 – I was going out on pass but the pass did not come so I had to stay in and amuse myself the best I could. I went to bed all day and in the evening I went down to Tom Von's and heard the news. Things are getting awfully dull and I am getting lazier every day.

April Saturday 29 1865 – Everything passed as usual. I slept all the morning and in the afternoon went down to Henry Levernes house and played three songs as follows: *Angelina Baker, Knickerbacker Line,* and

A Trip to the Moon. In the evening I took a few turns around the ring on the hill. This evening we drew flour instead of meat. Twenty four men escaped from here last night.

April Sunday 30 1865 – After breakfast our cook went to work and made some white bread and I stayed home to see the operation. We had beans and white bread for supper and dinner. In the afternoon I went down to Bill's and stayed a while. In the evening I took my usual turn around the ring. Fifty Three men got away last night. I think of trying it myself some day.

May Monday 1 1865 – Right after breakfast I lay down and went to sleep till dinner time. In the afternoon I lay under the shade talking. In the evening I went down to Henry Levernes. One year ago today I was at Alexandria and hadn't the slightest idea I should be here at this time, but it has fallen my lot and I must make the best of it.

May Tuesday 2 1865 – This morning I made up my mind to wash my clothes so I went to work and washed all my clothes except my pants and one shirt. The Colonel commanding this post issued a new order that every man must be inside his house at sunset and not show his nose out of it again till sunrise on the pain of being shot.

May Wednesday 3 1865 – Today has passed off the same as usual. I have been lying out under the shade napping and talking about rumors in camp. I feel quite lonely today. God grant that I may one day be released from this prison. Oh how I long to be with the Regiment; while I was there, I did not know how to appreciate it, but this trip to Texas has taught me a great many things.

May Thursday 4 1865 – This morning I laid in bed till dinner time as usual. Everything passed off as usual. In the afternoon Tom O'Brian went over to the Sutler's and sold his watch for $15.00 in specie and took it up to town. He got 56 lbs of flour, 2–1/2 dozen eggs and a bushel of meal. After this I think we shall not be hungary. We have been on short rations of Bacon.

May Friday 5 1865 – Today our cook has been making white bread all the forenoon. We have been living high on 5 meals today. I have been in bed the same as usual. My mind has been heavy all day and I have not felt very well in bodily health. I have got the Diareaha pretty bad but I hope I shall soon get over it. It is not very pleasant to have.

May Saturday 6 1865 – Last night Wm. McDonnell of Co. E of our Regiment was shot by the Patrol. He asked one of the Patrol to allow him to go outside the house to make water. When he got out, the guard told him to go back. As he turned to go he shot him in the rump. I have been in bed all day because it has been raining.

May Sunday 7 1865 – This morning it has commenced to rain again. As I had nothing to do I went to bed till afternoon, then I went down to Bill Pierces and got shaved. I then went to Hen's till the guards came in. I am getting to feeling worse every day. The rumor says that we shall be out of this by next friday. It will amount to shucks.

May Monday 8 1865 – Today passed off as usual in idleness and sleep. Oh how I wish I could employ my time in some usefullness. If I had a file I might make rings and such things. A man in this place will learn to be economical. I have learned that.

May Tuesday 9 1865 – Today I have been in bed all day except when there was water wanted, then of course I had to go after it. I am feeling much worse than yesterday. My bowels are unsettled and the diareahea much worse. I hope I am not going to be sick in here, for a man who is sick has hardly any chance of recovery.

May Wednesday 10 1865 – Today passed off as usual. I laid in bed all day. Oh that there might be some way provided for us to get away from here, not only for myself but for many that are in as bad a position as myself. But the time will come in time. The weather has turned wet and rainy.

May Thursday 11 1865 – Today I have been sick a bed all day till supper time. Then we had some soup for supper which eased my bowels right off. In the forenoon my bowels ached awfully but Lon managed to effect a cure. The day has been very fine. Yesterday was the anniversary of my compact with Zane Walker, three years more before the time of that compact expires.

May Friday 12 1865 – Today I am a little better than I was yesterday. Everything goes on as usual. No news.

May Saturday 13 1865 – Today I am much worse than yesterday. About 11 o'clock the Paroling Officer came in and sent in the news that he was going to parole the whole camp. If that is true I shall stand a good chance. This day passed off quite excellently. I took a turn around the ring in the evening.

May Sunday 14 1865 – The Paroling Officer has been paroling all day and we have been baking hard tack and getting ready for the march. I am getting to feel quite happy.

May Monday 15 1865 – Today there is much excitement. Yesterday Lon went out in the morning and was paroled. I got paroled this afternoon. The guards have all deserted, but Sweets men and they are all drunk, officers and all. In the evening the Band got together and went to Headquarters and played to the Rebs and our officers. The whiskey was passed around and I partook freely.

May Tuesday 16 1865 – This morning Capt. Joe Stephenson made me a present of a pair of good shoes. Today we have everything to ourselves. I went out with Bill Hercules and took a stroll around. In the evening big fires were built to cook with. Our cooking was all done, but we tore down our shade and built a big bonfire and had a midnight lunch.

May Wednesday 17 1865 – This morning we got up about 4 and got ready to start, but did not start till about 9. We passed through Starville during the afternoon and one of our men was seated on the meeting house steps. As we came along he rang the bell. We got along very well, but the day was hot. We camped about 4 miles from the Sabine. I am in good spirits.

May Thursday 18 1865 – I was quite sick last night, but I got over it before morning. We started early this morning and I of course fell in with the 1st Division. We crossed the Sabine. We went on and camped about 7 miles from the Sabine about 11 o'clock. A lot of Confederate prisoners (paroled) came along by camp on their way home.

May Saturday 20 1865 – This morning we got up at daylight and proceeded on our way. We passed by the Headquarters of General Tappan, and his brigade at Marshall. All the sick were put aboard the cars and we were turned over to some infantry. We went on about 5 miles, then camped for the night. We drew mutton instead of beef.

May Sunday 21 1865 – We started at daybreak and marched quite fast. Passed through Greenwood and camped a short distance from there. Today we passed a good many very nice hours and crossed the Texas line. I hope I shall never have occasion to cross it again.

The Indian Battle at Dove Creek

When James Buckner "Buck" Barry began writing his reminiscences late in his life, he was going blind. He was totally blind during the last months before his death in 1906, but his unfinished manuscript contains much interesting and worthwhile information concerning Civil War Texas. Barry's reminiscences are usually accurate because he had access to his private diary, his military records, much of his military correspondence, several post order books, and some personal letters.

Barry spent the Civil War years patrolling the central West Texas frontier under orders to prevent "Indians from coming in and driving off the cattle of the settlers" in his district. He and a volunteer company he had raised were mustered into military service at Fort Belknap in 1861. He served at Camp Cooper for a time and then assumed command of Fort Belknap in the First Frontier District, commanded by Brigadier General J. W. Throckmorton. Reports from the outlying outposts in his district were forwarded to him so his collection of documents contained information on practically every Indian "scare" in the entire central West Texas district.

Late in 1864, Barry received a message from a militia captain in Erath County that a large party of Indians had been sighted in the Brazos country moving southwestward toward the Rio Grande. The Indians were later found to be friendly Kickapoos from the Pottawatomie Agency in Kansas en route to Mexico. Thinking them out on a foray, Barry dispatched "what force [he] had available to act as scouts and assist the militia" in tracking down the Indians. The Texas frontiersmen descended upon the Kickapoos at Dove Creek, a stream about sixteen miles south of present-day San Angelo. The battle was the bloodiest and most tragic Indian fight in Texas during the Civil War. The Indians, armed with superior weapons but hampered because of their women and children, turned back the initial Texan attack inflicting heavy casualties. The battle was fought in bitter cold, and the Texans were held at bay by devastating musket fire for several hours. The Kickapoos, with inadequate clothing and a dearth of supplies, cared for their sick and wounded during the lull in the fighting. Sporadic skirmishes continued until nightfall, resulting in heavy casualties on both sides. Finally, just before dark, most of the Indians slipped away, leaving the frozen bodies of their dead on the eerie battleground.

The Indians, burdened by wounded warriors, sick squaws, and small children, continued their journey to the Rio Grande, but many of their number died along the way. The Texans, suffering from heavy casualties and depleted supplies, collected their wounded and dead and returned to the warmth of their cabins and forts. The Kickapoos who reached the relative safety of the Mexican interior evidently did not forget the hated Texans. This terrible and totally unnecessary incident probably explains the rash of devastating Kickapoo raids into South Texas from Mexico during the years following the Civil War.

Source: James Buckner Barry, *A Texas Ranger and Frontiersman,* ed. James K. Greer (Dallas: Southwest Press, 1932), pp. 185–196.

The details of the . . . [battle of Dove Creek] came to me through letters, special reports, company returns, and personal interviews, so that I had both oral and written accounts of what occurred. Perhaps it is sufficiently interesting to record here.

A letter from N. W. Gillentine, captain of a company of militia of Erath County in the Second Frontier District, on December 9, 1864, reached me a few days later and introduced the story. He was out on a scout with twenty men and had come to the Clear Fork of the Brazos at Phantom Hill. Asscending this river about thirty miles he found considerable horse sign. A brief examination revealed that a large party of Indians had camped. Apparently, there were nearly one hundred wigwams and some ten tents. The party was judged to total five hundred (it was later determined that there were over three times this number) and to have broken camp some forty-eight hours before. They had moved off slowly up the Clear Fork, leaving a trail some one hundred yards wide.

Following the trail they found a grave, which they opened in an attempt to identify the tribe of Indians. The grave contained the body of a female, just buried, and very richly adorned. Some articles in the grave and some of the decorative articles of dress were taken and the captain stated that he intended to send me one of the moccasins. He thought that the Indians were not aware that they were being followed and wanted me to join him with a sufficient force of men to make an attack. He wrote that he would wait for me on Paint Creek. Meanwhile, he gave the alarm throughout the settlements in the counties of Bosque, Brown, Comanche, Coryell, Erath, Hamilton, and one or two others, and the militia began to assemble to take the trail. But I could spare only a portion of my force, and the uncertainty of the strength and the identity of the Indians, together with other duties, did not seem to me to warrant my joining him. But I dispatched what force I had available to act as scouts and assist the militia in any possible engagement.

Out of the opening of the grave incident there came a story which came to be a tradition related around camp fires and firesides for many years afterwards. It was to the effect that some of Gillentine's men opposed the opening of the grave in which was found the body of the squaw. Finding their opposition to be of no avail, they protested against the taking of various trinkets, beads, and portions of clothing as souvenirs. But they were laughed down by some of their comrades who took the relics with which the body was so richly dressed. Those who were jibed for their protests asserted, with wry grins, that their trinkets might prove to be "bad medicine" for them. But the men encountered no visable results of their ghoulish act until the battle, a few days later, with these Indians they were trailing, when every possessor of a trinket met death in the fight.

This discovery of Indians in numbers I mentioned in a dispatch to General J. W. Throckmorton. In his reply, written from Decatur, he gave the opinion that these Indians were the same band of Kickapoos that had been reported to have left the Kansas border to depredate below the Red River. They probably intended to remain along the fringe of the border settlements during the winter and plunder, thought Throckmorton. It was his opinion that the forces we had to spare in attacking these invaders of the State would prove too small and that more men mounted on good horses might capture "the whole body."

The general was commanding the state forces of the First Frontier District with headquarters at Decatur, Wise County. He wrote two or three days later that everything was quiet in his section, but that he was anxiously waiting to hear of our success against the "band of Indians reported moving toward the Colorado." He was not to have to wait long to hear of the battle which occurred.

On December 23, I issued "Special Order, No. 31" to Lieutenant Giddens to take some men from the four companies, C-D-E-G, of my battalion, and others from the two companies of [Captain Henry] Fossett's Battalion and proceed hurriedly to Fort Chadbourne. At Chadbourne he was to meet with other forces of the two battalions and turn over his men to the senior officer of either Fossett's or my battalion. This order carried by Lieutenant Giddens also required the senior officer who assumed command to cooperate with any state troops that might be there, for the purpose of capturing or routing any Indians on our frontier. The senior officer in command was to return to my headquarters a correct roll of the officers and men who participated in the scout, with remarks of interest and information. In the meantime, I had ordered Fossett to Chadbourne.

Fossett arrived at Chadbourne the last day of the year with fifty from his battalion. He was joined by Lieutenants Brooks, Carpenter, and Giddens with sixty men from the Frontier Regiment. Captain [Jack] Cureton from Bosque County had seventeen militiamen and Lieutenant Morton of Brown County had thirty. Two days were devoted to waiting for the arrival of Captain Totten, commander of Company "A" of the Second Frontier District, who brought up several times more militia than those already assembled. Approximately four hundred men of the militia were present when all had arrived. Among the leaders of this last group of militia who arrived under command of Captain Totten, were Captains Rice of Hamilton County, James Cunningham of Comanche County and Culver of Coryell County. The two forces were not to march together, however, as Fossett and his small command of Confederate troops was to scout ahead. . . .

Fossett led out up the Colorado to find the Indian trail. Next day they found where the Indians had camped on the banks of the river. Two camps had been made; one with one hundred and fifteen wigwams and another large one a short distance up the river. Some two weeks had elapsed since the Indians had left these camps. As there was no grass along the river, the men decided to follow the trail to grass and water.

Some ten miles farther was found the site of another camp and at night, twenty miles distant, they came to where the redskins had had a camping place on the North Concho. Here were signs of some one hundred and sixty wigwams which were many more than had been supposed. The Indians had left this camp only a week before. Captain Fossett and his men waited here two days, sending spies ahead and waiting for the other division of the men, led by Captain Totten, to come up.

On the morning of the 7th, the spies returned to report that they had discovered the Indians encamped at Dove Creek. This stream emptied into the South Concho on the south side. It was about thirty miles distant. Captain Totten's men had not yet appeared. Fossett and his officers concluded that perhaps Totten had followed another Indian trail which was reported as being situated above theirs. So it was decided to advance and attack the camps at daylight the next morning with the forces in hand. A halt was made at two o'clock P.M., some twelve miles from the camp of the Indians, to eat dinner and put their arms in readiness. Lieutenant Mulkey and some men were sent forward to look over the plan of the camps and report back by night.

Just before night, as they were about to move forward, Captain Gillentine and Barnes came up. They reported that Captain Totten and his men were only fifteen miles behind. It was believed that he could arrive in time to assist in the planned attack. Men were sent back to guide him forward to those waiting, but he was farther back than supposed, and did not arrive until next morning, January 8th. . . .

Totten's men reached Fossett's camp about nine o'clock. The officers held a council of war. As the camp of the Indians, which was some three-fourths of a mile in length, was in a large thicket, accessible only by a few narrow paths, and along the creek, it was well fortified by nature. The horses of Totten's men were rather spent, and it was decided to have him attack the camps with his men dismounted. Fossett would lead the troops to cut off the Indians, in which he was to be assisted by the Tonk scouts, and try to intercept any Indians rushing from them or attempting to scatter from the camp. Fossett was to attack the upper and Totten the lower division of the camp.

When all was apparently in readiness and every eighth man was detailed to hold horses, because an effort was to be made to drive the Indians from the thicket, the attack was launched. To get at the Indians, it was necessary to wade Dove Creek which was from knee to waist deep, and afforded the Indians a fine opportunity to inflict severe losses. But Captain Totten and his force rushed bravely in and took possession, it seemed, of a greater part of the camp. For an hour the fight was fierce and bloody. However, as the militia held a portion of the camp, it seemed that they were winning. But now the Indians began to scatter through the brush, keeping up a rapid discharge of their arms, which were long ranged and of good make, and there was little chance of returning their shots with fatal results to many. Among those who fell before the fire of the redskins was Captain Culver of Coryell County. More of the men fell, and the others were becoming discouraged by seeing their comrades shot down by a foe it was impossible to reach.

Captain Totten saw the critical situation and shouted an order to his men to load their guns and prepare to retreat. The war chief of the Indians [No-Ko-Wat] heard and understood the order and ordered his braves to charge through the thicket and they came pouring back and sifting through the irregular line of whites. There was a moment of hand to hand fighting and then the men began to give back under the force of superior numbers. But among those men who were anxious to get in a fair shot at the foe which had paused to pour in a heavier fire and now remained hidden behind embankments as much as possible, was Captain Gillentine. Together with Captain Cunningham and John Anderson of Cunningham's men, he was firing from behind an embankment but realized that he was overshooting as he could see little to fire at. So he declared his intention of climbing on top of the bank and trying for just one shot. His companions attempted, without success, to restrain him from what meant certain death. He climbed to the top of the bank, took a step forward, and fired his gun. Then he turned to Anderson, who had asked him if he was hit, and handed him his gun, with the reply, "John, I am a dead man." Anderson helped him down and started to the rear with him but met some of the captain's men and was relieved of his burden. Captain Barnes and more of the men fell and the others were about to become panicky at the realization that when they started to retreat the fire of the wily foe had increased in effectiveness. Fossett's men were completely cut off from those of Totten. So when the retreat was begun, it was hard to keep the men in any kind of order, although Captain James Cunningham's men were attempting to act as a sort of rear guard of the retreat. The losses of the whites were kept down by the poor marksmanship of the Indians who overshot most of the time. The Indians flanked the retreating men on both sides and also attacked in the rear with their long range rifles. But Totten's men were determined not to be forced to endure this sort of retreat and they halted, rallied, and drove the Indians back into their camp. This last aggressive movement was then followed by a resumption of the retreat. After falling back to another creek some three miles distant, camp was made the end of the day. Just as the sun went down, the wounded Captain Gillentine died.

At the beginning of the fight, the Confederate troops of Fossett, aided by the militiamen of Cureton and Morton, and the Tonk scouts, made a mounted charge and captured most of the horses, nearly a thousand in number, which were near the camp. Skirmishes with the Indians were continuous as they wanted to recover their horses. As parties of them attacked, the men resisted bravely, killing them and driving them back into the thicket. But later, when the fighting at the camp had ceased, the Indians pressed forward in numbers, fighting furiously. For five hours the struggle raged, sometimes the troops giving ground and again driving the Indians back into the thicket. It was easily seen that these Indians had come into Texas with better guns and ammunition than the troops had. With their longer ranged and superior guns they tried to fight at long distances. The men would charge them bravely and when the Indians would sally after them, they would frequently manage to cut one of the braves off and kill him.

A large portion of the Indians now carried on the fight with Fossett's men, who were on the defensive, and the others were enabled to concentrate on stealing back their horses. This they were able to do. It was not realized by the troops at the time, but the Indians were no doubt preparing to begin a retreat and rear guard defense if driven to it. This they were not forced to do. Some two hours before night the Indians withdrew into the thicket, and the whites did not follow them. The fight had closed.

Fossett reported that his officers had acquitted themselves honorably, and many of the soldiers fought with marked courage. Armed chiefly with shot guns and common rifles, they were at a disadvantage. One officer of the troops, Lieutenant Giddens, a good officer and a splendid man, was mortally wounded and seven men were killed. (The lieutenant died later at [John] Chisum's Ranch on the Concho, and his effects at Belknap were turned over to the quartermaster for safe keeping.) Ten men were seriously wounded. Twenty-three Indians were known to be killed and it was believed they lost seven others.

Fossett had had no chance to unite his force with that of Totten, but he now came into Totten's camp at the close of the day. The combined losses were checked and showed twenty-three killed in the battle and some sixty seriously wounded, a few of whom died later. Sixty or seventy horses were killed or disabled in the fight. Plans were suggested concerning a renewal of the fight, if the Indians could be found. But, pack horses and provisions had been left behind when the last few hurried miles of marching to the battle had begun, so now there was no food. And about ten o'clock it began snowing. Next morning there was a nine- or ten-inch snow on the ground and there was no forage for the horses. So the only alternative seemed to be to seek the settlements at the mouth of the Concho. Captain Gillentine and the other dead would be buried there. Totten was to go back with twenty-five men and see if the Indians had left. He was to bury the dead left on the field of battle. With no food and deep snow to impede their return march, the men were becoming very hungary. So, for supper, they butchered some of the few Indian ponies which had not been recaptured by the Indians because the Tonks saw what was coming and pushed away toward the pack mules some seventy-five head of them.

After the snow had melted somewhat, next day, the wounded were placed on crude litters made of two poles strapped to horses, and the men moved on down the Concho. The pack mules were intercepted on the third day and enough provisions were had for one good meal. A detail was sent out to kill some beeves, when they reached the Colorado country. Eighteen head were secured and after some three days devoted to overtaking the men, despite the lack of trail which had been obliterated by additional snow, a good meal was had from the beef. When the Chisum ranch was reached, more provisions were secured and, after a night's camping, the men made their way home in scattered groups.

. . . .

When night descended on the scene of the battle, the Indians built up fires around their encampment, packed up, and marched in a southwesterly direction, as they had been traveling, toward Mexico. They traveled across the Staked Plains in the worst snow storm in the memory of the country's oldest settlers. They no doubt suffered terribly from the cold, as it was afterwards ascertained that they lost more from the march and exposure of their wounded and the children than they had in the battle.

When Totten went back to the battle ground he found and buried the dead whites, with the exception of one man whom he could not find. The dead were unscalped, although they had been stripped of most of their clothing. Wild animals had not molested them and the bodies were in a good state of preservation due to the cold weather. The Indians had left the night after the battle and also abandoned their dead, twenty-three in number, and much of their camp equipage and cooking utensils. Only two Indians were seen and they were gathering up the scattered horses that had been left.

Fossett's report estimated that there were several hundred warriors and that the Indians were from the vicinity of the Kansas River, Kansas. Perhaps this last opinion was influenced by the finding of a pass on the body of one of the Indians from the Potawatomie Agency in Kansas. There were a few white men with them, and it was supposed by Fossett and others that they were contemplating raids on the settlements.

Later we were to learn that these Indians were a band of Kickapoos who were journeying across Texas to join their tribe in Mexico. Early in the war they had fought under orders from the Federals against the civilized tribes of Indian Territory, who were partisans of the Confederacy. It may have been that they were merely migrating across Texas with no intention of raiding at this time. Certainly they robbed and killed plenty of Texans later, operating from the south side of the Rio Grande. But Indians, with a few well known exceptions, were not supposed to be within the boundaries of Texas since 1859. The long-suffering frontiersmen who were included in this group of attacking militia had appealed to me to help crush or drive out the strange redskins.

Mexico and the United States had agreed to the migration of the Indians, but the emigrants selected a poor time – during the War Between the States – for their crossing. General Throckmorton's information on the possible identity of these Indians was wider than mine and he thought that they were merely in our State for depredations. They had no recognition, and orders from the highest authorities were to treat them accordingly as wild Indians.

1865

Monotony and Excitement on the Texas Blockade

The following excerpt was taken from a paper published in 1883 by the Rhode Island Soldiers and Sailors Historical Society. The paper was read before the annual meeting of that organization on April 17, 1883, by William F. Hutchinson,

M.D. Hutchinson served as a surgeon in the U.S. Navy during the Civil War and was on board the flagship of a blockading fleet off Galveston Island late in the war.

Source: William F. Hutchinson, *Life on the Texan Blockade* (Providence: Rhode Island Soldiers and Sailors Historical Society, 1883), pp. 6–16.

In preparing this paper, I have drawn largely from a diary which I kept at the time, and take the liberty to transcribe the first page as a fitting introduction.

On board the United States steam sloop-of-war "Lackawanna," flagship of the second division of the West Gulf Blockading Squadron, I commence this record on the fifth day of February, 1865, proposing to keep a diary of such incidents in our monotonous life as shall seem worthy of being written; both for my own amusement and to fulfill a promise. . . .

It will seem that the scene opens at a time when the war was rapidly drawing to a close, when the victorious operations of our forces had placed almost the entire coast line again under the dominion of the old flag, and when Texas, with its isolated vast territory, was practically the only region yet unattacked. To the very last, its geographical position protected it from serious attack, and but for Banks' abortive Red River movement, the war was carried on by the Navy, operating by means of a more or less rigid blockade. A glance at the map will show that this was by no means so difficult a task as the mere extent of Texan coast line would seem to indicate; for there are few harbors on its whole length, and only one of these, Galveston, capable of affording entrance to vessels of moderate draught.

Let us, then, begin our story here, sitting in an open port, gazing listlessly across three miles of brown water, rolling athwart our hawse in short white-capped waves, to Galveston Point and Fort Magruder, with the Confederate banner streaming above it. To the left is the long white sand-beach in front of the town, along which are continually strolling parties to watch the Yankee men-of-war, or occasional horsemen, exercising their steeds. Behind the sand strip rise the red roofs and spires of the city, then numbering but a few thousand souls, and to the right the smoke-stacks and rigging of the "Harriet Lane," the "Matagorda" and "Isabel," all loaded with cotton, waiting a favorable moment to run out. Along the coast, stretching in a line ten miles long, were vessels of the division, eight in number, just far enough apart and far enough from the flag-ship to be reached by signals by night or day.

The current coming out of Galveston bay here meets the coast stream from the east, and the result is a long roll which gives the vessels a steady sway that used at first to drive us nearly frantic, but which, as one grew accustomed to the motion, became as essential to our slumbers as an infant's lullaby. Inboard, the white decks of the ships glittered in the hot sun, scored by brass tracks for gun carriages and dotted with piles of solid shot, standing handily in racks near each piece. Jack tars sat sailor fashion between them, looking over ditty boxes, making or mending clothing, or spinning interminable yarns. An occasional officer moved slowly about the deck, clad in white trowsers and undress jacket, generally bringing up under the top-gallant forecastle, our smoking-room. The watch officer paced backward and forward the starboard side of the quarter-deck, and to port the midshipman of the watch and an old quarter-master kept sharp lookout for signals from the gunboats on station, and upon the enemy shore. Below, the captain – flag officer by reason of seniority – kept solitary state in his cabin; the wardroom officers made themselves snug just forward, and the warrant officers and the engineers were in the steerage, one step further forward.

. . . .

There were two bright points in our life to be kept well in view – one the chase after the blockade runners, with its possibilities of rich reward of prize money; the other, our occasional visits to New Orleans for necessary repairs, and perchance to expend some of the money accumulated during months of hermitage at sea.

On the morning of the 20th of February, while lying quietly in my berth, reading, there came from on deck the quick, loud order from the officer on watch, "Stand by the cable! Steamer close aboard!" And as the heavy iron chain slid with a splash into the water, four bells in the engine-room started the ship ahead fast, with "Hard-aport!" away we went. In less time than I have written these words, I was on deck with almost every one else, and saw a small side-wheel steamer flying past us with a most extraordinary speed. Our long vessel took several minutes to turn around, and in that time the little steamer was a mile away, going so fast as to make the shots we sent after her as harmless as rain-drops. When we got fairly under way, and the sailing master had his course giving him "direct for Morro Castle Light," we knew we were in for a long chase. With our glasses we could plainly see the piles of cotton bales on deck, and, from the torrents of black smoke pouring from her funnels, understood the desperate efforts she was making to escape. Gradually, in spite of our utmost endeavors, she drew away from us, and, while all hands were speculating on how many bales she had on board, and dividing the prize money, even arranging how it should be spent, the chances of getting at it were decreasing. All day long we steamed hard after her, and at night lost her in a cloud in the eastern sky.

Still, steadily on we went, direct for Havana bay, and when grey dawn grew out of the night, were rewarded by finding her still in sight. She made another heroic effort to escape, throwing overboard bales of cotton in dozens, hoping, I presume, that the rapacious Yankees would stop and pick them up. But we resisted all temptation, although every bale was worth five or six hundred dollars, and kept after her. About noon she began to slack up, and then it would be hard to describe the excitement aboard us. From the grave old captain to the little messenger boy a dozen years old, all were perched upon the most eligible lookouts every nerve strained to the utmost as I have often thought a pack of hounds must feel in chase of a stag. In the engine and fire-room men were working thirty minutes' reliefs, for it was so hot down there that no human being could stand it longer; and the great furnaces were devouring coal at the rate of three tons an hour. The piston rods rose and fell with quick strokes, and the whole main deck danced so under the vibrating blows of the screw that to stand was difficult. Closer and closer we drew, until the first lieutenant sang out, "Clear away the forward rifle! Train on starboard bow! Luff a little, quarter-master! Fire!" and with a cheery howl the 300-pounder shell started after our prize money. Exploding just a little short, the rain of fragments of that iron messenger upon and around the steamer was so convincing that she gave up at once and hove to until we came up. When we got alongside, a boat was lowered and a lieutenant sent on board for the captain, supercargo and any passengers she might have, who were considered as prisoners and sent North to be confined, while the ship was placed under charge of one of our officers with a prize crew whose duty it was to take her to the nearest admiralty court for condemnation.

When Mr. Jones returned, his account of the state of things aboard was pitiful. Their efforts to escape had been so great that her fireroom crew were about dead. They had been compelled to work them all steadily, not having enough to change as we did, and they were lying on deck, several dead – so the lieutenant reported – and others dying. A visit on board made at once, resulted in saving all their lives, but the men were never good for anything afterwards. The ship was the "Isabel," from Galveston for Havana, with 600 bales of cotton and no passengers. The captain and supercargo, jolly good fellows, were sent to the North, and the vessel condemned at Key West. My share was $750, which made a nice day's work and a promise of many a nice day's play.

1861–1866

The Civil War Recollections of George Bernard Erath

George B. Erath, a native of Austria, came to America in 1832 and arrived in Texas just before the Texas Revolution. When he fought with Jesse Billingsley's volunteer unit at San Jacinto, he listed surveying as his civilian occupation, but he seemed destined to achieve significance in Texas politics. Erath served in the Texas Congress during the period of the republic and was a member of the state's first legislature after annexation in 1845.

When the clouds of secession and civil war descended upon the Lone Star State, Erath was serving in the state senate. Convinced that Texans were going to be forced to fight for self-determination, he resigned his seat in the senate and raised a company of infantry. His unit, attached to the Fifteenth Infantry Regiment, saw action in Louisiana in 1862, but Erath did not fight with his unit because of poor health. Early in 1864 Governor Pendleton Murrah appointed him commander of the Second Frontier District, created by legislation passed by the Tenth Texas Legislature. The Second District contained the counties of Erath, Bosque, Coryell, Hamilton, Comanche, Brown, Lampasas, San Saba, Mason, that part of Johnson County west of the Fort Belknap and Fort Graham Road, Eastland, Coleman, Runnels, Concho, McCulloch, Menard, Kimble, Callahan, and Taylor. The First Frontier District was to the north and was commanded by Brigadier General J. W. Throckmorton; the Third Frontier District was to the south and was under the direction of Brigadier General J. D. McAdoo. The primary purpose of this new system was to defend the frontier of the state against Indians, outlaws, and foreign invaders.

During the decades following the war, Erath's poor health severely limited his public service although he was elected to the Texas Senate again and served in the Fourteenth Legislature. Numerous editors and writers in Texas displayed an interest in the aging frontiersman's earlier activities as a soldier, statesman, and Indian fighter. They urged him to write his memoirs. Therefore, in 1886, just five years before his death, he began dictating his recollections to his daughter Lucy. He was seventy-three years of age at this time, but his daughter maintained that his mind was still vigorous and "the same as it had always been" even though he was totally blind. His extraordinary recollections were published by his daughter in 1916, twenty-five years after his death. The memoirs were published again in the *Southwestern Historical Quarterly* in 1923 in Volumes 26 and 27. Erath's grave may be seen today in the Oakwood Cemetery in Waco. The following excerpt from his memoirs deals with the Civil War years.

Source: George Bernard Erath, "Memoirs of Major George Bernard Erath," comp. Lucy A. Erath, *Southwestern Historical Quarterly* 27 (October 1923): 156–161. Reprinted by permission.

I was a candidate for the State senate in the general election of the summer of 1861 and was elected. My district comprised eight counties, two of them not organized; half the district extending out on the frontier. Hill County was the only one in which I did not receive a majority of the votes. A man from that county ran against me and received a few votes over me there.

But my health was failing. From early youth I had suffered from indigestion, but never lost much time from business on that account. My friends have considered me in a very dangerous condition from an attack on one day, and the next I would be up and riding forty miles. The privations and hardships I could endure had become a matter of comment. But after the spell of sickness I now suffered, I was never as well again. My constitution had been impaired by exposures and hardships. Barely recovering for the meeting of the legislature, I never recovered the old feeling of satisfaction of life again.

The Civil War had now fairly set in. We passed another bill for a regiment for the protection of the frontier; it was to be made up on the frontier, as the men in the lower counties were in the Confederate army. The Governor appointed Col. J. M. Norris commander. By the provisions of the law the men were stationed by companies at posts a day's ride apart in a line on the outer frontier edge to meet in scouts every few days. This plan had proved a failure in the first Indian war during the revolution, and it did not answer now. The regiment was organized early in the spring of 1862, and remained in service for a little over twelve months, when its place was supplied by men raised nominally under the Confederate government. There was but little variation in the depredations of the Indians.

The legislature of 1861 was in a great measure composed of men who had little experience in legislating; those who had experience had joined the army. I would like to speak of the ideas prevailing in that legislature and entertained by many of the people at that time. Almost all of the representatives, especially those from the eastern part of the State, were totally opposed to making appropriations for anything that in the course of government had been provided by the United States. They looked upon the new government as a fixture, like an old one, with plenty of money and means to furnish anything at any expense. They were very desirous, however, that everything purchased and all services rendered be paid for at once, and well paid for. Confederate money was looked upon as beyond any possibility of depreciation. The government was urged to spend it at a rate which could not prevent its decline in value far below par at an early day. There was a difference in the conduct of the masses now and in the time of the revolution against Mexico that made me apprehensive concerning the result. In our first revolution a soldier did not speak about pay. At some time way off he expected to receive pay at the rate of eight dollars a month. The farmer or citizen, who had anything to spare and often when he couldn't spare it, handed out his produce, perhaps, without even taking a receipt. If he happened to see the officer in charge, he probably asked for a receipt, thinking it might be well if a pay day should possibly come, but nothing more than the average price was expected. But the people of the Confederacy wanted money at once, and much of it. The soldier wanted his pay, and the candidate for legislative honors demanded more than the soldiers themselves for raising the soldier's pay. The people who remained at home were the ones who had most to say about the financial affairs of the government. There were many prominent men who held the view that secession once gone into, we could not be reconquered or under any circumstances merged again in the United States. Their idea of international law forbade that the Confederacy, once on the roll of nations, could be wiped out. At the surrender some of these still expressed a decided opinion that, being defeated, we might have to pay heavy damages, perhaps lose territory, but to be brought back into the Union without consent was impossible. The prospect in 1861 loomed gloomier more from prevailing mistaken ideas than from our actual lack of strength.

After the legislature adjourned I was too restless, from the prospect of the fate of war and also from my changed health, to remain at home. I joined the army, not believing much in any service I could render, but hoping that campaign life might benefit me. Our men wanted to go on horseback. There were plenty of horses in Texas. With men available, our State could have furnished a cavalry for the war that would have vied with that of Cassacks and Tartars, or the heavy armed knights of old; but infantry was then wanted. Richard Coke had just returned from Virginia, he reasoned with the people about their inclination to ride, and raised a company of infantry. I also raised one of infantry. They became a part of a regiment known as the 15th Texas, commanded by Colonel J. W. Speight. After being organized we were stationed, until the month of June, near Millican on the Central Railroad, so as to be convenient to Galveston or elsewhere when needed. In June we received orders to march east by way of Tyler, to be merged in some army corps of the Confederacy in Louisiana or Arkansas. As I was very weak, having to be transported sick much of the time, I offered my resignation while we delayed at Tyler. It was not accepted, but I was given a furlough for three months to recuperate. My eldest son, Edwin Porter Erath, not quite sixteen years old, was with me and was discharged nominally on account of his youth to accompany me home. Later he was in a volunteer cavalry regiment and, after going through the battle of Yellow Bayou, died of fever in camp in Louisiana, still under eighteen years of age. I again tendered my resignation in September, and it was accepted. My health was worse, but in 1863 I was recovered enough to transact business and to ride to town seven miles away.

On going into the army I had vacated my place in the legislature, which met three or four times during the year to devise means to help the Confederacy. The frontier was unprotected, and the legislature passed a law calling out the militia in the frontier counties. They were to act on the minute plan; that is a few were to be always scouting, the rest to be in readiness at any time called. They were to furnish everything themselves, except perhaps ammunition, and were to receive at some future time scant pay in Confederate money. The belt of frontier counties was divided into three districts, and a field officer with the rank, pay, and emoluments of major of cavalry, was placed in command of each district. In the first days of January, 1864, I was surprised by an express from the Governor tendering me a commission to command the middle district. I accepted and repaired at once to the frontier and established my headquarters in Gatesville, about central so far as east and west was concerned, San Saba being the extreme western and Johnson the eastern county. Palo Pinto and the counties due west belonged to the first or northern district. I had some six or eight counties in my district, containing in all fourteen companies and about a thousand men. This service was in the nature of local protection. Only in case of formidable invasion were the men to be taken out of their counties; but they frequently scouted in adjoining counties. I was to see the service performed, travel around through the different counties, inspect, and give directions. I still had frequent attacks of illness, which sometimes rendered me so weak I could not mount a horse without assistance, though often, once mounted, I rode the whole day.

The Indians had changed considerably. They were now dressed in clothes, were well armed and, with their usual activity and sagacity, moved faster than in old days and hid their tracks better. They could hardly be surprised, and when surprised, or in surprising our scouts, they were more daring and braver, at least at the onset, than of old. Small parties of my men had frequent encounters with small parties of Indians; the losses on each side were about equal.

About the time the Confederacy surrendered, the Indians were showing a disposition for peace, as evidenced by interviews between them and General Throckmorton, who then commanded the northern district. But the collapse of the Confederacy frustrated any plans, and after the surrender depredations were continued with more vigor than before. The Indians held to their old idea that the people of Texas were a different tribe from those of the United States, and that they could make war on the one without the other having a right to interfere.

At the close of the year, 1864, while I was at Austin, under orders to report there for a consultation, a party of about a hundred Kickapoos crossed Red River, on their way to emigrate to Mexico. They had with them their families and property, and seemed not disposed to molest any one on the way. They had roamed through Texas in early days, depredated in Mexico, and, at the request of Mexico, had been removed by the United States to the northern part of the Indian Territory about 1854. In the early days of the Civil War they had been employed by the Union against the civilized Indians of the Territory, who were taking part with the South. Tired of that strife they had now come to some arrangement with Mexico to settle in her territory. What they might have done later against Texas from Mexico is a matter of conjecture. Their entrance into Texas aroused the frontier at once; and the old inability to make distinctions between Indians remained as before. A small Confederate troop was started after them; messages were sent to all the counties in my district; everything available was put in motion under Captain Totten, senior officer in my absence. He fell in with Captain Forest of the Confederate force, who outranked him, and under the Confederate commander they reached the Indian camp on the Concho River. Without any reconnoitering the camp was charged at once. The Indians were armed with improved guns; they were good marksmen. The whites were repulsed; in vain they rallied two or three times, and were at last obliged to fall back to a sheltered place with their wounded. The Indians moved away in haste, crossed the Rio Grande, and continued to annoy western Texas for years afterward as the Comanches did the northern part. The affair might have been prevented. The Indians had talked to the settlers all along the route. A flag of truce should have been sent them; and if fighting had to be it should have been after they moved on from such a strong position. I would have allowed them to pass had I been there – that is if I could have controlled the frontiersmen, always crazed at the sight of Indians, and determined to kill.

The confusion after Lee's and Johnston's surrender threatened lawlessness. Men who called themselves soldiers rushed to Texas, probably because their war time misdeeds prevented their remaining at home. But the good, true soldiery, who had fought for the South, now came again to the front to maintain and quiet the country. Their declaration of a determination to yield to the laws of the land and to uphold order had its effect and much violence was prevented. A number of citizens, many of them our best, believing that they could not again live under the United States, tried Mexico, but they soon returned.

I was of the ranks of those broken financially. Like many another old Texan I had been careless of accumulating. Now prewar debts, incurred by going security for others, had to be paid. My own longstanding notes against others were paid in Confederate money at a late moment when one must take it or seem to throw doubt on the Confederacy. With ill health, old age, and new times to combat, I had to start again.

1861–1866

A Northern Impression of
Texas and Texans

Thomas North's *Five Years in Texas,* published in 1871, contains many of the author's observations, experiences, and impressions gained from his travels around the Lone Star State from January 1861 to January 1866. Although he resided in Brenham part of that time, he visited several major towns and made at least two railroad trips to Houston. These tours evidently led North to consider himself something of an authority on Texans because he was able to study the "native peoples" in several regions. The "we" he mentions may simply be the editorial "we" or could refer to his family, but, at any rate, he does not share with his readers any information concerning his traveling companions, if he had any. His having "officiated" at a funeral, his occasional reference to biblical concepts, and his frequent use of King James phraseology suggest that he was either a lay preacher or a Bible scholar. He found little in the rough and violent "dark corner" which he appreciated, and he encountered few Texans whom he liked or admired. He especially thought the lower classes contemptible and was horrified by the lack of concern for human life.

Source: Thomas North, *Five Years in Texas* (Cincinnati: Elm Street Printing Company, 1871), pp. 102–105, 155–161.

Unlike the other Southern States, Texas was never invaded and devastated by the Union armies. Considered in the light of a necessary evil, as a terrible educator, or rough civilizer for the barbarian element in Texas society; it might have been a good thing, perhaps, if she had been overrun, and this low element thoroughly subjugated, and made feel and understand that there was another force in the world besides Texas outlawry – that of law and order. But all things considered, it is probably as well she was saved from such a scourging. The innocent would have suffered with the guilty, and many lives and much property been sacrificed.

Texas was never whipped in spirit, only nominally whipped, in being surrendered by the official act of General E. Kirby Smith. Like "dog Tray," she was found in bad company. Indeed, so far from being whipped in spirit was she, that the proposition was seriously made and entertained, after Lee's surrender, that Texas could carry on the war by herself, and alone win what the whole South had failed to achieve together. General Magruder issued a bombastic proclamation to this effect. But the more sensible people understood it as a shrewd blind on his part, to facilitate his escape to Mexico, which he made immediately after.

By no means would we leave the impression that the whole population felt this way. The intelligent and better classes plainly saw, and admitted that their cause was irretrievably lost, and in justice to them we must say they were willing to accept the situation in good faith, and govern themselves accordingly. One of this class said to the writer: "I have fought the fight, been whipped, and now I submit and say, the United States Government is good enough for me, and hereafter I am as good a Union man as the best."

But we must say of the other class that swallowed Magruder's proclamation, that they did not accept the situation in good faith, Have not yet, and never will so long as they can keep the waters Muddy. For the benefit of this class, if they could have suffered alone, one could have desired Sherman's or Sheridan's army to pass through the country and give it a touch of devastation. You wish to know what class they were. We give the following description: They were a mixed class with very little of the good in the mixture. . . .

The masses of them wore spurs on their heels, generally the immense wheel-spur, and though they were not born with them on, yet they might as well have been, for they not only rode in them, but walked in them, ate in them, and slept in them. Their clanking as they walked was like a man in chains. They wore belts around the waist, suspending one or two revolvers and a bowie knife; were experts in the saddle, had a reckless dare-evil look, and were always ready for whiskey and a big chew of tobacco, and the handwriting of passion and appetite was all over them. They were cow-boys from the wild woods and prairies, and sons of the low class planters, with a strong sprinkling of the low white trash, clay-eaters, so plentiful in the Atlantic Southern States.

In such a flock the one that has killed his man or more is hero and leader. This class of desperadoes were tools of the more accomplished, genteel, oily-tongued, respectable scoundrels in society, who sat behind the screens in the green-room of iniquity, and were the wire-pulling promoters of crime – such as intimidation, robbery, assassination, and so on. Especially was this the case during the war. It is impossible to understand, without experience, the situation of unmitigated horror created by such surroundings. One can talk about it, and the hearer or reader can imagine, but experience alone realizes the full horror.

. . . .

In the summer of 1863, we were coming up the Texas Central Railroad, from Houston to Hempstead, a distance of fifty miles.

On reaching the latter place we stepped from the cars to the depot platform, and in a minute heard a pistol-shot on the opposite side of the train. Thought nothing strange of it till in a moment more some one remarked: "A man is shot." And even then thought nothing unusual of it. The feeling of terror was only a uniform matter of course. But stepping across the way we observed a crowd gathering at an unoccupied store building, went in and there saw a man on the counter, stretched at full length on his back, struggling in his blood, and breathing heavily, with a bullet-hole through his head and brains protruding. Near by him stood his murderer, Dr. O——r, with *nonchalance* and a smile of fiendish satisfaction.

The dying man had been overseer on his murderer's plantation. A difference had arisen between Mrs. O——r and the overseer about the management of the plantation. And the lady, true to Southern instinct, could not brook opposition from an overseer, so she writes herself "insulted" to the doctor in the army, and home he comes in a rage by the train we were on, and spying the unsuspecting offender through the car window, leaps out and shoots him down at sight without warning. No one looked strange or excited, or said a word. We walked back to the train in disgust, feeling it may be our turn next. Went home to B[renha]m, twenty-five miles, and the next morning a friend of ours – a druggest, Dr. F——g, from Paducah, Kentucky, at the opening of the war – was assassinated on the public streets. The writer officiated at his funeral from his widowed mother's house, who was thus robbed of her only son and support in old age. The sheriff of Washington County witnessed the transaction, and had foreknowledge of it, but did nothing officially to prevent or punish the crime. The name of the assassin was B——t, who, the writer learns, has since come to a similar end himself in the state of Mississippi, thus illustrating the innate reflex, as it were, of the law of retributive justice that neither sleeps nor slumbers till it has blood for blood, life for life! The murdered man's mother and only sister are since deceased, hurried out of the world by the great sorrow of his untimely and tragic end!

One night after the family had retired several pistol-shots were fired back of our house, attended with boisterous talking. Dressing, we went to the back window, and there saw a man in the moonlight falling to the ground. Just then a voice at the front of the house called: "Mr. N., Mr. N., come down here, I want to see you quick!" Descending the outside stairway leading from the upper to the lower gallery, we met our friend, Captain C., who instantly exclaimed: "Mr. N., I have shot my best friend all to pieces. Please go and look after him. I must leave. You will find me at Dr. B.'s or about there." We went to the dying man, and found several collected around him. He had two shots through the knee and thigh, the latter cutting a big artery, and he bled to death in a few minutes. . . .

We will now relate an incident, with which the writer was still more personally connected, to illustrate the bitter prejudices a Northern man had to meet living in that country. Yes, prejudice! a thing conceived in sin, born in iniquity, twin of jealousy, and equally cruel; one of the relics of barbarism still clinging to poor human nature, tormenting its waking hours and its dreams by night, lurking in the soul's deep recesses, and in the thoughts of the brain, displaying in its action all the bristling, snarling, growling, barking, and snapping suspicion of the canine race, ready to pitch on every strange dog passing the street. It may be further characterized as the blindest, most unreasonable, hateful and hating, and most desperately wicked passion of the human soul. It casts its blighting mildew over everything it touches.

. . . .

But why do we thus comment? Because in our five years' Texas experience we met this monster of the human heart in shapes and phases, deeper, and more vile than we had ever dreamed of before, or could have dreamed if we had never seen Texas. There is a barbarous element that assumes a more lawless and criminal form than in any other country we ever saw. There it hesitates not at doing personal violence to its object. And so much the more as they value human life less than other people. Comparatively, Northern people can scarcely imagine what prejudice means except in milder forms, and as defined in dictionaries, pulpit theories, and so forth.

A lady friend said to us on our return from that country: "Mr. N., you ought to be a wiser man for what you have seen in Texas." A gentleman was kind enough to say to us: "Served you right, you had no business to go there in the first place." Now we do not of course ask the alms of sympathy in our Texas experience, particularly from such as might feel harmed by the exercise of that noble grace, but simply appear as the writer of a little personal history. Perhaps no Northern man was more unfortunately situated in Texas than the writer. He had gone there just a few months prior to the war, which, to the eye of prejudice, was evidence, *prima facie,* that he was a spy, or something else inimical to the country's welfare.

1864–1866

"Forting Up" after the Elm Creek Raid

Even though the Confederate and Texas governments were fully aware of the need to protect residents of the Texas frontier from Indian depredations during the Civil War, little was done officially because of the shortage of both men and equipment. Local inhabitants thus had to establish their own makeshift defense systems. The "forting up" practice was developed early in the state's history and was used successfully until the end of organized Indian warfare in the 1870s.

The forting up system was logical and simple. Recognizing that there was safety and strength in numbers and seeking the advantages of inside lines in a well-fortified central location, residents of a community or perhaps an entire region constructed a communal fortress in a place accessible to all. Often this was done simply by converting several sturdy business houses or a massive church building into a defense complex, well stocked with arms, munitions, and supplies. An effective and sometimes elaborate alarm system was devised so that families of the area could retire to the centrally located defense establishment whenever the signal went out that Indians were in the region. Everyone had a specific duty or responsibility in the operation, and each was expected to do the job because the lives of everyone in the community might depend on it. Usually women and small children entrenched themselves in carefully designated locations, selected with maximum safety in mind, and were told to stay there until the danger had passed.

The system worked, but its continued effectiveness rested on local residents not becoming complacent. After a degree of safety was thought to exist in a region, residents sometimes allowed their defense systems to break down. This is essentially what happened in Young County in the fall of 1864.

In October a large band of Comanches and Kiowas attacked settlements along Elm Creek, a tributary of the Brazos some ten miles west of Fort Belknap. Men, women, and children – many caught completely unaware – were slaughtered in this unfortunate affair, and several white and black captives were carried off by Indians. Except for a young girl named Millie Durgan, most of the captives were eventually released through the remarkable efforts of an African American frontiersman who tracked down the marauders, gained their confidence, and bargained for the release of the captives. Millie Durgan married a Kiowa chief named Goombi and produced a sizable family. The black frontiersman, a slave named "Nigger Britt," who belonged to a Brazos country rancher, was killed by Indians in the spring of 1871 near present-day Newcastle on the old Butterfield Trail. The Indians left the hapless man with his genitals removed and stuffed in his mouth and his stomach slit open and a dead dog inside.

After the Elm Creek raid, residents of Young County took greater precautions to bolster their local defense system. The following excerpt contains an account of the raid and a description of the forting up activities that followed. It also provides glimpses into camp life at Fort Davis and Camp Cooper, scalphunting expeditions of Texas pioneers, and the ordinary day-to-day activities of frontier living. There can be no doubt that those who survived on the Indian frontier of Texas during the Civil War did so by remaining vigilant and prepared to fight to the death if necessary.

Source: Phin W. Reynolds, "Chapters from the Frontier Life of Phin W. Reynolds," comp. J. R. Webb, *West Texas Historical Association Year Book* 21 (1945): 113–120. Reprinted by permission.

For a few years after our arrival in Stephens County there were few Indian raids of any consequence until the big Indian raid down Elm Creek, in Young County, in 1864. Just prior to our arrival in the county, Jno. R. Baylor, who was a noted Indian fighter and hated the Indians, was desirous of avenging the death of the Browning boys; so he got up a party consisting of Tom Stockton (who was another noted fighter and who afterward established a ranch seven miles south of Raton, New Mexico, on the Santa Fe Trail), Min Wright, John Dawson, and two others and they went on an Indian hunt up in the Phantom Hill country and brought back about a dozen scalps. The Stockton family were neighbors of ours and there were three boys in the family, Tom, Rex and Thipe. A short time before their hunt the Indians had raided their place and killed around sixty sheep.

I remember well the big Indian raid down Elm Creek in Young County although I was but six years old at the time. A large force of warriors of the Comanche and Kiowa tribes, estimated by the settlers as between five hundred and one thousand men, swooped down the Elm Creek valley murdering and pillaging as they went. There were a number of men and women killed, and other women and children carried away into captivity. There was a man whose name I cannot recall whom you might call the Paul Revere of this raid and who was responsible for the saving of many lives. Seeing the approaching warriors in their war paint he rode furiously down the valley warning all in their path, thus enabling the men to make hurried preparations to fight and in most cases hide their women and children.

George Bragg and eight men stood the Indians off at his house. Uncle Bill Bragg had gone to Weatherford for supplies but his wife and their little boys and girls were at home. They were warned by the rider and hurried to a hideout, a shelving rock on the banks of a nearby creek. With them to this shelter they carried a little dog owned by the boys and there was dire fear that as the Indians approached their nearby home he might bark. Although they watched the Indians ramsack the house and tear apart and scatter the feathers from their pillows the little dog seeming to sense the danger, kept quiet even more so than the little boys. For one of the boys watching the pillaging and remembering that they had some unhulled pecans drying on the roof of the house whispered that he sure hoped they did not get those pecans. His mother warned him to be quiet, and that he would be lucky if they did not get his scalp. After thoroughly

pillaging the contents of the house and carrying away all they did not destroy, they started down the creek and directly toward this hideout. Although they passed along the bank above them close enough for the
tread of their mocassined feet to be heard, quiet prevailed under the protecting rock and they were not discovered. Upon receiving news of the
raid a number of men including my brother, George, went immediately
to the scene and helped bury the dead.

Two little girls, Lottie and Millie Durgan, and the wife of a negro
named Britt were captured and carried away by the Indians. Britt was
away at the time, having gone to Weatherford for supplies but upon his
return he trailed the Indians to the Indian Territory. He could talk their
language and he succeeded in trading with them for his wife and for Lottie Durgan, but Millie had disappeared. She was not heard of thereafter
until four or five years ago when she was discovered and identified in
Oklahoma, the squaw of an Indian and the mother of a number of half-
breed children. A short time after she was identified, she was in attendance [in 1932] at the Old Settlers Reunion in Young County, but has
since then died. When we lived at Fort Griffin the Durgans lived near
there and I went to school with Lottie and I well remember the tribal
brand, a red and blue circle on her forehead, which the Indians had
branded there while she was in captivity.

There was a great deal of excitement among the settlers after this raid
which occurred in the Fall of 1864, as it was realized that the families,
scattered as they were, were unable to protect themselves from the murderous bands of Indians prowling the country. Furthermore, we had no
rangers or soldiers on the frontier as there was an acute shortage of manpower in the Confederacy in the last years of the War. It was up to the
few settlers in the country to protect themselves. Many of the families
abandoned the frontier and left for the interior settlements. Those who
were determined to face the dangers and remain were called together for
discussion as to the ways and means of providing protection for their
families. It was decided to "fort up," that is, for the settlers in different
sections to come together and build their houses in close proximity so
that they would be gathered in groups, thus providing larger forces of
men to repel Indian raids. This was done and these communities of
houses were termed forts, though they were forts in no literal sense as
they had neither soldiers nor artillery. They did have men who were
called upon for guard duty and scouting purposes. The settlers who oc-

cupied these forts or communities spoke of having "forted up" during the War and it is so spoken of until this day. In our section were several such forts, one known as Fort Davis being the largest. . . .

Our family moved to Fort Davis which was built in the form of a square, and a picket stockade was started but never completed. It was to be constructed around all the houses, but as the scare died down somewhat work on it ceased. I can remember the houses and their owners and where each house was located. Our house was on the southwest corner of the hollow square; next door to the north was that of John Hittson who was the wealthiest man in the country; next was the home of Jim Thorpe; and next to his was the house of Matt Franz. He had been the stage line agent at Clear Fork Station of the Butterfield Stage Line until the stage line was abandoned at the outbreak of the Civil War. Next in order were the homes of Mich Anderson, A. Anderson, the Sutherlin family, and then the school house which was the northeast corner of the square. Sam Newcomb, my brother-in-law, who taught the school and kept a diary of events at the fort, occupied a house within the square. John G. Irwin who had a meat contract at Camp Cooper before the war also lived within the square. . . .

John Selman and his mother occupied the house on the east side of the square next to the school house. His mother gave me, while we were living at the fort, the first apple I ever saw. John Selman (pronounced Silman) was afterward to become a noted person and . . . killed the noted outlaw, John Wesley Hardin. . . . Next in order lived the families of T. E. Jackson, Alex Clark, January, Mich McCarty, Marion McCarty, Elgy Christenson, and last and next to our house was that of an old free negro known as Aunt Maria. When Joe Browning married Angelina McCarty at the fort the bride borrowed her wedding dress from Aunt Maria. After this wedding they had a big candy pulling and the candy was made from sorghum syrup boiled in a wash pot. Most all of the houses at the fort were constructed of pickets.

. . . .

At the outbreak of the Civil War, Camp Cooper, a well known government fort which was located on the Clear Fork near the mouth of Tecumseh Creek in Throckmorton County, was abandoned by the Federals, occupied for a short time by Texas rangers under Colonel Buck Barry and then was permanently abandoned as a fort. John and Bill Hittson moved into the fort and were occupying it at the time of the Elm Creek

Raid and continued to live there after most of the settlers had "forted up." A short while after this raid they were cow hunting on Tecumseh and only a few miles from the fort. With them were two cowboys, Press McCarty and a negro whose name I do not now recall. Suddenly and without warning a band of Comanches were seen charging down upon them. Outnumbered and taken by surprise, the Hittsons started a running fight and made for a well known bluff on Tecumseh Creek, where there was an overhanging rock which would provide some shelter. Before reaching it both Hittsons were wounded by arrows, Bill being pinned to his saddle by an arrow through his thigh, but both were able to dismount and get under the rock. The negro was further away but started racing for the same destination with the Indians in hot pursuit. In his haste he lost his hat. Instead of abandoning it to the Indians, he seemed to think more of it than he did the chances for his life; for he stopped, jumped from his horse to get it, and this move, or you might say the loss of that hat, cost his life. He was overtaken and killed before reaching the bluff. Press McCarty in the meanwhile, instead of joining the others and making for the bluff, left in the direction of Fort Davis, and succeeded in reaching there without harm. The Hittons, in spite of their wounds, backed up under the rock and fought off the Indians.

One of them told me that the Indians were afraid to make a frontal attack but made repeated attempts to roll big rocks down from above, trying to make them hit a tree just in front of the shelter and bounce back against them. In this they failed and withdrew from the fight. The Hittons reached the fort before a rescue party which was being formed had left there. After this they moved their family to the protection of the fort.

What has always been known in his section as the Old Stone Ranch was . . . built of stone by Captain Newt Givens, an officer at old Camp Cooper. The date it was built was 1856, or at least that date was carved in a keystone in the old ranch house. It is located on Walnut Creek three miles from the Clear Fork and in southwestern Throckmorton County. When Camp Cooper was abandoned at the outbreak of the Civil War the ranch house was vacated. During the War it was occupied for a short time by Knox and Gardner, a cow outfit, but they too abandoned it. In 1866 the settlers started leaving Fort Davis and returning to their ranches or starting new ones on the range. My father in that year moved his family to this old stone ranch house.

Reminiscences of a
Returning Confederate Veteran

The institution of slavery extinguished much of the African Americans' self-reliance and independent judgment. Compassion for the freedmen after the war was in short supply and came to be regarded as the leading cause of the conflict. Congressional Reconstruction, imposed on Texas and all other states of the old Confederacy except Tennessee, did little to improve the average Texan's disposition toward the newly enfranchised blacks or the "Black Republican" party. Many of these views are reflected in William Walton's *Reminiscences,* written in 1914 and published in 1965.

During the war, Major William M. "Buck" Walton served under General Henry E. McCulloch and General Richard Taylor in Arkansas, Mississippi, and Louisiana. Walton was with his unit near the Atchafalaya River in Louisiana in April 1865, when he learned that his wife was near death at their home in Austin, Texas. Although it had been rumored for several days that the war was over, Walton did not learn of Lee's surrender until he began his journey to Austin to attend his wife.

After his wife had experienced an almost miraculous recovery, Walton sent her and their four children to visit with friends in New Orleans while he remained in Austin to try to "straighten up things at home." The economic depression caused by the war made Walton's efforts to find employment and settle his debts extremely difficult, but he treated the freedmen with humanity and respect. Walton had much in common with David C. Nance, the author of the first excerpt in this volume. Both men displayed an intelligent attitude toward the blacks, possessed a well-above-average education, and served in the famous Parsons's Brigade in Arkansas and Louisiana.

Source: Major Buck Walton, *An Epitome of My Life: Civil War Reminiscences* (Austin: Waterloo Press, 1965), pp. 93–94. Reprinted by permission.

When I came home from the army, I had no money – no clothes – but one pair of gray pants and two flannel shirts – and my celebrated black buck skin suit – that was full of holes. Before I went to the army I had bought a house for $3000 – paid 1500 – and owed the balance – so when I was done soldiering – I had nothing but a wife and four children and a house with something like about $2200 due on it. My Negroes had all been freed, & they were poorer than I was. Two of the men wanted to stay with me, and work on as they had been – but I would not permit them. I could not afford to do it – I had nothing for them to do – and it was too bad for me to hire them out & live on the money coming therefrom. They were nothing but big black children – and had to knock against the world and learn something of life. I interested myself for them however – and got one a good place as a porter with Mssrs Sampson & Henricks at $50 a month – & the other I sent to the country to farm – and towed him along till he could make a crop. Both of these blacks lived a long time – did well, & were respected by all the people who knew them. Their names were Denmark & Bill Walton. They were good Democrats – and when candidates came to them, they would say, see Mass William – as he votes, we vote.

What did I do, just after the war – when I was so poorly off. I did anything that I could lay my hands to. I hunted – killed geese – ducks & squirrels & sold them. I fished, & brought the fish to market – was employed by Sampson & Henricks to go to Brenham – on some business – and walked back to save the stage charge ($15). I wrote for Frank Brown, District Clerk – bring up old records. I copied the opinions of the Supreme Court for publication in the Houston Telegraph. I did this – that – and – everything there was a dollar for me in. You must know I was disfranchised, and could not vote. I was disbarred as a lawyer, and could not practice my profession. The Federal authorities took my vote and licence away, I was in a very bad row of stumps. But I anticipate things as they happened. In August 1866, I was elected Atty. General of the State – and my affairs grew a little more agreeable. We had reorganized the State Government when Gov. Throckmorton was elected Governor, Geo. W. Jones, Lt. Governor – Col. Robards, Comptroller, and as I have said, I was Attorney General. The government worked smoothly, and all was beginning to be prosperous and to have a peaceful outlook – when in 1867 – the military of the United States took possession of everything – which was the beginning of the direct confusion to last seven years. We were all turned out of office, to the last man, State – District, and County – and the State put under military rule.

Appendix 1

List of Names Attached to the Texas Ordinance of Secession

In all, 171 Texans signed the ordinance of secession in Austin. These men were lawyers, soldiers, farmers, ranchers, merchants, physicians, preachers, and officers of the state and central governments. The name of the president of the convention, associate justice of the Texas Supreme Court O. M. Roberts, is the most prominent on the document, but those of Texas attorney general George M. Flournoy, former governor H. R. Runnels, and U.S. congressman John H. Reagan are also on the list. Other Texans of distinction who attached their signatures to the document were W. B. Ochiltree, William S. Oldham, William "Dirty-Neck" Scurry, Richard Coke, Benjamin F. Terry, "Ox-Cart John" Ireland, and John S. "Rip" Ford. The names of men of foreign as well as native birth, young men, old men, men of middle age, urban dwellers, rural folk, poor men, and men of great wealth were on the list. Almost all classes, professions, and religious affiliations were represented. The list reflects a cross-section of the white population of East Texas, where immigrants from the Deep South were predominant.

The 171 names attached to the Texas secession ordinance in 1861, including three that were added on or after March 2, appear below.

Source: Dudley G. Wooten, ed., *A Comprehensive History of Texas,* 2 vols. (Dallas: William G. Scarff, 1898), 2:104–106.

O. M. Roberts, President	James M. Anderson	S. W. Beasley
	T. S. Anderson	John Box
	James R. Armstrong	H. Newton Burdett
Edwin Waller	Richard L. Askew	James M. Burroughs
L. A. Abercrombie	W. S. J. Adams	John I. Burton
W. A. Allen	William C. Batte	S. E. Black

W. T. Blythe
Amzi Bradshaw
R. Weakly Brahan
A. S. Broaddus
John Henry Brown
Robert C. Campbell
Lewis F. Casey
William Chambers
T. J. Chambers
John Green Chambers
N. B. Charlton
George W. Chilton
Isham Chisum
William Clark, Jr.
J. A. Clayton
Charles L. Cleveland
A. G. Clopton
Richard Coke
James E. Cook
John W. Dancy
A. H. Davidson
C. Deen
Thomas J. Devine
Thomas C. Davenport
James L. Diamond
William K. Diamond
John Donelson
Joseph H. Dunham
Edward Dougherty
H. H. Edwards
Elbert Early
John N. Fall
Drury Field
John H. Feeney
George M. Flournoy
Spencer Ford
John S. Ford
Thomas C. Frost

Amos P. Gallaway
Charles Ganahl
Robert S. Gould
Robert Graham
Malcolm D. Graham
Peter W. Gray
John A. Green
John Gregg
William P. Hardeman
John B. Hayes
Philemon T. Herbert
A. W. O. Hicks
Thomas B. J. Hill
Alfred M. Hobby
John L. Hogg
J. J. Holt
James Hooker
Edward R. Hord
Russell Howard
A. Clark Hoyl
Thomas P. Hughes
J. W. Hutcheson
John Ireland
Thomas J. Jennings
F. Jones
W. C. Kelly
T. Koester
C. M. Lesueur
F. W. Latham
Pryor Lea
James S. Lester
John Littleton
M. F. Locke
Oliver Loftin
Thomas S. Lubbock
P. N. Luckett
Henry A. Maltby
Jesse Marshall

Manes M. Maxey
Lewis W. Moore
William McCraven
William McIntosh
Gilchrist McKay
Thomas M. McCraw
William Goodloe Miller
Albert N. Mills
Thomas Moore
Thomas C. Moore
Charles De Montel
B. F. Moss
John Muller
Thomas J. Nash
A. Nauendorf
T. C. Neel
Allison Nelson
James F. Newsom
W. M. Neyland
E. B. Nichols
A. J. Nicholson
E. P. Nicholson
James M. Norris
Alfred T. Obenchain
W. B. Ochiltree
William S. Oldham
R. J. Palmer
W. M. Payne
W. K. Payne
William M. Peck
W. R. Poag
Alexander Pope
David Y. Portis
D. M. Prendergast
Walter F. Preston
E. P. Price
A. T. Rainey
John H. Reagan

C. Rector

P. G. Rhome

E. S. C. Robertson

J. C. Robertson

J. B. Robertson

William P. Rogers

James H. Rogers

Edward M. Ross

John Rugeley

H. R. Runnels

E. B. Scarborough

William T. Scott

William Redi Scurry

James E. Shepard

Sam S. Smith

Gideon Smith

John D. Stell

John G. Stewart

Charles Stewart

F. S. Stockdale

William H. Stewart

Pleasant Taylor

B. F. Terry

Nathaniel Terry

E. Thomason

James G. Thompson

W. S. Todd

James Walworth

R. H. Ward

William Warren

James C. Watkins

John A. Wharton

Joseph P. Weir

John A. Wilcox

A. P. Wiley

Ben Williams

Jason Wilson

Philip A. Work

D. M. Stapp

John A. Chambers

Eli H. Baxter

Appendix II

Confederate Military Organization

The following information on Confederate military organization was compiled and written by Harold B. Simpson, noted author and publisher of Texas Confederate history.

Source: Harold B. Simpson in Marcus J. Wright, *Texas in the War,* ed. Simpson (Hillsboro: Hill Junior College Press, 1965), p. xviii. Reprinted by permission.

INFANTRY

Company (115 men at full strength)

Four officers captain, 1st lieutenant, 2nd lieutenant, 3rd lieutenant (or Jr. 2nd lieutenant or ensign).

Nine noncommissioned officers 1st or orderly sergeant, 2nd, 3rd, 4th and 5th sergeants; 1st, 2nd, 3rd and 4th corporals.

Two musicians (usually one drummer and one fifer).

One hundred privates.

Battalion

Any organization of two companies or more, or less than ten companies. Usually five companies.

Regiment

Usually ten companies. Occasionally eleven or twelve companies would be assigned together to make an overstrength regiment.

Brigade

Two to five regiments with four being the most common.

Division

Two to four brigades – occasionally five brigades. Four brigades to a division was the most common arrangement.

Corps

Usually two divisions.

Army

Usually two corps.

CAVALRY

Organization and strength for Texas Confederate cavalry units followed the infantry pattern. Occasionally the basic organization was referred to as a troop instead of a company.

ARTILLERY

Confederate field artillery batteries had both four and six guns assigned with the latter number being the most common. The gun batteries were generally of mixed caliber. There was no pattern to the organization or gun assignments of coastal, fixed or rocket batteries. The only formalized Texas artillery regiment, the 1st Texas Heavy Artillery, had eleven companies, one over strength. As a matter of fact, Texas Confederate artillery units except for a select few, were undermanned, poorly organized and deficient in both equipment and animals.

LEGION

In the Confederate army a legion generally consisted of one or two battalions of infantry (six to twelve companies), one battalion of cavalry (four to six companies), and a battery of light artillery (four to six guns).

Appendix III

Events Significant to
Texas and Texans

The following chronology was initially compiled by Professor John Duncan of Texas A & M University and was entitled "Important Events in Texas, 1861–1865." Since I have made extensive alterations in the original list to achieve a greater degree of congruity, the title has been changed to reflect my modifications. Many events that occurred beyond the borders of the Lone Star State and even outside the Confederate Trans-Mississippi Department have been added if they seemed to hold special significance for Texans. Confederate defeats at Antietam and Gettysburg, for example, were important to Texans because they altered the course of the war and involved relatives and friends fighting in Hood's Brigade and other Texas units. Many events described in the excerpts of this volume have been added even if they are of limited significance in the history of the state. Fremantle's arrival in 1863, for example, was inserted to indicate where it fit among the more important events that formed the essential currents of the war. Events on Professor Duncan's list that have been removed, although often significant, were either beyond the theme of this book or thought to be confusing or unnecessarily burdensome to the reader. Dates, places, and events discussed in the excerpts are sometimes slightly in error, but those included in this list are believed to be correct. It is my hope that this modified list will aid the reader in establishing the proper sequence of events, reveal how certain incidents fit together to form the larger picture of the war, and illuminate certain shadowy but noteworthy historical movements that make the story of Civil War Texas unique.

Source: Based on John Duncan's "Important Events in Texas, 1861–1865," in Marcus J. Wright, *Texas in the War,* ed. Harold B. Simpson (Hillsboro: Hill Junior College Press, 1956), pp. 197–204. Used by permission.

1861

January

5 Destruction of the printing office of *Die Union* in Galveston by a mob. Gigantic secessionist rally at flagpole at Hancock Corner in Austin.

9 Convention in Mississippi passes an ordinance of secession.

10 Convention in Florida passes an ordinance of secession.

11 Convention in Alabama passes an ordinance of secession.

19 Convention in Georgia passes an ordinance of secession.

21 The state legislature convenes in Austin in compliance with Governor Sam Houston's proclamation of December 17, 1860.

26 Convention in Louisiana passes an ordinance of secession.

28 The state legislature approves a joint resolution authorizing the impending state convention to act for the people of Texas on the question of secession.

The Secession Convention meets in Austin by request of prominent citizens (O. M. Roberts, George Flournoy, Guy M. Bryan, W. S. Oldham, and John Marshall) made on December 3, 1860.

30 The Committee of Public Safety appointed by the Secession Convention.

February

1 An ordinance of secession approved by the Secession Convention.

2 Committee of Public Safety directed to seize all Federal property in Texas.

4 The Secession Convention adjourns until March 2. Representatives of six Southern states (Texas not represented) meet in Montgomery, Alabama, to organize the Confederate government.

6 Address to the people of Texas by the opponents of secession (D. G. Burnett, E. M. Pease, E. J. Davis, A. J. Hamilton, J. W. Throckmorton, John and George Hancock).

9 Proclamation by Governor Houston ordering an election to be held on February 23 for ratification or rejection of the ordinance of secession.

The called session of the legislature adjourns until March 18.

16 The U.S. Army military post in San Antonio seized by representatives and forces under orders of the Committee of Safety.

General David E. Twiggs surrenders U.S. military posts in Texas.

R. E. Lee arrives in San Antonio from Fort Mason on his way to Washington, D.C.

19 Colonel Carlos A. Waite succeeds General Twiggs as U.S. Army commander, Department of Texas.

21 U.S. property at Brazos Santiago seized by Colonel John S. "Rip" Ford's volunteers upon orders of the Committee of Safety.

23 State election held to ratify or reject the ordinance of secession.

26 Camp Colorado, Coleman County, abandoned by U.S. troops.

March

1 General Twiggs dismissed from U.S. Army service.

2 John Butterfield's Southern Overland Mail Company terminates operation.

The Secession Convention reconvenes in Austin. Declaration of the state's separation from the United States.

The U.S. revenue schooner *Henry Dodge* seized by armed forces acting under orders from the Committee of Safety.

4 Votes canvassed on secession ordinance: for secession, 46,129; against, 14,697.

7 Fort Ringgold, Starr County, and Camp Verde, Kerr County, abandoned by U.S. troops.

12 Camp McIntosh, Webb County, abandoned by U.S. troops.

15 Camp Wood, Real County, abandoned by U.S. troops.

16 The Confederate oath of office administered to state officials in the presence of the Secession Convention; Governor Houston refuses to take the oath.

17 Camp Hudson, Val Verde County, abandoned by U.S. troops.

18 Governor Sam Houston is deposed for refusing to take the oath to support the Confederacy.

Edward Clark assumes the governorship of Texas.

19 Forts Brown, Cameron County; Inge, Uvalde County; and Lancaster, Crockett County, abandoned by U.S. troops. Governor Houston's farewell address published in newspapers.

20 Fort Brown, Cameron County, and Fort Duncan, Maverick County, abandoned by U.S. troops.

23 Fort Chadbourne, Coke County, abandoned by U.S. troops.

The permanent Constitution of the Confederate States of America ratified by the Secession Convention.

25 The Secession Convention adjourns.

Unionist A. J. Hamilton chosen state senator in a special election.

29 Fort Mason, Mason County, abandoned by U.S. troops.

31 Fort Bliss, El Paso County, abandoned by U.S. troops.

April

5 Fort Quitman, Hudspeth County, abandoned by U.S. troops.

9 The called session of the legislature adjourns.

11 Federal troops from Texas aboard the USS *Coatzacoalcos* arrive in New York.

12 Confederates open fire on Fort Sumter in Charleston, South Carolina.

13 Fort Davis, Jeff Davis County, abandoned by U.S. troops.

14 Fort Sumter surrenders to Confederates.

15 U.S. President Abraham Lincoln issues his first call for volunteers.

17 Texas volunteers under Colonel Earl Van Dorn, C.S.A., capture the *Star of the West* off the Texas coast near Indianola.

Confederate flag hoisted to the top of the flagpole at Hancock Corner in Austin.

Governor Edward Clark issues call for three thousand infantry troops.

Convention in Virginia passes an ordinance of secession.

19 President Lincoln declares a naval blockade of all Southern ports and coastlines.

W. P. Lane Rangers sworn into state service.

20 U.S. Coast Guard schooner *Twilight* seized by W. A. Jones, deputy customs collector, Aransas, Texas.

Austin City Light Infantry and the Capitol Guards organized on the capitol grounds in Austin.

21 Colonel Earl Van Dorn, C.S.A., assumes military command of Texas.

23 U.S. Army officers at San Antonio made prisoners of war; Eighth U.S. Infantry captured near San Antonio.

24 Governor Clark issues a second proclamation calling for an additional five thousand troops for service in the Confederate army.

25 U.S. forces surrender at Indianola.

Fort Stockton, Pecos County, abandoned by U.S. troops.

May

1 Adjutant General's office in Austin issues "Order Number One" stating number of officers and men required for Texas military organizations.

Federal forces capture the city of New Orleans.

5 Forts Arbuckle, Cobb, and Washita, Indian Territory, captured by Texas state troops commanded by Colonel W. C. Young.

Convention in Arkansas passes an ordinance of secession.

7 Convention in Tennessee passes an ordinance of secession.

8 W. P. Lane Rangers arrive in San Antonio on the way to Camp Wood.

9 U.S. troops captured near San Lucas Springs or Adam's Hill, fifteen miles west of San Antonio.

13–14 The *Alamo Express* office, San Antonio, burned by the Knights of the Golden Circle.

20 Convention in North Carolina issues an ordinance of secession.

June

? Organization in Virginia of the First Texas Infantry Regiment.

6 Ladies' Needle Battalion organizes in Austin to make uniforms for volunteer units.

8 Governor Clark issues a proclamation calling for the establishment of camps of military instruction in Texas.

13 The Third Regiment, Texas Cavalry, is organized.

14 W. P. Lane Rangers arrive at Camp Wood.

27 Tom Green Rifles leave Austin for a camp of infantry instruction on the San Marcos River in Hays County.

July

2 Blockading of Galveston initiated by the USS *South Carolina*.

4–12 Twelve vessels off Galveston destroyed and captured by the USS *South Carolina*.

Live Oak County residents hold mass meeting in Oakville to take the oath of allegiance to the state of Texas and the Confederacy.

8 Brigadier General H. H. Sibley receives orders to expel U.S. forces from New Mexico.

27 Fort Filmore near Mesilla, New Mexico, captured by the Second Regiment of the Texas Mounted Rifles under Lieutenant Colonel John R. Baylor, c.s.a.

August

1 Lieutenant Colonel Baylor issues a proclamation establishing the Confederate Territory of Arizona, which is to include that part of New Mexico and Arizona lying south of the thrity-fourth parallel.

Preparations begin for a Confederate invasion of New Mexico.

3 Confederate batteries at Galveston bombarded by the USS *South Carolina.*

11 Lieutenant R. B. May's detachment of fourteen men, Company D, Second Regiment, Texas Mounted Rifles, ambushed in a fight with Apaches near Fort Bliss.

14 General Paul O. Hébert apponted as commander of all Confederate troops in Texas.

16 Tom Green Rifles leave Houston for Niblett's Bluff, Louisiana.

17 General H. H. Sibley and Captain Tom Ochiltree arrive in Austin to recruit troops for service in Sibley's Brigade in New Mexico.

September

6 The Sixth Regiment of Texas Cavalry is mustered into service at Camp Bartow, Dallas County.

7 The *Solidad Cos,* with a cargo of coffee, is captured off the coast near Galveston.

9 Terry's Texas Rangers are mustered into service at Houston.

11 Terry's Texas Rangers leave Houston to join General Albert Sidney Johnston in Bowling Green, Kentucky.

12 David C. Nance enlists in W. H. Parsons's Twelfth Texas Cavalry in Collin County.

18 Command of Confederate troops in Texas transferred from General Earl Van Dorn to General Paul O. Hébert.

October

1–20 Secret organization in Cooke and adjacent counties, dedicated to the overthrow of Confederate authority in North Texas, is discovered.

2 Ninth Texas Cavalry is organized at Brogden Springs, twelve miles north of Sherman.

3 The *Reindeer* off San Luis Pass is captured by the USS *Sam Houston.*

5–8 Galveston is evacuated during a four-day truce.

10 The Second Texas Infantry is organized in Houston.

11–16 Military operations from Fort Inge, Uvalde County, against Indians.

22 Sibley's Brigade leaves San Antonio for the invasion of New Mexico.

27 The brig *Delta* off Galveston is captured by the USS *Santee.*

November

1 Skirmishing between Indians and a scouting party of the First Texas Regiment of Mounted Rifles near the Pease River.

John Hood's Texas Brigade formally organized at Dumfries, Virginia, comprised of the First, Fourth, and Fifth Volunteer Infantry regiments.

7 Francis R. Lubbock inaugurated as governor.

8 The *Royal Yacht* is captured by Federal sailors in Bolivar Channel.

12 The First, Fourth, and Fifth Texas Infantry regiments and the Eighteenth Georgia Regiment are organized into a brigade.

December

7 The Texas legislature suspends all laws providing for collection of certain debts and liabilities on bonds, promissory notes, bills of exchange, and contracts for money payments until January 1, 1864, or six months after the end of the war, except for those applying to enemy aliens.

20 The schooner *Gasonne* is captured off Galveston.

1862

January

6 The state legislature gives Anderson County permission to levy and collect taxes to pay for 128 Morse rifles.

The legislature appropriates $5,000 to pay the cost of transporting clothing or other contributions to Texans in the Confederate service.

8 The legislature provides for a hospital fund of $150,000 to care for the sick and wounded soldiers of Texas.

11 The legislature creates the State Military Board with authority to buy arms and munitions, to manufacture arms and munitions, and to establish foundries for the manufacture of ordnance and arms.

13 The legislature authorizes formation of county patrols.

14 The legislature appropriates $1 million for military purposes.

February

2 General H. H. Sibley defeats a large Federal force at Valverde and occupies Albuquerque and Santa Fe, New Mexico.

11–13 Aransas Bay policed by the U.S. Navy.

22 The U.S. Navy attacks Eighth Texas Infantry stationed at Aransas Pass.

March

22 Federal launches captured off Aransas Pass.

25 The Sixteenth Texas Volunteer Infantry Regiment organized at Camp Groce near Hempstead.

U.S. troops captured at Saluria (Matagorda Island).

U.S. forces surrender at Indianola.

26 Confederate supply train destroyed in battle of Apache Pass in New Mexico.

28 H. H. Sibley's Brigade is defeated at Glorieta Pass in New Mexico. Sibley's troops begin their return journey to Texas.

John R. Baylor's Confederate Territory of Arizona collapses.

April

5–6 Battle of Shiloh in western Tennessee.

Confederate General Albert Sidney Johnston from Texas is fatally wounded.

16 First Confederate conscription legislation is passed calling all able-bodied men from eighteen to thirty-five years of age for military service.

28 City of New Orleans captured by U.S. naval forces under command of David G. Farragut.

May

14–15 U.S. Navy demonstrations at Galveston.

26 The Confederate Trans-Mississippi Department is created.

28 Governor Lubbock dispatches Captain James Duff with two companies of Rangers to Fredericksburg to deal with anti-Confederate resistance among local Germans.

30 Martial law declared in Texas.

July

4 Attack on U.S. vessels at Velasco.

7 Parsons's Twelfth Cavalry engages the enemy in the battle of Cache River near Cotton Plant, Arkansas.

8–17 U.S. Navy increases patrol activity in San Luis Pass.

August

? Sibley's Regiment evacuates Fort Bliss after putting it to the torch. Federals occupy the Fort Bliss reservation.

4 Dr. Henry Childs, the first victim of the Great Hanging of Gainesville, is executed.

10 Sixty-five German Unionists, trying to make their way to Mexico, are attacked near Fort Clark by Captain C. D. McRae of the Second Texas Mounted Rifles and all but twenty of the Germans savagely slaughtered.

11 Action by the U.S. Navy at Velasco.

12 The *Breaker* captured and the *Hannah* destroyed at Corpus Christi.

16–18 Corpus Christi bombarded by the U.S. Navy.

29–30 Hood's Texas Brigade, fighting with R. E. Lee's Army of Northern Virginia in the second battle of Bull Run, suffers 638 casualties.

September

2 New Confederate conscription law raising the age limits to include all males from eighteen to forty-five years of age is enacted.

Martial law in Texas is repealed.

13–14 Operations at Flour Bluff, near Corpus Christi.

17 Hood's Texas Brigade, fighting with Lee's army in the battle of Antietam, suffers 519 casualties.

22 President Lincoln's preliminary Emancipation Proclamation is issued.

24 U.S. Navy bombards and captures Sabine Pass.

25 State legislature provides for enrollment and organization of state militia.

26 U.S. Navy captures Sabine City.

27 U.S. Navy burns railroad bridge across Taylor's Bayou in Jefferson County.

October

2 The railroad depot at Beaumont is burned.

5 Galveston captured by U.S. forces.

10 General John Magruder arrives to assume command of Confederate forces in Texas.

23 *New York Times* strongly urges a Federal invasion of Texas.

29 Confederate troops attack U.S. steamer *Dan* at Sabine City.

31 Port Lavaca bombarded by U.S. naval forces.

November

14 Lincoln commissions A. J. Hamilton brigadier general of Texas (Union) Volunteers and Federal military governor of Texas.

20 U.S. naval action near Matagorda.

29 General John Magruder assumes command of the District of Texas, New Mexico, and Arizona with headquarters in Houston.

December

12 Naval action against Confederate shore installations on Padre Island.

24 Galveston occupied by Federal forces.

31 Six hundred Texas Unionists hold a resistance rally in Austin County.

January   1863

1 Confederates use a combined land and water attack to capture Galveston.

The *Harriet Lane* is captured in the Galveston Harbor.

8 Martial law is declared in Colorado, Austin, and Fayette counties because of outbreak of organized anti-Confederate resistance.

11 Naval engagement near Galveston between the Federal *Hatteras* and the Confederate *Alabama*.

31 Confederate gunboats *Josia Bell* and *Uncle Ben* capture Union warships *Morning Light* and *Velocity* off Sabine Pass.

March

5 Legislature adds $200,000 to the State Hospital Fund and appropriates $600,000 for distribution among needy members of soldiers' families.

State tax rate is doubled.

7 State law provides that militia may be transferred to Confederate service for no more than one year.

April

2 Colonel A. J. L. Fremantle arrives at Bagdad, Mexico, from England.

15 Fremantle visits with John Magruder on the "cotton trail" north of Brownsville.

18 U.S. Navy arrives at Sabine Pass, but Federal landing party is captured by Confederates.

19 Fremantle visits with Mrs. Hamilton P. Bee at the King ranch.

27 Fremantle leaves San Antonio by stage for Alleyton.

29 The Confederate powder mill in Waxahachie explodes, killing William Rowen and Joshua G. Phillips.

30 Fremantle experiences his first ride on a Texas railroad and arrives in Houston at 4:30 P.M.

May

2 Fremantle meets Sam Houston on a train between Galveston and the city of Houston.

3 U.S. Navy landing party on Joseph Island is attacked and repulsed. Charles L. Pyron's Second Texas Cavalry leaves Galveston to intercept N. P. Banks at Niblett's Bluff.

8 Fremantle arrives in Shreveport, Louisiana, and calls on E. Kirby Smith.

22 The schooner *Stingaree* is captured on the Brazos River.

30 U.S. Navy attacks at Port Isabel.

June

13 First Federal prisoners of war are incarcerated at Camp Groce on Leonard W. Groce's Liendo Plantation about two miles east of Hempstead.

July

3 Hood's Texas Brigade, fighting with Lee's army at Gettysburg, suffers 597 casualties.

4 Vicksburg falls and E. Kirby Smith's Trans-Mississippi Department, including Texas, is isolated from the remainder of the Confederacy.

7 Kate Stone arrives in Texas.

August

10–13 Third Texas Infantry Regiment at Galveston mutiny and refuse to drill, and civilian sappers and miners assigned to the Galveston garrison refuse to work.

September

8 N. P. Banks's assault on Sabine Pass fails.

14 Two hundred twenty Union prisoners, captured at Sabine Pass, arrive at Camp Groce.

November

2–6 Brazos Island and Brownsville are occupied as a result of Federal combined army and navy action.

5 Pendleton Murrah inaugurated governor of Texas.

17 Confederate shore batteries at Aransas Pass are captured.

22 Skirmishing in Cedar Bayou, Matagorda County.

25 U.S. Navy captures Fort Esperanza, Matagorda Island.

December

1 A. J. Hamilton arrives in Brownsville to exercise his authority as military governor of Texas.

5 Confederate state government from Missouri, under the "governorship" of Thomas C. Reynolds, establishes residence in Marshall.

10 The legislature authorizes Governor Murrah to sell cotton bonds to secure $2 million in revenue.

15 A state law defining "sedition" and "disloyalty" and setting the punishment upon conviction before a jury is enacted.

The legislature appropriates $2 million for the State Hospital Fund.

The legislature appropriates $1 million to be spent in the next biennium for support and maintenance of families of Texas officers and soldiers.

16 The legislature appropriates $1 million in Confederate state treasury notes to be expended for the defense of the state's western frontier. Severe Indian raids in Montague and Cooke counties.

23 Indianola occupied by a Federal brigade.

29 Skirmishing between Confederates and Federals on Matagorda Bay.

1864

January

3 Major General Francis J. Herron assumes command of Federal forces on the Rio Grande.

8 Second Texas Infantry skirmishes with Federal gunboats at entrance of Caney Creek, Matagorda County.

February

6 An act of the Confederate Congress prohibits export of cotton, tobacco, and certain other commodities except under regulations issued by President Davis.

11 The town of Lamar, Aransas County, is bombarded and destroyed by the U.S. Navy.

17 Confederate conscription laws are changed to include all men aged seventeen to fifty and make all exemptions from military service subject to the approval of President Davis.

23 Naval fighting near Indianola.

March

12 Confederates evacuate Fort McIntosh, near Laredo. N. P. Banks's Red River campaign begins.

13 Skirmishing at Los Patricios or San Patricio by Federal and Confederate troops.

15 Banks's troops, ascending the Red River, occupy Alexandria, Louisiana.

16 Skirmishing at Santa Rose, Cameron County, by Federal and Confederate troops.

17 Confederates attack Corpus Christi.

19 Federal troops attack Laredo.

21 Union blockading ship attacks Velasco.

22 Federal detachment under E. J. Davis defeated near Laredo. Skirmishing at Corpus Christi.

April

8 Banks's troops routed near Mansfield, Louisiana, in the Red River campaign.

9 Federal forces defeat Confederates at Pleasant Hill, Louisiana, but General Banks decides to abandon the Red River invasion of Texas.

12–13 U.S. Navy expedition up Matagorda Bay.

14 Ralph J. Smith and the Second Texas Infantry arrive in Galveston to help bolster coastal defense.

May

18 Confederate forces attack Banks's retreating troops at Yellow Bayou, Louisiana, the final major battle of the Red River campaign.

28 The state legislature provides for the transfer of state troops to Confederate service but specifically exempts a large number of persons deemed not subject to Confederate conscription.

June

? Outbreak of yellow fever epidemic in Galveston.

15 U.S. forces evacuate Cavallo Pass.

19 Skirmishing at Eagle Pass.

26 Skirmishing at Los Rucias, twenty-four miles from Brownsville.

July

7 Expedition into Galveston Bay by ships of the U.S. Navy.

30 Brownsville reoccupied by John S. "Rip" Ford's Confederate troops.

August

4–15 Military operations off Brazos Santiago by Federal forces.

17 General John Magruder is transferred to the District of Arkansas and Major General John G. Walker assumes command in Texas. (See March 31, 1865, below.)

19 Skirmishing at Port Isabel.

September

2 Federal troops, commanded by general William T. Sherman, occupy Atlanta, Georgia.

6 Skirmishing near Fort Brown in South Texas.

October

13 Comanches and Kiowas raid frontier settlements along Elm Creek in the Brazos valley near Fort Belknap.

14 Skirmishing between Federal and Confederate forces at Boca Chica Pass.

14–20 Operations against Indians along Elm Creek.

November

12 A joint resolution passes in the legislature denouncing reunion with the United States even if the U.S. Constitution were rewritten to include guarantees favorable to the Confederate states.

15 The legislature appropriates funds for the annual use of six hundred thousand yards of cloth and excess thread manufactured by the state penitentiary to be distributed to indigent families and dependents of Texas servicemen.

December

? All prisoners at Camp Groce paroled and the camp abandoned.

15–20 Indian depredations in North Texas counties south of the Red River.

23 "Buck" Barry, commander of Fort Belknap, issues orders to intercept a band of Indians which had crossed the Clear Fork near the Fort Phantom Hill ruins moving southward.

1865

January

8 Texas troops defeated in the battle of Dove Creek, sixteen miles south of present-day San Angelo.

24 Sergeant Arthur E. Gilligan of the Third Rhode Island Cavalry is captured by a Confederate patrol near Bayou Goula, Louisiana.

February

10 U.S. government creates the Department of the Gulf, including Louisiana and Texas.

20 The *Lackawanna*, flagship of the second division of the West Gulf Blockading Squadron, runs down and captures the blockade runner *Isabel*, bound from Galveston to Havana.

March

31 General John Magruder replaces General John G. Walker as Confederate commander of the District of Texas, New Mexico, and Arizona.

April

3 Union troops occupy Richmond, Virginia.

9 General R. E. Lee surrenders to General U. S. Grant in the McLean house at Appomattox, Virginia.

14 Lincoln is shot at Ford's Theatre, Washington, D.C., by John Wilkes Booth.

19 Major General John Pope, commanding the Military Division of

the Missouri, offers the same surrender terms to E. Kirby Smith that Lee had accepted from Grant.

26 General Joseph E. Johnston accepts terms of capitulation similar to those accorded Lee.

May

9 E. Kirby Smith invites governors from the Confederate Trans-Mississippi Department to attend a conference in Marshall.

11 Federal forces on Brazos Santiago Island begin an expedition to reoccupy the South Texas mainland.

12 Last battle of the Civil War is fought at Palmito ranch house in South Texas.

13 Governors of the Confederate Trans-Mississippi Department, assembled in Marshall, recommend to E. Kirby Smith that the department be surrendered.

17 Last detachment of prisoners in the Confederate prison at Camp Ford are released.

25 Twenty-fifth U.S. Army Corps alerted for occupation duty in Texas.

26 Smith agrees to surrender the Trans-Mississippi Department to General E. R. S. Canby in New Orleans.

29 General Philip H. Sheridan, U.S.A., assumes command of the Military Division of the Southwest.

30 Smith informs Federal authorities that his army is disbanded and his department open for occupation.

June

2 Smith signs terms of surrender in Galveston.

11 Robbers loot the state treasury in Austin.

17 General Gordon Granger assumes command of all U.S. troops in Texas.

President Andrew Johnson issues proclamation naming A. J. Hamilton provisional governor of Texas.

19 General Gordon Granger arrives in Galveston and issues an order freeing all slaves in Texas and Louisiana.

27 General Philip H. Sheridan assumes command of the newly formed Military Department of the Gulf.

General E. R. S. Canby is named commander of the Department of Louisiana and Texas.

July

31 Arthur Gilligan is mustered out of service in New York City.

Appendix IV

An Essay on
Texas Civil War Historiography

The following bibliographical essay is comprehensive and contains valuable annotations and references on practically every phase of Texas's involvement in the Civil War. It was written by Professor Alwyn Barr when he was a social science research associate for the Texas State Historical Association at the University of Texas at Austin. To assist in the preparation of this third edition of *Texas, The Dark Corner of the Confederacy*, Professor Barr has brought his annotations up to date, added numerous bibliographical items, and revised and rewritten major sections. The result, presented in the excerpt that follows, is an even better, virtually definitive bibliographical essay, which once again makes a significant contribution to Civil War historiography. It is an indispensable tool for students, teachers, and writers with an interest in Texas during the Civil War. Professor Barr taught for several years at Purdue University and at Texas Tech University, where he was chair of the history department. He also served as president of the Texas State Historical Association. A respected and prolific writer, he received the 1971 Coral Horton Tullis Memorial Prize for his book *Reconstruction to Reform: Texas Politics, 1876–1906*, and his most recent book, *Texans in Revolt*, was awarded the 1990 San Antonio Conservation Society Award.

Source: Alwyn Barr, "Texas Civil War Historiography," *Texas Libraries* 26 (Winter 1964): 160–169. Used by permission.

Since the Civil War ended more than 125 years ago, historians have explored in detail many aspects of the conflict, including events in Texas, the Confederate frontier state farthest removed from the focal points of battle. A valuable bibliography of publications from the period is Ernest W. Winkler and Llerena Friend, eds., *Check List of Texas Imprints,*

1861–1876 (Austin, 1963). In this essay only the most important primary accounts will be mentioned for subjects on which secondary studies are available that include bibliographies or footnotes to older works. Articles have been omitted if they are chapters in books listed here. The most detailed account of Texas in the Civil War remains that of the president of the Texas Secession Convention, who was later a Confederate colonel, Oran M. Roberts, "Texas," in Volume 11 of Clement A. Evans, ed., *Confederate Military History* (12 vols.; Atlanta, 1899). More recent and better-balanced brief surveys of the period are Allan C. Ashcraft, *Texas in the Civil War: A Résumé History* (Austin, 1962); Stephen B. Oates, "Texas under the Secessionists," *Southwestern Historical Quarterly* 67 (October 1963); and Carl Newton Tyson, "Texas: Men for War; Cotton for Economy," *Journal of the West* 14 (January 1975).

As background for the secession of Texas in 1861, one should see Llerena Friend, *Sam Houston, The Great Designer* (Austin, 1954); and Earl Wesley Fornell, *The Galveston Era: The Texas Crescent on the Eve of Secession* (Austin, 1961). The supporters and opponents of secession and their views and actions are carefully analyzed in Walter L. Buenger, *Secession and the Union in Texas* (Austin, 1984). His conclusions are summarized in "Secession Revisited: The Texas Experience," *Civil War History* 30 (December 1984) and in "Texas and the Riddle of Secession," *Southwestern Historical Quarterly* 87 (October 1983). See also John Moretta, "William Pitt Ballinger and the Travail of Texas Secession," *Houston Review* 11 (1989); and John L. Waller, *Colossal Hamilton of Texas: A Biography of Andrew Jackson Hamilton* (El Paso, 1968).

The capture of United States military posts and units in Texas is the subject of J. J. Bowden, *The Exodus of Federal Troops from Texas* (Austin, 1986); Russell K. Brown, "An Old Woman with a Broomstick: General David E. Twiggs and the U.S. Surrender in Texas, 1861," *Military Affairs* 48 (April 1984); Jeanne T. Heidler, " 'Embarrassing Situation': David E. Twiggs and the Surrender of United States Forces in Texas, 1861," *Military History of the Southwest* 21 (Fall 1991); and Howard C. Westwood, "President Lincoln's Overture to Sam Houston," *Southwestern Historical Quarterly* 88 (October 1984).

About one out of four Texans voted against secession in 1861, and Unionism continued as a minority viewpoint throughout the war.

Unionist activities have been most fully considered in James Marten, *Texas Divided: Loyalty and Dissent in the Lone Star State, 1856–1874* (Lexington, 1990). That study should be supplemented by Marilyn M. Sibley, *George W. Brackenridge* (Austin, 1973); James Smallwood, "Disaffection in Confederate Texas: The Great Hanging at Gainesville," *Civil War History* 22 (December 1976); Vicki Betts, "'Private and Amateur Hangings': The Lynching of W. W. Montgomery, March 15, 1863," *Southwestern Historical Quarterly* 88 (October 1984); L. D. Clark, ed., *Civil War Recollections of James Lemuel Clark* (College Station, 1984); Randolph B. Campbell, "George W. Whitmore: East Texas Unionist," *East Texas Historical Journal* 28 (1990); J. S. Duncan, "Martin Hart, Civil War Guerrilla," *Military History of Texas and the Southwest* 11 (1973); James Marten, "The Diary of Thomas H. DuVal: The Civil War in Austin, Texas, February 26 to October 9, 1863," *Southwestern Historical Quarterly* 94 (January 1991); Richard Moore, "A Smuggler's Exile: S. M. Swenson Flees Texas," *East Texas Historical Journal* 25 (1987); Pete A. Y. Gunter, "The Great Gainesville Hanging, October, 1862," *Blue and Gray Magazine* 3 (May 1986); Floyd F. Ewing, Jr., "Origins of Union Sentiment on the West Texas Frontier," *West Texas Historical Association Year Book* 32 (1956), and "Unionist Sentiment on the Northwest Texas Frontier," ibid. 33 (1957); John W. Sansom, *Battle of Nueces River in Kinney County, Texas, August 10th, 1862* (San Antonio, 1905); Edward Schmidt, *1862–1912 Festschrift zur funfzigjahrigen erinnerungs-feier an das gefect am Nueces, 10 August 1862* (San Antonio, 1912); August Santleben, *A Texas Pioneer* (New York, 1910); George Adams Fisher, *The Yankee Conscript* (Philadelphia, 1864); and Alfred E. Mathews, *Interesting Narrative* (New Philadelphia, Ohio, 1861).

Defense of the Confederate military district of Texas centered primarily along the Gulf Coast. A general survey is Alwyn Barr, "Texas Coastal Defense, 1861–1865," *Southwestern Historical Quarterly* 65 (July 1961). Other accounts are James M. Day, "Leon Smith: Confederate Mariner," *East Texas Historical Journal* 3 (March 1965); and Ralph A. Wooster, "The Texas Gulf Coast in the Civil War," *Texas Gulf Historical and Biographical Record* 1 (November 1965). The battle of Galveston is discussed in Charles C. Cumberland, "The Confederate Loss and Recapture of Galveston, 1862–1863," ibid. 51 (October 1947); Philip C. Tucker III, "The United States Gunboat *Harriet Lane,*" ibid. 21 (April

1918); Dorman H. Winfrey, ed., "Two Battle of Galveston Letters," ibid. 65 (October 1961); Jonnie Lockhart Wallis, *Sixty Years on the Brazos: The Life and Letters of Dr. John Washington Lockhart, 1824–1900* (Los Angeles, 1930); Mitchell S. Goldberg, "A Federal Naval Raid into Galveston Harbor, November 7–8, 1861: What Really Happened?" *Southwestern Historical Quarterly* 76 (July 1972); and Maury Darst, "Artillery Defense of Galveston, 1863," *Military History of Texas and the Southwest* 12 (1974). For the battle of Sabine Pass there are Frank X. Tolbert, *Dick Dowling at Sabine Pass* (New York, 1962); Andrew Forest Muir, "Dick Dowling and the Battle of Sabine Pass," *Civil War History* 4 (December 1958); Jo Young, "The Battle of Sabine Pass," *Southwestern Historical Quarterly* 52 (April 1949); Alwyn Barr, "Sabine Pass, September, 1863," *Texas Military History* 2 (February 1962); Alwyn Barr, ed., "N. H. Smith's Letters from Sabine Pass, 1863," *East Texas Historical Journal* 4 (October 1966); Harold B. Simpson, "Sabine Pass," in *Battles of Texas* (Waco, 1968); W. T. Block, "Sabine Pass in the Civil War," *East Texas Historical Journal* 9 (October 1971); Block, "The Battle of Sabine Pass, Texas," *Blue and Gray Magazine* 4 (August–September 1986); and Henry S. McArthur, "A Yank at Sabine Pass," *Civil War Times Illustrated* 12 (December 1973). A later engagement by the Sabine Pass garrison is the subject of Alwyn Barr, "The Battle of Calcasieu Pass," *Southwestern Historical Quarterly* 66 (July 1962).

Activities on the coast from Galveston to Corpus Christi are covered by Lester N. Fitzhugh, "Saluria, Fort Esperanza, and Military Operations on the Texas Coast, 1861–1864," *Southwestern Historical Quarterly* 61 (July 1957); William H. Bentley, *History of the 77th Illinois Volunteer Infantry* (Paris, Ill., 1883); Ben F. Booth, *Dark Days of the Rebellion* (Indianola, Iowa, 1897); Charles B. Johnson, *Muskets and Medicine or Army Life in the Sixties* (Philadelphia, 1917); C. Richard King, "The Shadow and the Glory," *Texana* 9 (1971); and Norman C. Delaney, "Corpus Christi – The Vicksburg of Texas," *Civil War Times Illustrated* 16 (July 1977). The struggle for the lower Rio Grande is considered in Stephen B. Oates, "John S. 'Rip' Ford: Prudent Cavalryman, C.S.A.," *Southwestern Historical Quarterly* 64 (January 1961); Nannie M. Tilley, ed., *Federals on the Frontier: The Diary of Benjamin F. McIntyre, 1862–1864* (Austin, 1963); Stephen B. Oates, ed., *Rip Ford's Texas* (Austin, 1963); James S. Clark, *Life in the Middle West: Reminiscences* (Chicago, 1916); Samuel C. Jones, *Reminiscences* (Iowa City, 1907);

Richard P. Weinert, "Confederate Border Troubles with Mexico," *Civil War Times Illustrated* 3 (October 1964); Allan C. Ashcraft, "The Union Occupation of the Lower Rio Grande Valley in the Civil War," *Texas Military History* 8 (1970); and James A. Irby, *Backdoor at Bagdad: The Civil War on the Rio Grande* (El Paso, 1977).

Additional information on activities in the district of Texas may be found in Getulius Kellersberger, *Memoirs of an Engineer in the Confederate Army in Texas,* trans. Helen S. Sundstrom (Austin, 1957); Allen W. Jones, "Military Events in Texas during the Civil War, 1861–1865," *Southwestern Historical Quarterly* 64 (July 1960); Frank E. Vandiver and Eugene C. Barker, eds., "Letters from the Confederate Medical Service in Texas, 1863–1865," ibid. 55 (January, April 1952); Allan C. Ashcraft, "The Confederate 'Inspector of Railroads,'" *Texas Military History* 3 (Spring 1963), "Staff Function in the Confederate District of Texas," ibid. (Summer 1963), "Fort Brown, Texas, in 1861," ibid. (Winter 1963), and "The Defense of Houston, October, 1862," ibid. 4 (Fall 1964); J. D. Howard, comp., "William Pursley Letters, 1863," ibid.; Robert W. Williams and Ralph A. Wooster, eds., "A Texas War Clerk: Civil War Letters of Isaac Dunbar Affleck," ibid. 2 (November 1962); and Archie P. McDonald, "List of Men Enrolled for Camps, 1862–1864," ibid. 5 (Summer 1965). More specifically, efforts to supply the Confederate armies are discussed in Bill Winsor, *Texas in the Confederacy: Military Installations, Economy and People* (Hillsboro, 1978); Gary Wiggins, *Dance and Brothers: Texas Gunmakers of the Confederacy* (Orange, Va., 1986); William A. Albaugh, *Tyler, Texas, C.S.A.* (Harrisburg, 1958); Frank E. Vandiver, "Texas and the Confederate Army's Meat Problem," *Southwestern Historical Quarterly* 47 (January 1944); Allan Ashcraft, "Confederate Beef Packing at Jefferson, Texas," ibid. 68 (October 1964); and Michael Robert Green, "'So Illy Provided': Events Leading to the Creation of the Texas Military Board," *Military History of Texas and the Southwest* 10 (1972). Confederate military prisons are the subject of Leon Mitchell, Jr., "Camp Ford," ibid. 66 (July 1962), and "Camp Groce," ibid. 67 (July 1963); F. Lee Lawrence and Robert W. Glover, *Camp Ford, C.S.A.: The Story of Union Prisoners in Texas* (Austin, 1964); Robert W. Glover and Randal B. Gilbert, "Camp Ford, Tyler, Texas – The Largest Confederate Prison Camp West of the Mississippi River," *Chronicles of Smith County, Texas* 28 (Winter 1989); Randal B. Gilbert, "The Building of the Camp Ford Stockade," ibid. 24 (Winter

1985); Howard O. Pollan and Randal B. Gilbert, eds., "The Camp Ford Diary of Captain William Fortunatus McKinney," ibid. 25 (Summer 1986); Thomas Ludwell Bryan, "The Old Stockade," ibid. 12 (Summer 1973); Gary Wilson, "The Ordeal of William H. Cowdin and the Officers of the Forty-second Massachusetts Regiment: Union Prisoners of War," *East Texas Historical Journal* 23 (1985); and Aaron T. Sutton, *Prisoner of the Rebels in Texas* (Decatur, Ind., 1978).

Frontier defense during the war has been most fully studied in David Paul Smith, *Frontier Defense in the Civil War: Texas' Rangers and Rebels* (College Station, 1992). Additional accounts include Rupert N. Richardson, *The Frontier of Northwest Texas, 1845–1876* (Los Angeles, 1963); W. C. Holden, "Frontier Defense in Texas during the Civil War," *West Texas Historical Association Year Book* 4 (1928); D. S. Howell, "Along the Texas Frontier during the Civil War," ibid. 13 (1937); Marilynne Howsley, "Forting Up on the Texas Frontier during the Civil War," ibid. 18 (1941); J. R. Webb, "Chapters from the Frontier Life of Phin W. Reynolds," ibid. 21 (1945); John Thomas Duncan, ed., "Some Civil War Letters of D. Port Smythe," ibid. 37 (1961); Floyd F. Ewing, Jr., "Suggestions for the Observance in West Texas of the Civil War Centennial," ibid. 36 (1960); E. E. Townsend, "The Mays Massacre of 1861," *West Texas Historical and Scientific Society Publications* 5 (1933); William C. Pool, "Battle of Dove Creek," *Southwestern Historical Quarterly* 53 (April 1950); Lucy A. Erath, ed., *Memoirs of Major George Bernard Erath, 1813–1891* (Waco, 1956); James K. Greer, ed., *A Texas Ranger and Frontiersman: The Days of Buck Barry in Texas, 1845–1906* (Dallas, 1932); T. R. Havins, *Camp Colorado: A Decade of Frontier Defense* (Brownwood, 1964); Kenneth Neighbors, "Elm Creek Raid in Young County, 1864," *West Texas Historical Association Year Book* 40 (1964); David Marshall, "A Civilian Fort on the Confederate Frontier," ibid. 61 (1985); and Larry C. Rampp and Donald L. Rampp, "The Phillips Expedition: The Abortive Federal Invasion of Texas, January–February, 1864," *Military History of Texas and the Southwest* 9 (1971). The war in the trans-Pecos is the subject of J. L. Waller, "The Civil War in the El Paso Area," *West Texas Historical Association Year Book* 22 (1946); W. W. Mills, *Forty Years at El Paso*, ed. Rex Strickland (El Paso, 1962); Richard K. McMaster, "Fort Bliss Diary, 1845–1868," *Password* 11 (Spring 1966); Martin H. Hall, "Planter vs. Frontiersman: Conflict in the Confederate Indian Policy," in William E. Holmes and

Harold M. Hollingsworth, eds., *Essays on the American Civil War* (Austin, 1968); and Wayne R. Austerman, "The San Antonio–El Paso Mail, C.S.A.," *West Texas Historical Association Year Book* 58 (1982).

The activities of the state government may be followed in Nancy Head Bowen, "A Political Labyrinth: Texas in the Civil War," *East Texas Historical Journal* 11 (Fall 1973), a summary of her more elaborate dissertation; Ralph A. Wooster, "Texas," in W. Buck Yearns, ed., *The Confederate Governors* (Athens, Ga., 1985); Oran M. Roberts, "The Political, Legislative, and Judicial History of Texas for Its Fifty Years of Statehood, 1845–1895," in Dudley G. Wooten, ed., *A Comprehensive History of Texas, 1685–1897* (2 vols.; Dallas, 1898), vol. 2; C. W. Raines, ed., *Six Decades in Texas; or, Memoirs of Francis Richard Lubbock, Governor of Texas in War-time* (Austin, 1900); James M. Day, ed., *Journals of the Ninth Legislature of the State of Texas* (4 vols.; Austin, 1963–1964), and *Journals of the Tenth Legislature of the State of Texas* (4 vols.; Austin, 1965); E. T. Miller, "The State Finances of Texas during the Civil War," *Southwestern Historical Quarterly* 14 (July 1910); Charles W. Ramsdell, "The Texas State Military Board, 1862–1865," ibid. 27 (April 1924); and William Frank Zornow, "Texas State Aid for Indigent Soldiers, 1861–1865," *Mid-America* 37 (July 1955). The Confederate courts in Texas are studied in T. R. Havins, "Administration of the Sequestration Act in the Confederate District Court for the Western District of Texas, 1862–1865," *Southwestern Historical Quarterly* 48 (January 1940); Nowlin Randolph, "Judge William Pinckney Hill Aids the Confederate War Effort," ibid. 68 (July 1964); Alwyn Barr, ed., "Records of the Confederate Military Commission in San Antonio, July 2–October 10, 1862," *Southwestern Historical Quarterly* 70 (July, October 1966, April 1967), 71 (October 1967), 73 (July, October 1969); and Brian Dirck, "'Administered in Much Discretion': William Pinckney Hill and the Confederate Grand Jury in Galveston, Texas, 1861–1862," *Houston Review* 13 (1991).

Trade through Mexico is the subject of James W. Daddysman, *The Matamoros Trade: Confederate Commerce, Diplomacy, and Intrigue* (Newark, 1984); Ronnie C. Tyler, *Santiago Vidaurri and the Southern Confederacy* (Austin, 1973); Robert Delaney, "Matamoros, Port for Texas during the Civil War," *Southwestern Historical Quarterly* 58 (April 1955); Brother Avila Larios, "Brownsville-Matamoros: Confederate Lifeline," *Mid-America* 40 (April 1958); Mitchell Smith, "The

'Neutral' Matamoros Trade, 1861–65," *Southwest Review* 37 (Autumn 1952); Thomas Schoonover, "Confederate Diplomacy and the Texas-Mexican Border, 1861–1865," *East Texas Historical Journal* 11 (Spring 1973); and Fredericka Meiners, "The Texas Border Cotton Trade, 1862–1863," *Civil War History* 23 (December 1977). Trade through Texas ports is described by L. Tuffly Ellis, "Maritime Commerce on the Far Western Gulf, 1861–1865," *Southwestern Historical Quarterly* 77 (October 1973); Thomas E. Taylor, *Running the Blockade* (London, 1896); William Watson, *The Adventures of a Blockade Runner* (London, 1892); David P. Martin, "The Harriet Lane," *Southwestern Historical Quarterly* 39 (July 1935); H. A. Trexler, "The Harriet Lane and the Blockade of Galveston," ibid. 35 (October 1931); William F. Hutchinson, *Life on the Texas Blockade* (Providence, 1883); Frederic S. Hill, *Twenty Years at Sea* (New York, 1893); and M. B. Glascock, "The Last Cruise of the General Rusk (Blanche)," *Military History of Texas and the Southwest* 13 (1975). Behind the lines Texans struggled with a variety of economic, social, and political issues at the local level. These are discussed in Randolph B. Campbell, *A Southern Community in Crisis: Harrison County, Texas, 1850–1880* (Austin, 1983); Vicki Betts, *Smith County, Texas, in the Civil War* (Tyler, 1978); Ralph A. Wooster and Robert Wooster, "A People at War: East Texans during the Civil War," *East Texas Historical Journal* 28 (1990); Jack Stoltz, "Kaufman County in the Civil War," ibid. 28 (1990); Ronald B. Jager, "Houston, Texas, Fights the Civil War," *Texana* 11 (1973); Tony E. Duty, "The Home Front: McLennan County in the Civil War," ibid. 12 (1974); Gilbert M. Cuthbertson, " 'But the Corn Stands Rather Well': Smith County, Texas, 1862," *Chronicles of Smith County, Texas* 12 (Summer 1973); Andrew L. Leath, ed., "News from Flora, 1863: The Carter Letters," ibid. 25 (Summer 1986); Vicki Betts, ed., "The Horace Chilton Memoirs, 1858–1873," ibid. 30 (Summer 1991); David C. Humphrey, "A 'Very Muddy and Conflicting' View: The Civil War as Seen from Austin," *Southwestern Historical Quarterly* 94 (January 1991); and Leila R. Eads, *Defenders: A Confederate History of Henderson County, Texas* (Athens, Texas, 1969). Chapters on the war period are in Kenneth W. Wheeler, *To Wear a City's Crown: The Beginnings of Urban Growth in Texas, 1836–1865* (Cambridge, 1968); Brownson Malsch, *Indianola: The Mother of Western Texas* (Austin, 1977); David G. McComb, *Houston: The Bayou City* (Austin, 1969); and McComb, *Galveston: A History* (Austin,

1986). Descriptions of the home front came from a visiting British army officer, J. A. L. Fremantle, *The Fremantle Diary*, ed. Walter Lord (Boston, 1954); a Northerner, Thomas North, *Five Years in Texas, 1861–1865* (Cincinnati, 1870); and Texans, Mrs. E. M. Loughery, *War and Reconstruction Times in Texas, 1861–1865* (Nacogdoches, 1897, reprinted Austin, 1914); William Abraham Bowen, *Uncle Zeke's Speculation: A Story of War and Reconstruction Days in Texas* (Arlington, 1910); Merle Mears Duncan, ed., "An 1864 Letter to Mrs. Rufus C. Burleson," *Southwestern Historical Quarterly* 64 (January 1961); and Lois Wood Burkhalter, *Gideon Lincecum, 1793–1874: A Biography* (Austin, 1965). Louisiana refugees to Texas are the focus of Mrs. Francis (Hewitt) Fearn, ed., *Diary of a Refugee* (New York, 1910); and John Q. Anderson, ed., *Brokenburn: The Journal of Kate Stone, 1861–1868* (Baton Rouge, 1955).

Additional information on internal affairs is provided by Ralph A. Wooster, "Life in Civil War East Texas," *East Texas Historical Journal* 3 (October 1965); Grover C. Ramsey, comp., *Confederate Postmasters in Texas, 1861–1865* (Waco, 1963); Hank Bieciuk and H. G. "Bill" Corbin, *Texas Confederate County Notes and Private Scrip* (Tyler, 1961); and William R. Geise, "Missouri's Confederate Capital in Marshall, Texas," ibid. 66 (October 1962). Cultural activities receive attention in Guy Nelson, "Baylor University at Independence, The War Years: 1861–1865," *Texana* 2 (Spring 1964); Lota M. Spell, "Music in Texas," *Civil War History* 4 (September 1958); E. H. Cushing, pub., *The New Texas School Reader* (Houston, 1864, reprinted Austin, 1962), an example of a Southern-oriented school text that included information on Texas troops in the war; Lawrence L. Brown, *The Episcopal Church in Texas, 1838–1874* (Austin, 1963); Robert A. Baker, *The Blossoming Desert: A Concise History of Texas Baptists* (Waco, 1970); Walter Vernon et al., *The Methodist Excitement in Texas* (Dallas, 1984); and Frederick J. Dobney, "From Denominationalism to Nationalism in the Civil War: A Case Study," *Texana* 9 (1971). Immigrants and minorities are considered in Jody Feldtman Wright, *Czechs in Grey and Blue, Too!* (San Antonio, 1988); Carland Elaine Crook, "Benjamin Theron and French Designs in Texas during the Civil War," *Southwestern Historical Quarterly* 68 (April 1965); Howard N. Martin, "Texas Redskins in Confederate Gray," ibid. 70 (April 1967); Jerry Don Thompson, *Vaqueros in Blue and Gray* (Austin, 1977), and *Mexican Texans in the Union Army* (El

Paso, 1986). Newspaper editors receive attention in Emory M. Thomas, "Rebel Nationalism: E. H. Cushing and the Confederate Experience," *Southwestern Historical Quarterly* 73 (January 1970); Randy J. Sparks, "John P. Osterhout, Yankee, Rebel, Republican," ibid. 90 (October 1986); and Max S. Lale, "Robert W. Loughery: Rebel Editor," *East Texas Historical Journal* 21 (1983).

The impact of war on Texas slaves is considered by Randolph B. Campbell, *An Empire for Slavery: The Peculiar Institution in Texas, 1821–1865* (Baton Rouge, 1989); James Marten, "Slaves and Rebels: The Peculiar Institution in Texas, 1861–1865," *East Texas Historical Journal* 28 (1990); Cecil Harper, Jr., "Slavery without Cotton: Hunt County, Texas, 1846–1864," *Southwestern Historical Quarterly* 88 (April 1985); Vicki Betts, "'I Found the Country Greatly Excited': A Civil War Letter," *Chronicles of Smith County, Texas* 17 (Summer 1978); and John Gauss, "Give the Blacks Texas," *Civil War Times Illustrated* 29 (May–June 1990).

Several Texans became prominent leaders of the Confederate cause. Government leaders are the subjects of Ben H. Proctor, *Not without Honor: The Life of John H. Reagan* (Austin, 1962), the Confederate postmaster general whose *Memoirs* (New York, 1906) were edited by W. F. McCaleb; Mary S. Estill, ed., "Diary of a Confederate Congressman [F. B. Sexton], 1862–1863," *Southwestern Historical Quarterly* 38 (April 1935), 39 (July 1935); Alma Dexta King, "The Political Career of Williamson Simpson Oldham," ibid. 33 (October 1929), a Texas senator; Deolece Parmalee, "Forgotten Prologue – Fletcher Summerfield Stockdale," *Texana* 2 (Fall 1964), a lieutenant governor; and Alvy King, *Louis T. Wigfall, Southern Fire-eater* (Baton Rouge, 1970). W. C. Nunn, ed., *Ten Texans in Gray* (Hillsboro, 1968), includes essays on four military leaders, John Bell Hood, John B. Magruder, John R. Baylor, and Richard Dowling; and six political figures, Edward Clark, Francis R. Lubbock, Pendleton Murrah, W. S. Oldham, Louis T. Wigfall, and John H. Reagan. A second volume, W. C. Nunn, ed., *Ten More Texans in Gray* (Hillsboro, 1980), contains chapters on one government figure, James Webb Throckmorton, and nine military officers, John S. Ford, Thomas Green, Albert Sidney Johnston, Samuel Bell Maxey, Ben Mc-Culloch, Oran Milo Roberts, Lawrence Sullivan Ross, Henry Hopkins Sibley, and Benjamin Franklin Terry. Studies and reminiscences of Texas generals include Charles Roland, *Albert Sidney Johnston: Soldier of*

Three Republics (Austin, 1964); William Preston Johnston, *The Life of General Albert Sidney Johnston* (New York, 1878); John P. Dyer, *The Gallant Hood* (Indianapolis, 1950); Richard O'Connor, *Hood: Cavalier General* (New York, 1949); John B. Hood, *Advance and Retreat* (New Orleans, 1880, reprinted Bloomington, 1959); Richard M. McMurry, *John Bell Hood and the War for Southern Independence* (Lexington, 1982); Victor M. Rose, *The Life and Services of General Ben McCulloch* (Philadelphia, 1888, reprinted Austin, 1958); Jack W. Gunn, "Ben McCulloch: A Big Captain," *Southwestern Historical Quarterly* 58 (July 1954); Edward M. Coffman, ed., "Ben McCulloch Letters," ibid. 60 (July 1956); William W. Grace, "Major General John A. Wharton," ibid. 19 (January 1916); Walter Paye Lane, *The Adventures and Recollections of General Walter P. Lane* (Marshall, 1928); Odie B. Faulk, *Fightin' Texan: General Tom Green* (Waco, 1963); Alwyn Barr, "Tom Green: The Forrest of the Trans-Mississippi, *Lincoln Herald* 88 (Summer 1986); Hugh H. Young, "Two Texas Patriots," *Southwestern Historical Quarterly* 44 (July 1940), one of whom was William Hugh Young; Claude Elliott, *Leathercoat* (San Antonio, 1938), the life of J. W. Throckmorton, a brigadier general of state troops; Louise Horton, *Samuel Bell Maxey: A Biography* (Austin, 1974); Judith Ann Benner, *Sul Ross: Soldier, Statesman, Educator* (College Station, 1983); Jerry Thompson, *Henry Hopkins Sibley: Confederate General of the West* (Natchitoches, 1987); and William N. Bate, *General Sidney Sherman: Texas Soldier, Statesman and Builder* (Waco, 1974).

Texan field and line officers are the subject of Ernest Wallace, *Charles DeMorse: Pioneer Editor and Statesman* (Lubbock, 1943); Elizabeth Silverthorne, *Ashbel Smith of Texas: Pioneer, Patriot, Statesman, 1805–1886* (College Station, 1982); John L. Waller, "Colonel George Wythe Baylor," *Southwestern Social Science Quarterly* 24 (January 1943); Marcus J. Wright, "Colonel Thomas P. Ochiltree," *Southern Bivouac* 2 (July 1884); W. J. Hughes, *Rebellious Ranger: Rip Ford and the Old Southwest* (Norman, 1964); George P. Garrison, "Guy M. Bryan," *Southwestern Historical Quarterly* 5 (October 1901); Dudley G. Wooten, "Oran M. Roberts," ibid. 2 (July 1898); Lois Foster Blount, "Captain Thomas William Blount and His Memoirs," ibid. 39 (July 1935); Francis Robertson Sackett, *Dick Dowling* (Houston, 1937); George Wythe Baylor, *John Robert Baylor: Confederate Governor of Arizona,* ed. Odie Faulk (Tucson, 1966); and Langston James Goree V,

The Thomas Jewett Goree Letters, Volume I: The Civil War Correspondence (Bryan, 1981). Biographical collections include Mamie Yeary, comp., *Reminiscences of the Boys in Gray, 1861–1865* (Dallas, 1912); Sidney Smith Johnston, *Texans Who Wore the Gray* (Tyler, 1907); W. D. Wood, *A Partial Roster of the Officers and Men Raised in Leon County, Texas* (San Marcos, 1899, reprinted Waco, 1963); Thomas F. Harwell, *Eighty Years under the Stars and Bars* (Kyle, 1947); and Harold B. Simpson, "West Pointers in the Texas Confederate Army," *Texas Military History* 6 (Spring 1967).

The most accurate list of Texas Confederate troops is Lester N. Fitzhugh, *Texas Batteries, Battalions, Regiments, Commanders, and Field Officers, Confederate States Army, 1861–1865* (Midlothian, 1959). Other lists, which include sketches of some units, are Wooten, *A Comprehensive History of Texas,* vol. 2; Harry M. Henderson, *Texas in the Confederacy* (San Antonio, 1955); and Marcus J. Wright, *Texas in the War, 1861–1865,* ed. Harold B. Simpson (Hillsboro, 1965). A good introductory article on Texas soldiers is Ralph A. Wooster and Robert Wooster, "'Rarin' for a Fight': Texans in the Confederate Army," *Southwestern Historical Quarterly* 84 (April 1981). Accounts of Texas artillery units include Alwyn Barr, "Texas' Confederate Field Artillery," *Texas Military History* 1 (August 1961); P. D. Browne, "Captain T. D. Nettles and the Valverde Battery," *Texana* 2 (Winter 1964); Richard K. McMaster and George Ruhlen, "The Guns of Valverde," *Password* 5 (January 1960); William E. Woodruff, Jr., *With the Light Guns in '61–'65: Reminiscences of Eleven Arkansas, Missouri and Texas Light Batteries in the Civil War* (Little Rock, 1900); [William Edgar Hughes], *The Journal of a Grandfather* (St. Louis, 1912), by a member of the Good-Douglas battery; David B. Gracy II, ed., "New Mexico Campaign Letters of Frank Starr, 1861–1862," *Texas Military History* 4 (Fall 1964); Paul C. Boethel, *The Big Guns of Fayette* (Austin, 1965), on the Creuzbaur-Welhausen battery; Lucia Rutherford Douglas, ed., *Douglas's Texas Battery, C.S.A.* (Tyler, 1966); June P. Trop, "The Douglas Letters: An Update," *Chronicles of Smith County, Texas* 22 (Summer 1983); Marc B. Smith, Jr., "A Southern Victory: Civil War Letter by Marcus Fleishel," ibid. 22 (Winter 1983); Lester Newton Fitzhugh, ed., *Cannon Smoke: The Letters of Captain John J. Good, Good-Douglas Texas Battery, C.S.A.* (Hillsboro, 1971); and Edgar E. Lackner, "Civil War Diaries of Edwin F. Stanton, U.S.A., and William Quensell, C.S.A.,

'Yank and Reb' under One Cover," *East Texas Historical Journal* 18 (1980), on Haldemann's battery.

Of the infantry units from Texas, the best known is Hood's Brigade, which served in the Army of Northern Virginia. Harold B. Simpson, *Hood's Texas Brigade* (4 vols.; Waco, 1968–1977), replaces Joseph B. Polley, *Hood's Texas Brigade* (New York, 1910), as the most complete account of the command. Other studies of value are John Spencer, *From Corsicana to Appomattox: The Story of the Corsicana Invincibles and the Navarro Rifles* (Corsicana, 1984); O. T. Hanks, *History of Captain B. F. Benton's Company, Hood's Texas Brigade, 1861–1865* (Austin, 1984); Elvis E. Fleming, "Some Hard Fighting: Letters of Private Robert T. Wilson, 5th Texas Infantry, Hood's Brigade, 1862–1865," *Military History of Texas and the Southwest* 9 (1971); Dayton Kelley, "The Texas Brigade at the Wilderness, May 6, 1864," *Texana* 11 (1973); Ann Dempster and Homer L. Kerr, eds., "The William L. Edwards Letters, 1862," *Texas Military History* 7 (Spring 1968), by a member of the fourth Texas Infantry; and S. B. Bedinger, "Chaplain Nicholas A. Davis: A Man of Action and Accomplishment," *East Texas Historical Journal* 26 (1988).

The largest unit of Texans in the war was Walker's infantry division, which is the subject of Joseph P. Blessington, *The Campaigns of Walker's Texas Division* (New York, 1875), by a member of the Sixteenth Texas Infantry; Fred Carleton, *Roll of Company G, 16th Texas Infantry* (Austin, 1899); John Q. Anderson, *A Texas Surgeon in the* C.S.A. (Tuscaloosa, 1957), about a member of the Twenty-eighth Texas Dismounted Cavalry; Thomas Reuben Bonner, "Sketches of the Campaign of 1864," *The Land We Love* 5 (October 1868), 6 (November 1868); Robert W. Glover, ed., "The War Letters of a Texas Conscript in Arkansas," *Arkansas Historical Quarterly* 20 (Winter 1961), by members of the Eighteenth Texas Infantry; Leon Durst, comp., "A Confederate Texas Letter: Bruno Durst to Jet Black," *Southwestern Historical Quarterly* 57 (July 1953), from a member of the Thirteenth Texas Dismounted Cavalry; Alwyn Barr, ed., "The Battle of Bayou Bourbeau, November 3, 1863: Colonel Oran M. Roberts' Report," *Louisiana History* 6 (Winter 1965), by the commander of the Eleventh Texas Infantry; Norman D. Brown, *Journey to Pleasant Hill: The Civil War Letters of Captain Elijah P. Petty, Walker's Texas Division, C.S.A.* (San Antonio, 1982); Max S. Lale, "A Letter from Leonard Randal to His Son," *East Texas Historical Journal* 23 (1985); and "New Light on the Battle of Mansfield," ibid. 25

(1987); Jon P. Harrison, "The Confederate Letters of John Simmons," *Chronicles of Smith County, Texas* 14 (Summer 1975); and Thomas W. Cutrer, ed., "'Bully for Flournoy's Regiment, We Are Some Punkins, You'll Bet': The Civil War Letters of Virgil Sullivan Rabb, Captain, Company I Sixteenth Texas Infantry, C.S.A.," *Military History of the Southwest* 19 (Fall 1989), 20 (Spring 1990).

In the Army of Tennessee there were two Texas infantry brigades, a separate regiment, and the infantry portion of a legion. For Ector's brigade see Howard L. Meredith and James L. Nichols, "Letters of a Confederate Soldier: The Andrew Fogle Collection," *Library Chronicle* of the University of Texas 8 (Spring 1965), by a member of the Ninth Texas Infantry; Steve Peters, "The Murder of Col. Joseph M. Bounds, Eleventh Texas Cavalry, Young's Regiment, C.S.A.," *Texana* 12 (1974); Judy Watson McClure, *Confederate from East Texas: The Civil War Letters of James Monroe Watson* (Quanah, 1976); Jon H. Harrison, "Tenth Texas Cavalry, C.S.A.," *Military History of Texas and the Southwest* 12 (1974); and Vicki Betts, ed., "The Civil War Letters of Elbridge Littlejohn," *Chronicles of Smith County, Texas* 17 (Winter 1978), 18 (Summer 1979). Granbury's Brigade, which also served a short time in the Trans-Mississippi, is discussed in James M. McCaffrey, *This Band of Heroes: Granbury's Texas Brigade* (Austin, 1985); W. O. Wynn, *A Brief Sketch of the Life . . . of an ex-Confederate Soldier* (Garland, 1927), by a member of the Tenth Texas Infantry; Sandra Myres, ed., *Force without Fanfare: The Autobiography of K. M. Van Zandt* (Fort Worth, 1969), a member of the Seventh Texas Infantry; Norman D. Brown, ed., *One of Cleburne's Command: The Civil War Reminiscences and Diary of Captain Samuel T. Foster, Granbury's Texas Brigade, C.S.A.* (Austin, 1980); Andrew L. Leath, "Company F, Seventh Texas Infantry, C.S.A.," *Chronicles of Smith County, Texas* 30 (Summer 1991); and R. W. Ford, "I Fear . . . We Must Go Up," ed. Russell Surles, *Civil War Times Illustrated* 25 (February 1987), from a detachment at Port Hudson.

The two Texas units that fought at Vicksburg are considered in Edwin C. Bearss, *Texas at Vicksburg* (Austin, 1961); Joseph E. Chance, *The Second Texas Infantry: From Shiloh to Vicksburg* (Austin, 1984); Wayne Flynt, "The Texas Legion at Vicksburg," *East Texas Historical Journal* 17 (1979); by four members of the Second Texas Infantry: Ralph J. Smith, *Reminiscences of the Civil War* (San Marcos, 1911, reprinted Waco, 1962); Sam Houston, Jr., "Shiloh Shadows," *Southwestern His-*

torical Quarterly 34 (April 1931); Eleanor Damon Pace, ed., "The Diary and Letters of William P. Rogers, 1846–1862," ibid. 32 (April 1929); and Walter H. Mays, ed., "The Vicksburg Diary of M. K. Simons, 1863," *Texas Military History* 5 (Spring 1965); and by two members of Waul's Legion, John Duff Brown, "Reminiscences," *Southwestern Historical Quarterly* 12 (April 1909); Leonard B. Plummer, trans., "Excerpts from the Hander Diary," *Journal of Mississippi History* 26 (May 1964); and Camilla Davis Trammell, *Seven Pines, Its Occupants and Their Letters, 1825–1872* (Dallas, 1986).

In the Trans-Mississippi, a unit that began as a cavalry brigade and was converted to infantry service is the subject of Alwyn Barr, *Polignac's Texas Brigade* (Houston, 1964); Alwyn Barr, ed., "James Allen Hamilton's Civil War Diary," *Texana* 2 (Summer 1964), by a member of the Fifteenth Texas Infantry; F. Lee Lawrence and Robert W. Glover, eds., "A Smith County Confederate Writes Home: Letters of Z. H. Crow," *Chronicles of Smith County, Texas* 4 (Fall 1965), by a member of the Seventeenth Texas Cavalry; Robert S. Weddle, *Plow-Horse Cavalry: The Caney Creek Boys of the Thirty-fourth Texas* (Austin, 1974); J. S. Duncan, "Alexander Cameron in the Louisiana Campaign, 1863–1865," *Military History of Texas and the Southwest* 12 (1974), 13 (1975); Norman C. Delaney, "Diary and Memoirs of Marshall Samuel Pierson, Company C, 17th Regt., Texas Cavalry, 1862–1865," ibid. 13 (1975); Douglas Hale, "One Man's War: Captain Joseph H. Bruton, 1861–1865," *East Texas Historical Journal* 20 (1982); Charles R. Walker, "Spaight's Battalion, C.S.A.," *Texas Gulf Historical and Biographical Record* 8 (November 1972); K. D. Keith, "The Memoirs of Captain Kosciuszko D. Keith," ibid. 10 (November 1974); and John Calvin Williams, "A Rebel Remembers the Red River Campaign," *Civil War Times Illustrated* 17 (January 1979). Accounts of the brigade's most renowned commander are Roy O. Hatton, "The Prince and the Confederates," ibid. 19 (August 1980); and Hatton, "Polignac Diary," ibid. 19 (August, October 1980). A general article on Texas cavalry units is Stephen B. Oates, "Recruiting Confederate Cavalry in Texas," *Southwestern Historical Quarterly* 64 (April 1961). The best-known Texas cavalry unit was Terry's Texas Rangers, the Eighth Texas Cavalry, which served with the Army of Tennessee. Accounts of its service include William A. Fletcher, *Rebel Private: Front and Rear;* C. C. Jeffries, *Terry's Rangers* (New York, 1961); Ephraim S. Dodd, *Diary* (Austin, 1914);

L. B. Giles, *Terry's Texas Rangers* (Austin, 1911); H. J. H. Rugeley, ed., *Batchelor-Turner Letters, 1861–1864* (Austin, 1961); Lester N. Fitzhugh, *Terry's Texas Rangers* (Houston, 1958); Margaret B. Jones, comp., *Bastrop ... With Letters Written by Terry Rangers* (Bastrop, 1936); J. K. P. Blackburn, *Reminiscences of the Terry Rangers* (Austin, 1919); A. P. Harcourt, "Terry's Texas Rangers," *Southern Bivouac* 1 (November 1882); Kate Scurry Terrell, "Terry's Texas Rangers," in Wooten, *A Comprehensive History of Texas*, vol. 2; Ralph A. Wooster and Robert W. Williams, Jr., "With Terry's Texas Rangers: The Letters of Dunbar Affleck," *Civil War History* 9 (September 1963); David B. Gracy II, "With Danger and Honor: George Washington Littlefield, 1861–1864," *Texana* 1 (Winter, Spring 1963); Henry William Graber, *A Terry Texas Ranger* (1916; reprinted Austin, 1987); Thomas W. Cutrer, ed., "'We Are Stern and Resolved': The Civil War Letters of John Wesley Rabb, Terry's Texas Rangers," *Southwestern Historical Quarterly* 91 (October 1987); Ralph A. Wooster, "With the Confederate Cavalry in the West: The Civil War Experiences of Isaac Dunbar Affleck," ibid. 83 (July 1979); Paul R. Scott, "Shannon's Scouts: Combat Reconnaissance Detachment of Terry's Texas Rangers," *Military History of Texas and the Southwest* 15 (1977); Paula Mitchell Marks, "The Ranger Reverend," *Civil War Times Illustrated* 24 (December 1985); Paul Scott, ed., "On the Road to the Sea: Shannon's Scouts," ibid. 21 (January 1983); and Maury Darst, "Robert Hodges, Jr., "Confederate Soldier," *East Texas Historical Journal* 9 (March 1971).

Another Texas cavalry brigade that served with the Army of Tennessee was Ross's Brigade. Accounts of the command by or about members of the Third Texas Cavalry are Victor M. Rose, *Ross' Texas Brigade* (Louisville, 1881, reprinted Kennesaw, Ga., 1961); Samuel B. Barron, *The Lone Star Defenders* (New York, 1908, reprinted Waco, 1964); Lawrence Sullivan Ross, "Sherman's Campaign in Mississippi," *Southern Historical Society Papers* 9 (1881); Douglas John Cater, *As It Was: Reminiscences of a Soldier of the Third Texas Cavalry and the Nineteenth Louisiana Infantry* (Austin, 1990); Max S. Lale, "The Boy-Bugler of the Third Texas Cavalry: The A. B. Blocker Narrative," *Military History of Texas and the Southwest* 14 (1976), 14 (1977); Douglas Hale, "The Third Texas Cavalry: A Socioeconomic Profile of a Confederate Regiment," *Military History of the Southwest* 19 (Spring 1989); Tom Hogg, "Reminiscences of the War: The Last Day at Corinth," ed. Robert

C. Cotner, *East Texas Historical Journal* 20 (1982); Douglas Hale, "Life and Death among the Lone Star Defenders: Cherokee County Boys in the Civil War," ibid. 29 (1991); and "Company K: A Composite Portrait of Smith County Boys in the Civil War," *Chronicles of Smith County, Texas* 27 (1988); by members of the Sixth Texas Cavalry: Joe M. Scott, *Four Years Service in the Southern Army* (Mulberry, Ark., 1897); Max Lale and Hobart Key, Jr., eds., *The Civil War Letters of David R. Garrett* (Marshall, 1964); and William Clyde Billingsley, ed., "Such Is War: The Confederate Memoirs of Newton Asbury Keen," *Texas Military History* 6 (Winter 1967), 7 (Spring, Summer, Autumn 1968); and, by members of the Ninth Texas Cavalry: E. L. Dohoney, *An Average American* (Paris, Texas, 1907), Allison W. Sparks, *The War Between the States as I Saw It* (Tyler, 1901); and Homer L. Kerr, ed., *Fighting with Ross' Texas Cavalry Brigade, c.s.a.: The Diary of George L. Griscom* (Hillsboro, 1976).

In the Trans-Mississippi, the Sibley-Green Brigade became the best-known Texas cavalry command. The only complete histories of the unit are Theophilus Noel, *Campaign from Santa Fe to the Mississippi* (Shreveport, 1865, reprinted by Martin H. Hall and E. A. Davis, Houston, 1961), and J. H. McLeary, "Green's Brigade," in Wooten, *A Comprehensive History of Texas,* vol. 2. Accounts of its invasion of New Mexico are numerous, however, and include Martin H. Hall, *Sibley's New Mexico Campaign* (Austin, 1960), and *The Confederate Army of New Mexico* (Austin, 1978); Ray C. Colton, *The Civil War in the Western Territories* (Norman, 1959); Robert L. Kerby, *The Confederate Invasion of New Mexico and Arizona* (Los Angeles, 1958); Martin H. Hall, ed., "The Journal of Ebenezer Hanna," *Password* 3 (Spring 1958), a member of the Fourth Texas Cavalry; "A Confederate Soldier's Letter from Fort Bliss, July 6, 1861," ibid. 25 (Spring 1980); "An Appraisal of the 1862 New Mexico Campaign: A Confederate Officer's Letter to Nacogdoches," *New Mexico Historical Review* 51 (October 1976); and "The Taylor Letters: Confederate Correspondence from Fort Bliss, 1861," *Military History of Texas and the Southwest* 15 (1977); Odie B. Faulk, "Confederate Hero at Val Verde [Tom Green]," *New Mexico Historical Review* 38 (October 1963); Ernest A. Archambeau, Jr., "The New Mexico Campaign, 1861–1862," *Panhandle Plains Historical Review* 37 (1964); Thomas Benton Collins, "A Texan's Account of the Battle of Valverde," ibid.; George Cook, "Letter from the Front,"

New Mexico Magazine (September 1965); Kenneth A. Goldblatt, "The Confederate Capture of Arizona," *Texas Military History* 8 (1970); and David Westphall, "The Battle of Glorieta Pass: Its Importance in the Civil War," *New Mexico Historical Review* 44 (April 1969); Don E. Alberts, ed., *Rebels on the Rio Grande: The Civil War Journal of A. B. Peticolas* (Albuquerque, 1984); Jerry D. Thompson, ed., *Westward the Texans: The Civil War Journal of Private William Randolph Howell* (El Paso, 1991); Michael L. Tate, "A Johnny Reb in Sibley's New Mexico Campaign: Reminiscences of Pvt. Henry C. Wright, 1861–1862," *East Texas Historical Journal* 25 (1987), 26 (1988); and Stanley S. Graham, "Campaign for New Mexico, 1861–1862," *Military History of Texas and the Southwest* 10 (1972). Personal narratives that extend through the entire war include Oscar Haas, "The Diary of Julius Giesecke," *Texas Military History* 3 (Winter 1963), 4 (Spring 1964); Theophilus Noel, *Autobiography* (Chicago, 1904), by members of the Fourth Texas Cavalry; and C. C. Cox, "Reminiscences," *Southwestern Historical Quarterly* 6 (January 1903), by a member of Waller's Battalion.

A unit connected with the Sibley-Green Brigade to form a cavalry division was Major's Brigade, which may be considered through Rebecca W. Smith and Marion Mullins, eds., "The Diary of H. C. Medford, Confederate Soldier, 1864," ibid. 34 (October 1930, January 1931); Jerry D. Thompson, ed., *From Desert to Bayou: The Civil War Journal and Sketches of Morgan Wolfe Merrick* (El Paso, 1991); and J. S. Duncan, "A Soldier's Fare Is Rough: Letters from A. Cameron in the Indian Territory, Arkansas Campaign, 1862–1864," *Military History of Texas and the Southwest* 12 (1974). Another little-known cavalry command that served in the Trans-Mississippi, Gano's Brigade, is discussed in Wallace, *Charles DeMorse;* Allan C. Ashcraft, "Confederate Indian Territory Conditions in 1865," *Chronicles of Oklahoma* 42 (Winter 1964–1965); Bradford Felmly and John Grady, "The Death of Private McDermott," *Civil War Times Illustrated* (December 1969); and Felmly and Grady, *Suffering to Silence: 29th Texas Cavalry C.S.A.* (Quanah, 1976); and Robert Horn, *The Annals of Elder Horn: Early Life in the Southwest* (New York, 1930). Parsons's Brigade, which also fought west of the Mississippi, is described in Anne J. Bailey, *Between the Enemy and Texas: Parsons's Texas Cavalry in the Civil War* (Fort Worth, 1989); and B. P. Gallaway, *The Ragged Rebel: A Common Soldier in W. H. Parsons' Texas Cavalry, 1861–1865* (Austin, 1988).

In 1864, several Texas cavalry regiments were organized into a division under General H. P. Bee for the Red River campaign in Louisiana. The histories of those units include Alwyn Barr, ed., "William T. Mechling's Journal of the Red River Campaign, April 7-May 10, 1864," *Texana* 1 (Fall 1963), by a division staff officer; Hamilton P. Bee, "Battle of Pleasant Hill," *Southern Historical Society Papers* 8 (1880); Fredericka Meiners, "Hamilton P. Bee in the Red River Campaign of 1864," *Southwestern Historical Quarterly* 78 (July 1974); Xavier B. Debray, *A Sketch of the History of Debray's 26th Regiment of Texas Cavalry* (Austin, 1884, reprinted Waco, 1961, and Pasadena, Texas, 1964); Thomas H. Edgar, *History of Debray's (26th) Regiment of Texas Cavalry* (Galveston, 1898); H. A. Graves, *Andrew Jackson Potter* (Nashville, 1881), about a member of the Twenty-sixth Texas Cavalry; Thomas C. Smith, *Here's Your Mule: The Diary of Thomas C. Smith, 3rd Sergeant, Company "G," Woods' Regiment, 32nd [36th] Texas Cavalry, C.S.A.* (Waco, 1958); Carl L. Duaine, *The Dead Men Wore Boots: An Account of the 32 [36th] Texas Volunteer Cavalry, C.S.A., 1862–1865* (Austin, 1966); John Spencer, *Terrell's Texas Cavalry* (Burnet, 1982); Davis Bitten, ed., *The Reminiscences and Civil War Letters of Levi Lamoni Wright* (Salt Lake City, 1970); and Minetta Altgelt Goyne, ed., *Lone Star and Double Eagle: Civil War Letters of a German-Texas Family* (Fort Worth, 1982).

For a look at cavalry service in the Trans-Mississippi through the eyes of a Texan see Robert W. Williams, Jr., and Ralph A. Wooster, eds., "With the Confederate Cavalry in East Texas: The Civil War Letters of Private Isaac Dunbar Affleck," *East Texas Historical Journal* 1 (July 1963), and "Camp Life in Civil War Louisiana: The Letters of Private Isaac Dunbar Affleck," *Arkansas Historical Quarterly* 21 (Autumn 1962).

Additional studies that provide information on Texas and Texans in the western theater of the Civil War are Robert L. Kerby, *Kirby Smith's Confederacy: The Trans-Mississippi South, 1863–1865* (New York, 1972); Joseph H. Parks, *General Edmund Kirby Smith* (Baton Rouge, 1954), the commander of the Trans-Mississippi Department; Stephen B. Oates, *Confederate Cavalry West of the River* (Austin, 1961), on the same area; James L. Nichols, *Confederate Quartermaster in the Trans-Mississippi* (Austin, 1964); Richard Taylor, *Destruction and Reconstruction*, ed. Richard Harwell (New York, 1955), by the commander of the district of western Louisiana adjoining Texas; Alwyn Barr, "Confederate Artillery in the Trans Mississippi," *Military Affairs* 27 (Summer

1963); Lester N. Fitzhugh, "Texas Forces in the Red River Campaign, March–May, 1864," *Texas Military History* 3 (Spring 1963); Alwyn Barr, "Texan Losses in the Red River Campaign, 1864," ibid. (Summer 1963), and "The Battle of Blair's Landing," *Louisiana Studies* 2 (Winter 1963), fought entirely by Texas troops during the Red River campaign; and Albert Castel, "Quantrill in Texas," *Civil War Times Illustrated* 11 (June 1972).

Final scenes in Texas and the flight of some Texans into Mexico are described in Charles W. Ramsdell, "The Last Hope of the Confederacy: John Tyler to the Governor and Authorities of Texas," *Southwestern Historical Quarterly* 14 (October 1910); Noah Andre Trudeau, "The Story of the War's Final Days," *Civil War Times Illustrated* 29 (July–August 1990), especially chapter 4; William W. White, "The Disintegration of an Army: Confederate Forces in Texas, April–June, 1865," *East Texas Historical Journal* 26 (1988); Edwin Adams, *Fallen Guidon: The Forgotten Saga of General Jo Shelby's Confederate Command, the Brigade That Never Surrendered, and Its Expedition to Mexico* (Santa Fe, 1962); Alexander Watkins Terrell, *From Texas to Mexico and the Court of Maximilian in 1866* (Dallas, 1933); and John N. Edwards, *Shelby's Expedition to Mexico* (Kansas City, 1872; reprinted Austin, 1964).

From an analysis of the foregoing discussion, it seems that, although much has been written on Texas and Texans in the Civil War, some topics remain to be explored. Although considerable detailed work has been done, summaries are lacking on the activities of the state government and several aspects of civilian life in Texas. There are political and military leaders of the period who have not yet found biographers, and some military units are marching off the pages of history for lack of a historian. Finally and most important, there remains no summary of the state and its citizens and soldiers during the conflict.

Index